Sociology of the
Global System

Sociology of the Global System

Leslie Sklair

The Johns Hopkins University Press
Baltimore

First published, 1991, by
The Johns Hopkins University Press
701 West 40th Street
Baltimore, Maryland 21211

ISBN 0–8018–4186–0
    0–8018–4220–4 (pbk)

Cataloging-in-Publication Data for this book
is available from the Library of Congress.
LC 90-21658

Sociology of today . . . reminds one of the
visitor at a zoological garden in Krylov's
fable who reports enthusiastically to his
friend on the wonders he has seen: marvelous
insects, gnats, butterflies, bugs, mosquitoes,
and similar creatures. But when his friend
asks him what he thought of the elephants, the
visitor confesses with embarrassment that he
had not noticed any elephant. It is all right to
study the little socio-cultural creatures, but
such a research does not justify neglecting a
study of socio-cultural elephants. (Pitirim Sorokin,
American Journal of Sociology, 1966, p. 492)

Contents

Preface   xi

1   A sociology of the global system   1
The global system and the nation-state   2
Transnational practices   5
Classifying the global system   10
   Income-based classifications   11
   Trade-based classifications   15
   Resource-based classifications   16
   Quality of life   18
   Bloc-based classifications   20
Conclusion   22

2   Towards a theory of transnational practices   26
Theories of the global system   27
   Imperialism   28
   Modernization   29
   Neo-Marxist theories   30
   World system theory   33
   Modes of production theory   35
The politics of development   36
Economy, polity, culture-ideology   40

History and theory of the transnational
corporation (TNC) 43
    Research on the TNCs 43
    TNCs and foreign direct investment 45
    TNCs and Third World governments 48

3. Corporations, classes and consumerism 52
The conceptual space for transnational practices (TNP) 52
Economic transnational practices 54
    Jobs 55
    Linkages 58
Political transnational practices 60
The transnational capitalist class 62
    Labour and capital 63
    Downgrading of domestic practices 65
    'Comprador' mentality 68
    Counter movements 69
    Protectionism 70
    The Green movement 71
Cultural-ideological transnational practices 72
The culture-ideology of consumerism 75
    Informatics and consumerism 77
The theory of the global system: a summary 81

4. Transnational practices in the Third World 85
Economic TNPs in the Third World 86
    The Volta Dam and linkages 87
    Transnational corporations in the Third World 91
    TNC employment 93
    The sexual division of labour 96
    Transnational pressures on TNCs 101
    Training and technology 105
Transnational corporations and Third World food 107
    Women and food production 108
    Agribusiness 110
The transnational capitalist class in the Third World 117
    The African bourgeoisie 120

Indigenization in Nigeria 122
Triple alliances and transnational capitalist classes 125

5. The culture-ideology of consumerism in the Third World 129
Consumerism and producerism 129
Cultural imperialism and media imperialism 132
Latin American research on the media 137
A new world information order 140
Control of global media markets 143
Advertising and the spread of consumerism 148
Global exposure 150
Delivering the goods 153
Case studies in global consumerism 155
The baby bottle-feed case 155
Drugs, health and profits 157
Cola wars 162
Conclusion 165

6. Socialist societies in the global system (1) 170
Communism and socialism defined 170
Choices for socialist societies 173
New China 178
The opening door 178
The labour market 184
'Classes' in the New China 187
New consumption needs 195

7. Socialist societies in the global system (2) 205
Transnational practices and East Europe 205
TNCs in East Europe 208
The socialist Third World 212
Cuba 212
Nicaragua 214
African socialism 215
Tanzania 217

Mozambique 220
Conclusion 223

8. Conclusion 227
TNCs and development 229
Democratic feminist socialism: a Third Way? 232
Democracy 232
Feminism 233
Socialism 235

References 240
Index 260

Preface

The idea for this book began to germinate in 1986 when I was asked to write a background paper for the 1988 edition of the United Nations Centre on Transnational Corporations Quinquenniel Survey, *Transnational Corporations in World Development*. My brief was to discuss the political and socio-cultural impact of the TNCs in the developing countries. Frankly, this was not an entirely satisfactory experience on either side. I could never really understand what they were getting at, and I suspect the feeling was mutual. However, I am grateful to Manuel Agosin at UNCTC for the opportunity it gave me to start thinking systematically about how the TNCs work globally.

The problem, of course, is that it is not possible to discuss coherently the political and socio-cultural impact of anything in the absence of a theoretical framework, even a rather schematic one of the type presented in this book. This framework grew gradually, sometimes painfully, out of the mass of theory, data and opinion on the TNCs and their operations all over the world that I have been collecting for almost 10 years. It has also helped me to organize the material of my ongoing research project on export led industrialization (specifically in export oriented zones) in China, Egypt, Ireland and Mexico, and this is reflected at various points in the book.

This has actually been an exciting book to research and to write. The increasing visibility of the global practices of the TNCs and the unfolding of events in China and East Europe (a mixture of the tragic and the unprecedentedly hopeful) gave the text an immediacy which is usually denied the sociological analyst. For example, as I write this preface, one of the two new quality newspapers to have appeared in Britain in the last few months (*The Independent on Sunday*, Business Section, 25 March 1990), includes three relevant articles. The first (p.14) argues that the idea of a US or any other country owned company is 'an obsolete notion in a world increasingly without economic borders' (see Chapter 1) and 'It is only beginning to be realised that the rise of the global company is ongoing and inevitable' (see Chapters 2 and 4). The second (p.14) tells the story of a Hungarian skilled worker and inventor turned entrepreneur (see Chapter 7). And the third (p.28) details the proposed 'fairy-tale marriage' between Nestlé and Disney (see Chapter 5). It would be foolish of me to claim that everything that has happened recently confirms clearly the theory put forward in this book, but enough of it does to give me confidence that the arguments are worth making.

I have been very fortunate in having had opportunities to discuss the book with friends and colleagues. Some of these discussions have been brief but nevertheless important for clarifying my thinking on specific questions. Although none should be implicated, I would like to thank Larry Herzog, Herbert Schiller and Carlos Waisman (in San Diego), John Friedman and Richard Sklar (in Los Angeles), Vivienne Bennett and Paul Lubeck (in Santa Cruz) and Jeff Henderson, Philip Schlesinger and the members of the Historical Sociology seminar in London. I should also like to acknowledge the debt I owe to the postgraduate students whose research I have supervised at the London School of Economics over the past few years. In particular, Barry King, Jane Kelly, Dawn Currie, Hamida Kazi, Brigitte Dumas, Inderjeet Parmar, Lucie Dumais, Huang Ping and Leith Dunn probably do not realize how much I have learned from them. The same goes for the students in my undergraduate and graduate courses on the 'Sociology of Development'.

All through the research and the arduous writing and rewriting of the book Doro Marden combined loving support and a critique of my literary style, and our children Jessie, Aphra and Tillie, provided countless delightful distractions. Clare Grist at Harvester Wheatsheaf has been an enthusiastic and helpful publisher and, as always, Yvonne Brown has been a wonderful secretary.

London, March 1990.

1

A sociology of the global system

We are always being told that the world is shrinking and that the new technology is bringing the inhabitants of planet earth ever closer together, whether they like it or not. With few exceptions, however, social scientists have not yet come to regard the whole world as a legitimate object of knowledge. There are very good reasons for this. The study of even a single society is considered to be extraordinarily difficult because of the complexity of social relations and the obvious problems of trying to generalize about people, their groupings and the structures within which they act.

Comparative sociology is supposed to be the attempt to gener-ate universal propositions on the basis of systematic comparisons of a variety of different societies, and so it might have been ex-pected to stimulate thinking about the global system. In fact the opposite happened. Due to the obsession of most comparative sociologists with problems of measurement, all sight of a global system was lost in the mists of dubious generalization about a host of discrete variables from societies all over the world. Their only conceptual connection was that someone (often a foreign ob-server) had produced numbers about one phenomenon that could be correlated with numbers from other societies purporting to be about the same phenomenon. This drew attention away from the whole and focused it on the part, as all empiricist research tends to do. So the social sciences groan under the weight of occupational, educational, demographic, gender, ethnic and many more categories of data collected cross-culturally, but offering little if any insight into the global system as a whole.

Does the *global system* really exist? Like all ideas it exists in the minds of people who think it, but it is further from the world of everyday immediate experience than other ideas such as power or friendship. Some ideas are found, or intended, to have no scientific validity at all. The point of this book is to demonstrate that the concept of the global system does have genuine scientific validity and, indeed, that it is increasingly necessary for the analysis of a growing number of rapidly changing phenomena. Naturally, people who choose to ignore these phenomena will have no need for the idea (just as those who choose to ignore societal phenomena have no need for an idea of society) but in both cases this leads to a dramatic impoverishment of their views of the real world.

The global system and the nation-state

What, then, does the idea (or concept, or abstraction) of the global system refer to? Because the world is divided into sovereign states, most with relatively clear and unified national cultures, it is convenient to identify these states as the basic elements of the global system. This is what the thriving academic discipline of international relations tends to do. Nevertheless, even here the notion that there are some important international relations that are not necessarily between states is generally accepted.[1]

This is the position of the British scholar, John Burton, an influential figure in the creation of the modern discipline of international relations. In a series of books from the 1960s he searched for a theory of world society. Burton argued that: 'We are choosing an approach when we choose to speak of world society and not international relations.' Studies based on states 'cannot give us that understanding we seek of world society' either within or between states (1972, pp.19, 20). What he labels the 'billiard-ball model' only recognizes governmental interaction. Historically, world society has become a believable idea only in the last few hundred years, and science, technology, industry, and universal values are creating a twentieth century world that is different from any past age. The geographical image of states must be replaced by the behavioural image of systems. However, 'world society appears to be at a transition stage at which it is neither a world comprising only of states, nor a world comprising only systems' (p.51).

Burton's approach can be seriously criticized on the grounds that he pays little attention to such problems as the globalization of capital, class struggle or ideology, and that he often appears to confuse society and system at both the descriptive and the conceptual levels. This is a consequence of the primacy he gives to *communications* over *power*. Nevertheless, his attempt to move international relations from the study of relations between nations to the study of 'world society' (leaving aside the essential vagueness of this latter idea), did represent a progressive problem shift for all those interested in the elephants rather than the little creatures.

In parallel, but quite independent of Burton, a group of North Americans began to make an explicit attempt to replace the 'state-centric' model, with a 'transnational relations' model, focused more on transnational interactions and organizations. In an important collection of essays, Keohane and Nye disclosed that they began to think along these lines under the influence of the French sociologist, Raymond Aron, who introduced the idea of 'transnational society'. They found this unsatisfactory because 'it did not direct attention to governmental manipulation of transnational relations . . . [and they have] grown progressively more interested in the interaction between governments and transnational society and in transnational coalitions among subunits of governments' (Keohane and Nye, 1973, p.vii).[2]

The 'transnational relations' approach, therefore, is not a specific theory but more of an injunction to researchers to pay more attention to non-governmental entities, particularly when they are interacting with governments. This is an important point but, as with Burton's 'world society', there is an essential vagueness about the central concept, transnational relations. One consequence of this is that no systematic research programme has resulted from this approach. Its eclecticism is what attracts many scholars. The proponents of the transnational relations approach have a tendency to analyze interactions within systems rather than effects of practices and, though they claim to be transcending the state-centric model, they more often than not permit the state to set the agenda for them. This is because, for the most part, they conceptualize the state and its agencies as by far the most important actors in the global system. In this they may or may not be correct, empirically, and they may or may not be theorizing in the most fruitful manner, but the very structure of the approach suggests an ambiguity about this key issue. And this persists in the work of political scientists, sociologists and others who have been impressed by the approach.[3]

Classical Marxists refuse to accept, either empirically or theoretically, that the state is the most important actor in the global system. For Marxists, the global system is the capitalist global system, and the most important actors are the capitalist classes in the most powerful states. In practice, however, most contemporary Marxism is state-centred to a greater or lesser extent. This is illustrated by the ongoing debate about the 'relative autonomy of the state'. Few Marxists now hold to the traditional claim that the state is nothing but the executive committee of the bourgeoisie. Apparent contradictions between state actions and the interests of the capitalist class can be explained in terms of the struggles of the competing fractions of the bourgeoisie and the bureaucracy. To some extent, this is obviously true. Neo-Marxists have gone much further and tend to claim that, in advanced capitalist societies, the state and its various bureaucracies have distinctive levels of relative autonomy from the different fractions of the bourgeoisie and, indeed, on occasion state functionaries can successfully play off one section of the bourgeoisie (as well as competing classes) against others, domestically or transnationally, in their own interests. Again, this is obviously true, to some extent.

Both of these apparently contradictory statements are *obviously* true, but only at the level of empirical observation. Theoretically, they can only both be true if we can demonstrate that they truthfully reflect a genuinely contradictory reality, in terms of their competing contributions to the structure and dynamic of a complex system of ideas and propositions, established to theorize that reality. For example, between 1970 and 1990 the distribution of income on a per capita basis in some Third World countries became more unequal, the top 10 per cent got relatively more and the bottom 10 per cent got relatively less, while the average per capita income (gross national product divided by population) roughly doubled in this period. Were these countries becoming richer or poorer?

The rich in these societies certainly became richer, on both measures. On the first measure the poor were becoming poorer, while on the second measure they were becoming richer, though not to the same extent as the rich. How can this be explained? Some theorize that income distribution is mainly a result of government action (wage policy, taxation, etc.) while per capita income is mainly a result of transnational forces (for example, the price that exports bring on the world market). Government actions may be responsive mainly to the interests of the capitalist class or the interests of a political class dependent on popular or sectional support to maintain its position of power. Alternatively (as happened in many Third World countries in the 1980s) they may be responsive to the interests of transnational capital in the shape of the World Bank and the IMF imposing 'restructuring' policies in order to ensure repayment of Third World debts. Similarly, transnational forces may be mainly responsive to these international financial organizations, or to the governments of the countries who control them, or to 'disinterested' international bureaucrats trying to sort out the mess. The reality is clearly very complex.[4]

Where a country is largely isolated from the rest of the world, the state-centred approach does seem more plausible than where it is located within an identifiable system of global relationships. Nevertheless, state-centrists, transnational relations advocates and Marxists of several persuasions, while acknowledging the growing importance of the global system in one form or another, all continue to prioritize the system of nation-states, they all fall back on it to describe what happens in the world, and to explain how and why it happens. The renaissance of historical sociology since the 1970s, for example, is largely powered by the idea of 'bringing the state back in' (see Evans *et al.*, 1985). My argument is that state-centrism, whether in its directly state-centrist form or in indirect forms, takes us quite far but not far enough.

Transnational practices

This book argues that we need to take a step towards a *sociology of the global system*. State-centred, transnational relations and neo-Marxist approaches, while often interesting and fruitful, tend to close off other interesting and fruitful avenues of theory and research. We cannot ignore the nation-state, but this book attempts to offer in addition a conception of the global system based on *transnational practices* (TNPs).

TNPs are analytically distinguished on three levels, economic, political and cultural-ideological, what I take to constitute the sociological totality. In the concrete conditions of the world as it is, a world largely structured by global capitalism, each of these TNPs is typically, but not exclusively, characterized by a major institution. The transnational corporation (TNC) is the major locus of transnational economic practices; what I shall term the transnational capitalist class is the major locus of transnational political practices; and the major locus of transnational cultural-ideological practices is to be found in the culture-ideology of consumerism. Not all culture is ideological, even in capitalist societies. The reason why I run *culture* and *ideology* together to identify the institutionalization of consumerism is that consumerism in the global system can only be fully understood as a cultural-ideological practice.[5] When we buy something that has been imported we are engaged in a typical economic transnational practice. When we are influenced to vote or support a cause by those whose interests are transnational we are engaged in a typical political transnational practice. When we experience the need for a global product we are engaged in a typical cultural-ideological transnational practice.

The TNPs make sense only in the context of the global system. The theory of the global system based on transnational practices is an attempt to escape from the limitations of state-centrism. In order to do this, it is necessary to spell out exactly what these limitations are.

The global system is marked by a very great asymmetry. The most important economic, political and cultural-ideological goods that circulate around the globe tend to be owned and/or controlled by small groups in a relatively small number of countries. Until recently it was both convenient and accurate to use the term 'Western' to describe this asymmetry, and the idea of 'Western imperialism' was widely acknowledged as a way of analyzing the global system. However, the present global status of Japan makes these terms obsolete. In this book I shall use the awkward but evocative term *hegemon* to describe the asymmetry in the global system. The hegemon is the agent of the key TNPs, it can be a representative individual, organization, state or class, whose interests prevail in the struggle for global resources. Other terms, such as 'superpower', and the triad of centre, semi-periphery and periphery states (see Wallerstein, 1984) are also common. These terms are less useful for the purposes of this analysis. The first tends to refer mainly to the military context which, while obviously important, is not what this book is about; and the second is clearly state-centrist, and does not fully convey the sense of hegemony where it does not directly involve the state, which I take to be crucial. While there is only one country, the United States, whose agents, organizations and classes are hegemonic in all three spheres, other countries and agents, organizations and classes are hegemonic, or realistically claim to share hegemony, within each sphere.

The nation-state, therefore, is the spatial reference point for most of the crucial transnational practices that go to make up the structures of the global system, in the sense that most transnational practices intersect in particular countries and come under the jurisdiction of particular nation-states. But it is not the only reference point. The most important is, of course, the global capitalist system, based on a variegated global capitalist class, which unquestionably dictates economic transnational practices, and is the most important single force in the struggle to dominate political and cultural-ideological transnational practices. There are several other systems, regionally important, ethnically, culturally and/or theologically based but none has, as yet, had the pervasive success that capitalism has enjoyed in the twentieth century.

The success of a system is often bound up with the success of the state that is its main proponent. Britain in the nineteenth century was, and the United States of America in the twentieth century is, the hegemon of global capitalism, though of rather different versions of it. Through their (respective) straightforward colonial and convoluted imperialist trajectories the transnational practices of these two countries etched the forms of capitalism onto the global system. It was this hegemonic combination of a mighty domestic economy, a progressive ruling class (in comparison with most others actually existing), and at least some desirable cultural-ideological features particularly attractive to 'modernizing' elites, that opened the global door to them and ensured the creation, persistence and often aggrandisement of social classes in countries all over the world willing and eager to adopt their transnational practices.

These classes are widely known by the label 'comprador' though this term has attracted a great deal of criticism. Here, I shall convert the idea into a concept of the *transnational capitalist class* (TCC). This class consists of those people who see their own interests and/or the interests of their nation, as best served by an identification with the interests of the capitalist global system, in particular the interests of the countries of the capitalist core and the transnational corporations domiciled in them. The TCC holds certain transnational practices to be more valuable than domestic practices. It is quite possible for a fraction of it to identify more with economic transnational practices than with political or cultural-ideological ones, or vice versa. Indeed, the fundamental in-built instability of the global system, and the most important contradiction with which any theory of the global system has to grapple, is that the hegemonic ideology of the system is under constant challenge, particularly outside the First World. The substantive content of the theory, how the transnational corporations harness the transnational capitalist classes to solidify their hegemonic control of consumerist culture and ideology, is the site of the many struggles for the global system. Who will win and who will lose these struggles is not a foregone conclusion.

The place of Britain and the United States in the history of capitalism and the very existence of the TCC that the British and US (and some other) capitalist classes helped create, have historically built in the asymmetries and inequalities that now characterize the global system. Just as hegemon nation-states (whether acting directly in the interests of the capitalist class or not) can call on superior economic, political and cultural-ideological resources in their dealings with other nation-states, so some transnational agents can command greater resources than others.

Sociologists, economists, political scientists, historians, geographers, anthropologists and everyone else whose work demanded a global perspective had long been accustomed to perceive the world as split into modern and traditional, advanced and backward, progressive and stagnant societies, to mention only the most commonly used distinctions. All of these were more or less subsumed under the rubric of the developed (advanced industrial) societies and the developing (usually a euphemism for undeveloped or, more radically, underdeveloped) societies. With the rise of theories purporting to identify this phenomenon of *under*development and to explain it as an active process in the global strategy of capitalist exploitation, First, Second and Third Worlds, despite the emphasis on the nation-state, were usually conceptualized as relatively undifferentiated objects. Though there have always been differences between countries outside the First World, for a long time it did appear to make sense to speak of *The Third World*, the title of Worsley's very influential book (1973) on the subject. Perhaps some countries were exploited rather more for their natural resources and others for their cheap labour, but they all fitted in to a global pattern in which the capitalist-imperialist centre underdeveloped the rest of the world. The implication of this line of reasoning was that if they could be left alone, insulated from the capitalist global reach, Third World countries would be better off, and would actually be able to develop themselves.

The experiences of some of the Second World (communist) countries, those who had escaped from the grip of global capitalism, particularly the Soviet Union and then China, seemed to lend support to the argument. The theory was most exhaustively worked out for countries in Latin America, where it swept the board among academics, politicians, bureaucrats and militants for some time under the general rubric of the *dependency* approach. It did for a time seem to explain the trajectories of development and underdevelopment in some countries of Latin America, but when it was applied to Africa and Asia it was much less successful. This led some writers to suspect that the Third World, like the First World, was not of a piece, but that there might be substantial differences of kind as well as the obvious differences of degree between countries. It is a short step from this view to the position that there are several Third (and First) Worlds and that each of these Worlds has a specific set of relations with global capitalism, or even that there is no such thing as global capitalism but that there are several capitalisms operating nationally and internationally in different ways with different Third Worlds. One of the problems of the dependency approach is precisely that its proponents too often speak about one country as dependent on another in a vague and unhelpful fashion. In order to clarify this issue, it is necessary to begin to think about how to classify the constituent parts of the global system.

Classifying the global system

Although most writers warn against the dangers of explaining the plight of contemporary Third World societies in terms of the historical experiences of the advanced industrial societies, it is nevertheless true that the classifications of the three Worlds are mainly based on these historical experiences. For example, the distribution of the labour force between agriculture and industry has always been regarded as an important indicator of economic growth, if not precisely development, because most of the present advanced industrial societies, in particular the United Kingdom and the United States, exhibited a marked tendency to reduce their agricultural labour force while increasing their industrial labour force. This is, of course, why industrialization is seen to be so important in most theories of development. The standard of living is another key measure which has its origins in the same source. Whether measured by per capita GNP (gross national product), calorific intake or any other indicator, it gives a quick, if not always entirely accurate or meaningful, basis on which to rank societies.

It is important to be aware of the fact that, however obvious and relevant these measures might seem to us, they are all 'theory-laden' in the sense that they all assume, usually without argument or justification, a particular theory of economic growth and/or development. I do not make this point to suggest that all these theories are wrong in every detail, but to underline the importance of looking behind the apparently innocent measures on which so much of the global-system literature is based. We must know what we are letting ourselves in for, theoretically, when we use such measures. This is far from an argument that we should avoid such measures (let alone empirical research itself) but rather an argument for a continual critical assessment of them, and perhaps a call for better measures.[6]

While the global system is most commonly classified in terms of First, Second and Third Worlds, and these are very convenient and for many purposes useful labels, it is certain that they conceal as much as they reveal. If we are to begin to describe the global system in a more theoretically fruitful manner we will have to look behind these labels. There are at least five main classifications of the global system in current usage and they are all state-centred.

These can be roughly characterised as follows:

1. Income-based.
2. Trade-based.
3. Resource-based.
4. Quality of life-based.
5. Bloc-based.

Income-based classification

This is the simplest, most widely used, and in some ways the most misleading of the classifications. Economists and economic historians have been interested in measuring poverty and wealth on a per capita basis for some time, and such data have been available for some of the advanced industrial countries for many years. The lack of statistical services in most Third World countries has meant that population figures, let alone GNP per capita figures, have been very sparse and unreliable. This situation improved somewhat in the 1970s, and international agencies have been systematically organizing the collection of such data. Since 1978 the World Bank has been publishing an annual *World Development Report* with a growing number of 'world development indicators' tables (eighteen tables in 1978, twenty-seven in 1983, thirty-three in 1988), based for the most part on UN and internal World Bank data sources. This is certainly the most useful, easily accessible and up-to-date compilation of figures, and it is the one I shall mainly rely on in this book. A new and probably more reliable set of data from the University of Pennsylvania (see Summers and Heston, 1988) may well displace the World Bank tables as the best available source.

The World Bank ranks all the countries of the world according to their GNP per capita, though countries with populations of less than 1 million (of whom there were 35 identified in the 1988 Report) are excluded from the main tables. All World Bank financial data are converted into US dollars, and this is, indeed, one serious problem with them as the bank itself acknowledges (see, for example, *World Development Report*, 1988, pp.290–1). The 1978 Report has 125 countries with GNP per capita figures ranging from $70 (Bhutan) to $15,480 (Kuwait). The countries are divided into 6 categories as follows: low-income with GNP per capita up to $250 (34 countries); middle-income over $250 per capita (58 countries); industrialized countries (19); capital surplus oil exporters (3); and centrally-planned economies, communist countries (11). There are several anomalies in this classification. In the first place, while countries listed from 1 to 92 are in strict GNP per capita order, countries 93, 94 and 95 (South Africa, Ireland and Italy) all have lower per capita figures than 92 (Israel). No fewer than 14 middle-income countries have higher per capita figures than 'industrialized' South Africa, and 5 of these are 'richer' than Ireland. Further, the per capita figures for the oil exporters and the centrally-planned economies would distribute the countries in these categories fairly widely throughout the list.

By 1983, the categories had changed somewhat, though the anomalies remained. The poorest 34 countries were still identified as low-income economies; the next 60 countries were divided into 39 lower-middle-income and 21 upper-middle-income economies. Four high-income oil exporters, 19 industrial market economies and 8 East European non-market economies completed the list of 125 countries. The main differences between the 1978 and the 1983 lists were definitional (the splitting up of the middle-income group) and political (South Africa expelled from the industrial group and relegated to the upper-middle-income group and replaced, incidentally, by Spain; Taiwan expelled altogether from the list and the People's Republic of China integrated into the low-income group at number 21). The two most populous countries in the world, China and India, in the low-income economies group, were also separated out from the rest of this group for averaging purposes; as were oil exporters and oil importers in the middle-income economies group.

By 1988 the total number of countries had risen to 129, split into 39 low-income, 34 lower-middle, 24 upper-middle, 4 high-income oil exporters, 19 industrial market, and 9 centrally-planned economies, renamed 'nonreporting nonmembers' (aptly, as there was little information on them outside the demographic and social indicators tables). Again, a certain amount of category switching had taken place. For example, Hungary, Poland and Romania were inserted into the upper-middle-income group, where their apparent per capita income scores would locate them in any case, whereas Angola, Cuba and North Korea were transplanted from lower-middle-income to nonreporting nonmembers. Further, all the low and middle-income groups were also categorized as 'developing economies' subdivided into oil exporters, exporters of manufactures, highly indebted countries, and sub-Saharan Africa (new sub-categories of great ideological significance), for the purposes of averaging.

It is not only the anomalies in these tables to which I wish to draw attention but the assumptions on which they are based. These assumptions are as follows:

1. GNP per capita can be determined for all of the countries concerned in such a way that meaningful comparisons can be drawn.
2. The per capita income is the basic criterion for drawing comparisons.
3. In some cases other criteria will override the per capita income basis of the classification.

Economists at the World Bank and elsewhere have laboured hard and long to put international data on a sound footing and the 'Technical Notes' that follow the tables in the Reports are full of acknowledgements of the difficulties involved. These difficulties, however, are not simply technical, in the sense of translating one country's GNP or GDP into terms that will bear comparison with those of other countries. They are also a matter of political economy, in the sense that some measures best represent some socio-economic systems while they discriminate against, perhaps by undervaluing the products of, other socio-economic systems or classes of people within a system. A glaring example of this is the neglect of the domestically-consumed products of farmers (particularly women) in the Third World. Such economic activity is excluded from World Bank data.

Women's work in the countries of the Third World is generally rendered 'invisible' by normal national accounting procedures because it usually takes place outside the conventional sphere of wage labour, mostly on the family farm and in the home. This 'invisibility' results in serious understatement of the great economic significance of female labour, especially in the production, collection, preparation and processing of food. Thus, male-dominated organizations like national statistical services and the World Bank, underestimate the real economic activity of Third World countries (see Boserup, 1970).[7]

It is no accident that the global standard used by the World Bank and most other organizations is the US dollar. It is a simple indication that the US economy is the most powerful in the world (despite the fact that it is in relative decline) and that global economic activity does tend to be measured in comparison with the sorts of economic activities with which the United States is mainly involved. Lurking behind these measures, therefore, is a congerie of theories of economic growth and/or development most applicable to the United States and other similar industrial economies.

Income-based classifications of 'developing' and non-market economies are therefore inherently problematic. Where they are used as the basis of inter-country comparisons, which is by far the most common use that is made of them, they predispose the results of such comparisons to certain conclusions which are usually prejudiced by unspoken theory-laden assumptions. However, as long as we are aware of these provisos, and are able to correct the most crass biases at the empirical and conceptual levels, there is clearly a use to which such classifications can be put. For example, the countries of the world can be split into groups according to population as well as per capita income. The logic behind this is obvious. One important basis of comparison between countries is their size, and it is clearly very relevant to an appreciation of the relative levels of economic growth and development achieved by any country, to know roughly among how many people the social product, however large or small, has to be divided. The absolute size of a country is a relatively neglected question in the study of the global system.[8]

If we correlate population categories (1–20 million, 20–50 million, 50–100 million, and 100 million plus) with World Bank GNP per capita categories (roughly lower-, middle-, and higher- income countries) we find that two-thirds of countries are relatively small (up to about 20 million in population) and two-thirds of these are quite poor (GNP per capita of less than $1,570), while almost half the relatively rich countries (GNP per capita of more than $8,000), have relatively large populations (over 50 million). The only real conclusion that we can draw from such an exercise is that there appears to be no simple relationship between population and the wealth of a nation-state. This might give a little pause to those who dogmatically believe that poverty is a direct consequence of 'overpopulation'.

Trade-based classifications

Though clearly important, income and population size are not the only important characteristics of countries. The structure of the economy and society can be broken down in a variety of ways for a variety of purposes. Those who have investigated the factors that seem to accompany economic growth and development in the second half of the twentieth century have often looked to the historical experiences of the contemporary advanced industrial societies for clues, and they have generally found that patterns of foreign trade are very important. The quantity, value and type of goods and services traditionally exported and imported by most of the contemporary rich nations, indeed, fell into fairly clear patterns. Briefly, they exported manufactured goods and capital, and they imported raw materials. The so-called terms of trade, more accurately labelled 'unequal exchange' (see Edwards, 1985, ch. 4), ensured that for the most part the prices of raw materials were falling relative to the prices of manufactured goods.[9] A further and central feature of this system of trade was that while those countries exporting manufactures were usually involved in many diverse lines of business, the raw-material exporters were often engaged in the production of one or two major staples. Mono-crop economies are particularly vulnerable to the instabilities in the world market directed, not by the hidden hand of the market, but by the actions of a global collection of profit-maximizing capitalists, usually based in hegemon countries and often acting in unison.

Even those writers who specifically warned against using the historical experiences of contemporary rich countries as a guide for the Third World could not resist drawing some conclusions from the realm of foreign trade. It seemed very obvious, first of all, that a country does not get rich by importing manufactured goods if it can possibly manufacture them itself. This truism was elevated to the status of a theory of and a strategy for development, particularly in Latin America, and became known as 'import substitution industrialization' (ISI). But though they no longer imported some categories of finished products, many Third World manufacturers found they were importing the components, materials and technology for these products instead. When ISI began to fail, or at least brought with it as many problems as it was solving, a new theory and strategy began to emerge, based this time not on imports but on exports. The idea behind this was the mirror image of ISI. What had enriched the rich was not their insulation from imports (rich countries do, in fact, import massively all sorts of goods) but their success in manufactured exports, where higher prices could be commanded than for Third World raw materials. This thinking led to the theory and strategy of 'export-led industrialization' (ELI).

ISI and ELI have been used as complementary and contradictory developmental strategies. Let it suffice to say, at this point, notwithstanding the criticisms that have been made of the assumptions on which both ISI and ELI theories are based, export–import structure is now a key characteristic of the economic growth and by implication developmental prospects of Third World countries. That this should be so is not simply a matter of cognitive theory choice, but also a matter of the economic, political and cultural-ideological interests of theoreticians and practical actors in rich and poor countries. This is not entirely unconnected to another feature of the economies of many Third World countries that has become of great salience in recent years, namely their foreign debt and the effect that servicing that debt, particularly in times of rising and unpredictable interest rates, has on economic and social planning.

Resource-based classifications

No country in the world is entirely self-sufficient in all the materials it uses. Even the largest and most richly resource-endowed countries, such as the United States and the Soviet Union, must import some of the raw materials they use, for example rare metals. The United States is particularly vulnerable in this respect, both because it is lacking in some valuable resources, and because its vast productive machine uses so much of everything. In a book significantly entitled *American Multinationals and American Interests*, Bergson and his colleagues worked out the percentage of key minerals and metals supplied by imports in 1976 (Bergson *et al.*, 1978, Table 5.1). The list includes columbium, sheet mica, strontium (100 per cent); manganese, cobalt, tantalum, chromium (90 per cent plus); asbestos, aluminium, fluorine, bismuth, platinum (80 per cent plus); and tin, mercury, nickel (70 per cent plus). It is no wonder that the United States keeps such a large navy patrolling the trade routes of the world. The United States is still resource-dependent to an appreciable degree.[10]

The list leaves out what many consider to be the single most important US import, namely oil. This, at least, is the view of Gail (1978), who reports that a Gallup Poll in May 1978 showed that 40 per cent of Americans did not know that the United States imported oil at all, and that hardly any of them knew that it imported about half its crude oil and refined products at that time. Knowledge on the issue was increased by the Iranian hostage crisis and subsequent events, but the fact remains that the 'U.S. economy is now absolutely dependent on imported oil [and has] sharply increased its dependence on Arab oil imports since 1973' (p.18). This is why the United States pays a good price for half of Mexico's oil.

It is not only the United States that has become dependent on imports of oil. Lucky chance put massive reserves of oil within the national boundaries of some barren and desolate desert kingdoms and political will has, through the organized power of OPEC, turned some of their rulers into the richest men in the world. But however important the possession of oil is for a country, oil exporters such as Nigeria, Mexico and Egypt demonstrate that oil alone is no guarantee of general prosperity. The effect of having to rely on imported oil is of great significance for development. So clear did this become after the 1974 oil crisis, when the upward spiral of oil prices began, that international agencies invented a new category of country: the most seriously affected nations (MSANs), i.e. those countries, mainly in Africa, who could no longer afford to buy oil. Inability to buy oil is widely interpreted to mean inability to sustain even the very low level of industrialization already achieved. Prospects for such countries are extremely bleak.

While it is clearly one very important natural resource on the world stage at present, and for the foreseeable future in the absence of entirely new energy sources, oil is not the only important natural resource. Another is food, and for the hungry it is infinitely more important than oil. Some countries choose to import food items that they could easily grow for themselves because they find it commercially advantageous to grow industrial raw materials for export and to import the food they need, which tends to be less costly relative to their exports. There are few countries which choose to rely on imports of basic cereals (wheat, rice etc.) if they can avoid it. More or less all the countries in the world which are heavily dependent on cereal imports on a per capita basis are poor countries, or rich countries with relatively little arable land (like Japan).

It would, therefore, be instructive to classify the nations of the world in terms of their oil and cereal resources, as measured by the degree to which they are self-sufficient or seriously dependent on others for their supplies. We must be careful not to speak of oil and cereal *needs* which may be very different from *consumption*. This point is made not in the interests of pedantry, but because it bears directly on the criticisms of current approaches to the global system that lie at the heart of this book. To anticipate the argument a little, my view is that consumption patterns of the majority of people (not only in the Third World) are ill-matched to their needs because both consumption and needs are generally dictated by transnational practices. When we begin to appreciate more clearly and with greater precision how and why so many Third World countries are locked into a global system that is so patently against the interests of the majority of their peoples, we may find one of the keys to the development puzzle, and a valuable clue as to how the global system currently works. A resource-based classification of the nations of the world represents a step towards this goal (see Cole, 1988).

Quality of life

The structure of the economy is clearly the basis on which to build a classification of the countries of the world in terms of their economic growth, or lack of it. Development in the global system implies something more. For many years national and international agencies have been collecting data on some significant social indicators, and it is now possible, with all the provisos about the nature of the data that I have already made, to make some, albeit rough and preliminary ranking of the nations of the world on the most widely accepted social and welfare criteria. The point of this exercise is to begin to derive a picture of how economic growth and development, as they have been generally defined, are related to the extent that the measures available permit us to draw some conclusions about the relative positions on a world scale of different groups of countries. The social welfare indicators that are most commonly agreed to be of relevance here are the degree of literacy, the distribution of health and educational services, the infant mortality rate and the life expectancy of the population. To this list it would be very desirable to add the status of women and the distribution of income, housing and consumer durables, but there is, as yet, not much reliable information available on these for the poorer countries of the world.

Scholars from various disciplines have been working on these problems since the mid-1940s. The first substantial efforts came from international organizations, particularly United Nations agencies and the OECD (see, for example, UNESCO, 1976). Morris (1979) published a 'Physical Quality of Life Index' but as this was exclusively based on health and educational criteria, it is of limited utility. In an attempt to extend the scope of quality of life methodology, Estes (1988) has constructed an 'Index of Social Progress' based on forty-four welfare-relevant social indicators, which includes items normally ignored by economically based measures (like the status of women and children, politics, effects of disasters, cultural diversity, and defence expenditures). The changing distributions between 1970 and 1980 on this index have been calculated for over 100 countries, with some surprising results. For example, some of the countries of East Europe and Costa Rica, rank higher than the United Kingdom and the United States (Estes, 1988).

Gonzalez (1988, Table 4.2), usefully compares four different indexes for a large sample of countries. He finds, not surprisingly, that the two based mainly on economic indicators tend to rank the United States very high (first and second), while the other two, more widely based, classifications rank it lower (sixth and twenty-fourth). This is clearly a very controversial question, and it has been much discussed in the context of the 'basic needs' approach to development. Basic needs theorists argue that it is more fruitful to stress results rather than inputs in order to measure the adequacy of development policy. For example, life expectancy is a better measure of health services than numbers of doctors per person, and calorie supply per capita is a better measure of nutrition than total production of food. Thus, the basic needs approach switches attention from '*how much* is being produced . . . to *what* is being produced, in *what ways*, for *whom* and with what *impact*' (Hicks and Streeton, 1979, p.577).[11]

As I suggested at the beginning of the discussion on classifying the global system, all measures are theory laden. This is particularly the case for quality of life, for the ways in which quality of life is measured, and specifically the role and definition of basic needs, virtually define our conceptions of development within the global system.

Bloc-based classifications

The final type of classification is one that appears to be less rather than more relevant for the 1990s than previously. This is sociopolitical blocs. The major bloc-based classification reflects the economic, political and cultural-ideological struggle between capitalism and communism for control over the global system. So important is it, that the decades since the end of the Second World War are commonly referred to as the epoch of the 'Cold War' between capitalism and communism.

It is interesting to note that in the 1978 World Bank Report some communist countries were given a special category, 'centrally-planned economies'. In the 1983 Report this was changed to 'East European non-market economies' and by 1988 the communist countries were either scattered in the 'developing economies' groups or under the anodyne label of 'nonreporting nonmembers'. These changes were partly to handle the massive, though poor, People's Republic of China, incorporated into the 'low-income economies' and the dropping of the geographical reference is a nod of recognition in the direction of the African and Asian and other countries who claim to be socialist.

Irrespective of the decisions of the World Bank classifiers, however, it is an undeniable fact that in the 1990s most hitherto self-proclaimed socialist or communist countries are rapidly coming to an understanding with transnational capitalism, and that the scope and volume of the transnational practices of such states with the states and institutions of the capitalist system have increased dramatically in the last decade. As I shall argue in Chapters 6 and 7, this does not necessarily mean that the socialist or communist countries are 'going capitalist', though it does highlight changing relationships between the global capitalist system and its alternatives.

Communism found its first means of expression in the various international organizations (the *Internationals*) that were established by Marx and Engels and their followers from the 1860s on. However, it is not until the Bolshevik Party, the first communist party to seize state power, ushers in the birth of the Soviet Union that we can realistically speak of a communist bloc. In 1949, the Soviet Union organized the Council for Mutual Economic Aid (Comecon), paralleling the Organization for European Economic Cooperation, which had been formed in 1948 as a framework within which the United States could distribute aid to rebuild the war-shattered West European economies. This body was renamed the Organization for Economic Cooperation and Development (OECD) in 1961, and its membership and functions were extended to promote the global leadership of the capitalist 'Western' democracies. It has the reputation of a 'rich countries' club, though some poorer European countries have now joined.

The most visible public presence of the communist and capitalist blocs, however, is through their military alliances. The Warsaw Pact of East European communist countries is a Soviet-dominated military alliance, established in 1955 in response to the entry of West Germany into US-dominated NATO (North Atlantic Treaty Organization). NATO had been formed after the Second World War in order to tie North America and Western Europe together in a military alliance against the perceived threat of world domination by the Soviet Union. The opposition of these two blocs has had a profound effect on the geopolitics of the global system in the second half of the twentieth century. However, both the Warsaw Pact and NATO have changed since the 1950s, and although their military hegemony, based largely on phenomenal nuclear overkill capacity, remains unsurpassed, other blocs have arisen to challenge them on a variety of strategic issues.

One such alternative bloc, identified by the World Bank and the rest of the world, is the oil exporters, organized through OPEC. They deserve to be listed in this context, as they often operate in unison even if they do not always do so. This idea of collective economic and political action is exactly what is meant when we speak about blocs. There are also several economic unions which operate more or less in a bloc-like manner. Prime amongst these, at the present historical juncture, is the European Community (EC), whose progress towards economic and political integration has been slow, a fact which does not dismay its competitors in world trade. A more fundamental integration is promised in 1992. Other economic unions, some short-lived and some longer-lived, in Africa, Asia and the Americas, have had a modicum of influence locally, but none can be said to have had a major influence in global terms. This is largely explained by the realization that most, if not all, of these unions begin from a position of economic and political weakness.[12]

The feeble achievements of the Non-Aligned Movement (NAM) and the Group of 77 confirm this in the political sphere. NAM originated in the Bandung Conference of 1955, where a large number of poor African and Asian countries called for a better economic deal from the rich countries of the world. The Group of 77, named for 77 underdeveloped southern countries, unaligned with either the Soviet or the US camp, came together in 1964 through their common membership of the United Nations (Sauvant, 1981). The Group, now with over 100 members, also presses for a better deal from the rich countries of the world, mainly in the north. The only common interest of these 'southern' countries is their general view that they are being more or less exploited by the rich countries of the 'north'. An expression of this was the call for a 'New International Economic Order'. This produced a torrent of words but little effective action. Such practical failures make it difficult to sustain economic solidarity, political unity or cultural-ideological sympathy.

Blocs are being seen as increasingly irrelevant today largely because the global capitalist system is perceived as increasingly salient. As the countries of the world, irrespective of bloc, appear to become more and more bound up with one another through the extension of transnational practices, some of which are directly identifiable as practices of global capitalism and some of which not, the fact of the global system becomes more and more obvious to ever more people, though the nature of the global system might still appear extremely difficult to grasp.

Conclusion

These five classifications, based on nation-state classifications of income/population, trade, resources, quality of life and blocs, serve different purposes in theory and practice. They can be used, for example, to organize the evidence for and justify morally one or other theory of development or the lack of development. As I have emphasized, it is very important to be aware of the assumptions that lie behind these classifications and the theories based on them. These theories often guide the practice of those who make and carry out the policies which have led to so little actual economic growth and development in most Third World countries.

These classifications, then, give us a wealth of empirical data, but the result is conceptual confusion and general inconclusiveness when we try to explain anything in terms of such state-centred categories. The tremendous variation in the experiences of First, Second and Third World countries in terms of income, population, foreign trade, resources, quality of life and blocs might lead the faint-hearted to conclude that the global system either does not exist or that it is so hopelessly complex that there is no point in trying to conceptualize it at all. This is precisely the limitation of state-centrist approaches and why all analyses that begin and end with nation-states have such difficulty in finding explanations of what is going on in the global system. To illustrate this point, let us return to the phenomenon that motivates so much research on the global system, namely the gap between rich and poor.

What some writers now term the 'widening gap' between the rich and the poor, both within countries and between the First and the Third Worlds, might tempt us to subscribe pessimistically to the view that the countries of the Third World are passive victims of the exercise of First World hegemon countries' power. This view is a direct consequence of the state-centrist approach, and has to be rejected on the grounds that it is theoretically mechanical and empirically false. There are underprivileged individuals and groups in the First World, as well as in the Third and Second Worlds. It is not a geographical accident of birth that determines whether an individual or group is going to be rich or poor, but a question of class location. Of course, there are relatively as well as absolutely very many more poor people in the Third World than in the First World but this is not only a question of geography but also of transnational class location.

The poor in all countries struggle against the domestic and global forces that oppress them and their resistance takes many forms. Where this involves opposition to those who run the global system in their own interests it will naturally involve transnational practices in the economic, political and cultural-ideological spheres. It is important to recognize how the global capitalist system uses the myth of the nation-state, sometimes in the form of reactionary nationalist ideologies, to deflect criticism and opposition to its hegemonic control of the global system onto the claims of competing nations. Dividing the world up into nation-states, as it is for most practical purposes for most people, is therefore a profoundly ideological strategy. It is not common sense, and the fact that for most people it is one of the fundamental taken-for-granted assumptions of daily life is a measure of the tremendous success and power of the capitalist global system project.

In contrast, ideologies not based on the nation-state tend to be more genuinely transnational in scope. These are of two types, namely those that necessarily exclude outsiders and create an in-group; and those that are inclusively internationalist, and promote the common human characteristics of all who share the planet. A powerful example of the first type is ethnic exclusivism, whose extreme form is found in the fascist idea of 'race pride'. Similarly, some religious fundamentalisms classify all non-believers (generally an ascribed rather than an achieved status) as devilish.

The second type includes the several versions of democratic socialist internationalism (as opposed to bureaucratic communist chauvinism). An integral part of this global project is its feminist goal. Therefore it is best labelled democratic feminist socialism. Its ideal of international comradeship is based on the belief that the survival of humanity is incompatible with capitalist exploitation, imperialism and the patriarchal nation-state. Many tactical and strategic differences separate those who hold these views, particularly between women and men, and between libertarians and those who attach great importance to the construction of organizations and institutions. It is certainly the case that the global capitalist project is a great deal more consistent at this point in time than any democratic feminist socialist project. It is also certainly the case that the global capitalist system has brought to hundreds of millions of people a standard of living that their parents would never have believed possible. In this sense it is a proven success, while democratic feminist socialism is, to most people in the world, an obscure jumble of aspirations. A central feature of this book is to show how global capitalism produces the material conditions for socialism, but closes down the political and cultural-ideological space for it.

In the next two chapters a theory of the global system based on economic, political, and cultural-ideological transnational practices will be introduced to explain this.

Notes

1. International relations is, of course, an increasingly complex and multifaceted discipline. The following paragraphs attempt only to draw out some sociological implications of developments in this area.
2. See also the special issue of the *International Social Science Journal* (1974, Vol. 26, no. 1), 'Challenged paradigms in international relations'. Mansbach and Vasquez (1981), amongst others, announce the end of the old paradigm and stake a claim to establish a new one.
3. In addition to the multitude of US and Euro-centred contributions to this literature, see Chan's interesting 'view from Africa' (1987); and the promising, though as yet tentative 'local–global nexus' of Alger (1988).
4. Two interesting studies that conclude against the primacy of the state, Biersteker (1980) on Nigeria, and Moaddel (1989) on Iran, both illustrate how difficult it is to escape state-centrism.
5. For further elaboration of this argument see Chapter 3, pp.72–7; and Chapter 5, *passim.*
6. Polly Hill convincingly points up the 'poor quality of official statistics' in her iconoclastic critique of development economics (Hill, 1986, ch.3), and I shall follow her contradictory example in making use of them while expressing scepticism!
7. The World Bank (1979) belatedly acknowledged.
8. Interesting contributions to the question, from entirely different perspectives, are Thomas (1975) and Goodman (1987).
9. This is a rather simplistic expression of what is a complex and somewhat controversial set of theses. For an excellent review, see Spraos (1983, ch.1–3).
10. For a thoughtful critique of the concept of resource dependence see Russett (1984). See also Barnet and Müller (1974, pp.123–7)
11. The journal *World Development*, particularly the issue of June 1979, contains several interesting articles on 'basic needs'. See also Burki and Ul Haq (1981). The essays in Norwine and Gonzalez (1988) locate these issues in a wider context.
12. As Vaitsos (1978) argues, both countries and TNCs can structure regional economic unions in their own interests.

2

Towards a theory of transnational practices

The impact of transnational practices in the global system at the level of immediate observation is plain for all to see. The tourist or business or conference traveller will more often than not travel on a plane manufactured by one of the few aerospace TNCs that dominate the civil airline industry, occupy a hotel room subcontracted to or owned or managed by the local affiliate of one of the few chains that dominate the global hotel industry, hire a car from an agency of one of the international firms that dominate the car rental industry, and will pay for all this with one of the credit cards issued by the few TNCs that control global personal finance.

Within most First, Second and Third World countries the traveller will be able to watch television programmes and films of hegemon origin, will be able to buy hegemon branded goods, at a price, and will usually be able to get around using English, the major hegemon language. The traveller is also liable to be bombarded with advertisements for global consumer goods placed by the local affiliates of the transnational advertising agencies. While the TNCs from the United States no longer dominate these sectors as they once did, they are still the leaders in a wide variety of fields and even when they are not the leaders it tends to be 'American' cultural products or local adaptations of them that are on offer.

This much is obvious at the level of perception. However, it would be simplistic to conclude that the two Mcs (McLuhan and McDonald's) have succeeded in shaping the global village in the form of a fast food outlet or that the 'real' world is in the process of being reconstructed as a universal theme park along the lines of Disneyland. The reality is much more complex than this, though we would be well advised to remember the central insight of McLuhan, that the world is becoming a global village, and of McDonald's, that global packaging creates global desires.

In the first chapter I dealt briefly with some of the major ways in which the global system has been categorized. Now is the time to look at how some theories specifically address the question of development within the global system. Lying behind my summary evaluations of these theories is the conviction that most of them are fixated around the unhelpful idea that hegemon states exploit other states. The view that is propounded here is that it is more fruitful to conceptualize the global system in terms of transnational practices. The agents and institutions of transnational practices in one country may exploit or indeed may facilitate the development of those in other countries. The state-centrist approach leads to empirical enlightenment, as I tried to show in the previous chapter, but at the expense of some theoretical confusion.

Theories of the global system

There are many classifications of theories of the global system and I claim no great privilege for the classification adopted here. It does, however, cover the main theories that have attracted a following in the twentieth century. This book is not intended as a textbook of theories, so there will be no detailed exegetical analysis of each one. My purpose here will be to give a very brief sketch of what each of the theories attempts and to direct the interested reader to a few of the many other books that do give detailed accounts and critiques of them. The theories are classified as follows:

1. Imperialist and neo-imperialist.
2. Modernization and neo-evolutionist.
3. Neo-Marxist (including various dependency theories).

4.   World system (and new international division of labour theory).
5.   Modes of production theory.

Imperialism

The theory of imperialism (or colonialism) tries to explain the structure of the modern world in terms of the struggles between the major powers to find new markets, sources of raw materials, investment opportunities, and to extend their political and cultural influence. It puts the necessity for capitalist expansion at the centre of the theory. Although Marx himself did discuss the issue of colonialism in various places, it was twentieth-century Marxists like Lenin, Rosa Luxemburg, Hilferding and Bukharin who laid the foundations for a Marxist theory of imperialism. As is often the case in the creation of new ideas, there were many scholars working along the same lines as these theorists, particularly those trying to analyze the experience of the British Empire at the end of the nineteenth century, pre-eminently the 'social-liberal' J.A. Hobson.

The Marxist theory of imperialism has been robustly challenged and robustly defended from many directions[1] and it has left its mark on most subsequent theories of the global system. It raises two questions crucial for the understanding of the modern world. First, is the theory historically true in the sense that the phenomenon of imperialism is best explained in terms of the expansion of the world capitalist system? This is still a crucial question because, with the end of direct colonial rule (political imperialism) in most of the Third World by the 1970s, the idea that imperialism was finished was widely believed. However, if imperialism is a consequence of capitalist expansionism and not simply a colonial system of government, then some form of economic neo-imperialism could persist after independence for ex-colonies (see Abel and Lewis, 1985). Second, if this is true, can capitalism develop the Third World? Bill Warren, a self-styled orthodox Marxist, took this question by the scruff of the neck in his book *Imperialism: Pioneer of Capitalism* (1980), and argued, to the consternation of a wide variety of antagonists, that the problem with the Third World is not that there is too much capitalist influence, but that there is too little. We shall return to these issues below when the neo-Marxist theories are discussed.

Modernization

Modernization theories of the global system are largely based on the distinction between the *traditional* and the *modern*. The central idea of the theory is that development revolves around the question of attitudes and values (rather than the material interests entailed in capitalist expansionism). Traditional societies are run by traditionally-minded individuals, typically those who are inward-looking, not prepared to innovate and influenced by magic and religion; while modern societies are run by modern-minded individuals, outward-looking, keen to try out new things, influenced by rational thought and practical experience. This theory is partly derived from Max Weber's attempts to relate the rise of capitalism (the epitome of modern society) with the Protestant ethic and to show how other different belief systems (like the religions of the Orient) inhibited the rise of modern society. Modernization theory, like the Weber thesis, has its strong supporters and its strong detractors. Despite recent efforts to strengthen it, modernization theory has few academic supporters today.[2] There are two main problems with the theory, now generally acknowledged. The first is that the distinction between *traditional* and *modern* is too crude to be theoretically useful, and that there may well be clear material interests behind at least some 'traditional' as well as some 'modern' attitudes and values. The second main criticism is that modernization theory tends to ignore the role that class and other interests play in the promotion or inhibition of development.

The main strength of the theory is that it directs attention to the entrepreneurial or innovative personalities who seem to be so important in the developmental process, but even here the theory does tend to ignore the inconsistencies and contradictions that are inherent in explanations based on individual characteristics. The search for a theory that will combine structural explanations in terms of societal forces and psychological explanations in terms of individual attributes is as far from success in this as in all other fields of sociological research.

The idea of neo-evolutionism is often coupled with the theory of modernization. Neo-evolutionism provides an historical context for the analysis of traditional and modern societies, in the sense that modern societies are said to evolve from traditional ones through the processes of social differentiation. For example, in so-called traditional societies the political, economic and educational functions all tend to be fulfilled by the same umbrella institution, whereas in so-called modern societies we have separate social structures and organizations to deal with politics, the economy, education and so on. Modern societies are therefore institutionally differentiated, on the analogy of biological organisms, from the relatively simple to the relatively complex. This is called neo-evolutionism, because the nineteenth-century evolutionism which tended to insist that there was a single path along which societies would evolve (usually from the primitive to the civilized states), was considered unacceptable. Neo-evolutionism rejects this uni-linear dogma, and argues that there are many possible paths from the traditional to the modern, though there is a strong supposition that the capitalist road via pluralist democracy resulting in something like the contemporary United States and Western Europe, is the best and most efficient of the alternatives.[3] In the 1950s and the 1960s, as an offshoot of the sociological functionalism of Talcott Parsons, theories of modernization and neo-evolutionism dominated the social science study of development and the global system (see Parsons, 1977). However, by the mid-1960s, with anti-imperialist wars raging in Africa, Asia and Latin America, various neo-Marxist theories were beginning to challenge the functionalist orthodoxies.

Neo-Marxist theories

Marx did not himself create a systematic theory of the global system, though his work certainly guided Lenin and others in their attempts to construct a theory of imperialism. The Leninist theory of capitalist expansionism is generally considered to be the orthodox Marxist position. But even if Lenin was correct in his analysis of the capitalist-imperialist roots of the First World War, by the 1950s and 1960s the capitalist global system and the Third World had both changed so much that many Marxists felt the need to generate new theories to explain what was happening and to show the way forward from a political point of view. This is why these theories are labelled *neo-Marxist*.

The single most influential neo-Marxist conceptual innovation for the analysis of development within the global system in general in the last few decades has been *dependency* theory, or what might be more accurately termed the dependency metatheory. The dependency metatheory, created by a group of Latin American social scientists, came to prominence in the 1960s and, despite formidable criticism since then, has obstinately refused to disappear. It is useful to distinguish three theories connected with the metatheory. These are the theories of dependent underdevelopment, dependent development and dependency reversal (see Sklair, 1988a).

The *dependentistas* argued that the global capitalist system, largely but not exclusively through transnational corporations (TNCs), operated actively to underdevelop the Third World and that no genuine development was possible as long as this system survived. While substantial general support for the dependency approach was accumulated, most scholars now acknowledge that the *dependentistas* were never able to explain satisfactorily the economic growth and social and industrial development that had clearly taken place in some Third World countries.[4] The widespread acceptance of a new nomenclature for these, the Newly Industrializing Countries (NICs), was undoubtedly an implicit recognition of the inadequacy of Frank's (1967) version of dependency theory as the development of underdevelopment, dependent underdevelopment (but see Frank, 1984). Other writers in the dependency tradition saw this, but were unwilling to discard the dependency approach entirely. Cardoso called what was plainly 'development' to pragmatists, 'associated dependent industrialization' (see Cardoso and Faletto, 1979), and in the hands of Evans (1979) this evolved into a more general theory of dependent development.

Dependency theorists, therefore, were still trying to answer the question that had troubled Marxists since the turn of the century, namely 'can capitalism develop the Third World?' Frank, and those who agreed with his theory of the development of underdevelopment, unequivocally denied that capitalism could ever develop the Third World. The best it could do would be to permit a small degree of enclave development, which only reproduced First World–Third World exploitation within the Third World. Dependent development theorists, on the other hand, acknowledged capitalist development in the Third World, particularly in the NICs, but it was development of a peculiar kind, namely dependent development. The problem is that *dependent development* seems to be possible not only in the Third World but also in underprivileged areas within the hegemonic countries of the First World. This conceptual inflation tends to reduce the effectiveness of the idea by playing into the hands of critics who maintain that the concept of dependency is unviable because it closes off the theoretical space for explaining growth and development, however limited, where it does occur. To those who argue along these lines, the idea of dependent development seems entirely *ad hoc*, dragged in to explain away phenomena that the theory seems to forbid.

One possible exit from this cul-de-sac may be the idea (it is not yet a fully articulated theory) of dependency reversal. This suggests that certain Third World countries, or institutional sectors within them, which were once in the thrall of dependency, can escape and reverse their previous disadvantage.[5] This is an interesting and, in the case of institutions rather than countries, an eminently testable idea. For example, there has been a good deal of solid research on the changing nature of the mining industries in the Third World, once entirely and now less entirely dominated by First World TNCs. Some of this research suggests that in certain cases, for example the bauxite and aluminium industry, the global disposition of power is still very much in favour of the First World TNCs, while in other cases, for example petroleum and perhaps copper, the balance of power has shifted in recent decades, and the First World TNCs have to be content with a smaller share of the revenues.[6]

One problem with dependency reversal is that it tends to take development strategies for granted while it assesses the benefits, or costs, of particular activities. The price that an institution (or a whole country) might have to pay for success in reversing a particular state of dependency might in the long run not be worth paying. For example, a Third World producer might win the battle to process a mineral or an industrial crop on site, but if this leads to a crisis in foreign currency because the machinery and the technology necessary for the task have to be imported, then it may eventually result in greater dependence. Nevertheless, if there is any sense in which capitalism can develop the Third World, and there is evidence that this is happening in some countries or in some sectors, then the theoretical elaboration of the idea of dependency reversal may be useful.

World system theory

In parallel with the dependency framework, but distanced theoretically and empirically from it by conceptual innovations and
differences of interpretation, is the 'world system' approach whose
origins can be found in the works of Immanuel Wallerstein, particularly his volumes on the modern world system (see Wallerstein,
1974). The world system theorists, who publish regularly in *Review*, the journal of the Braudel Center at the State University of
New York at Binghamton, of which Wallerstein is the intellectual
inspiration, have developed a systematic and far-reaching analysis
based on a dynamically changing division of labour between the
core, peripheral and semi-peripheral countries within the orbit of
the capitalist world system.

At least two main shortcomings of Wallerstein's work have been
critically exposed. He is accused of first, neglecting the class struggle, and second, distorting the history of capitalism and thus the
progressive role of capitalism in development (Brenner, 1977; Corbridge, 1986, ch.2). Though argument continues on all these points,
for almost twenty years this school of thought has been the most
systematic available for the analysis of the global system, and those
working within its orbit have produced an impressive volume of
theoretical and substantive research.[7] Nevertheless, there are signs
that the paradigm is approaching exhaustion.[8]

A key indication of this is that the world system approach, like
the dependency approach, is having increasing difficulty in dealing
with the development, or at least industrialization, of non-
hegemon countries. Wallerstein elaborated the concept of the
semi-periphery to describe such countries, and this idea has been
picked up by many scholars as a useful tool in analyzing the NICs
and, increasingly, those countries that are on the fringes of the
First World, but not exactly in the Third World, like Ireland, Portugal, and the Balkan states (for example, Mouzelis, 1986). Critics
of world systems theory have suggested that the idea of the semi-
periphery is an *ad hoc* invention to deal with those cases that do
not fit neatly into the core–periphery framework. This criticism is
strengthened to some extent by the observation that much creative
work in this genre in recent years has been precisely in the elaboration of dependent development in the countries of the semi-
periphery.

An implicit attempt to make connections between the dependency metatheory and world systems has been formulated on the basis of an influential conceptual innovation, the *new international division of labour* (NIDL) theory, particularly as elaborated by Fröbel *et al.* (1980). This theory draws attention to the consequences of the changes in global production strategies of the TNCs in recent decades. In common with Wallerstein and the 'world systems' theorists the proponents of the NIDL share a general conception of the capitalist world system divided into core, semi-periphery and periphery in which a division of labour has evolved to maximize the profits of transnational corporations and/ or to solve the problems of the major capitalist societies. In common with the *dependentistas* the NIDL theorists see no prospects whatsoever for any genuine Third World development in these changes in global capitalist strategies. The idea of the new international division of labour has excited a great deal of research interest (for example, the volumes edited by Nash and Fernandez Kelly, 1983; Sanderson, 1985 and Caporaso, 1987).

The theory of the new international division of labour has been criticized for its uncompromising condemnation of TNC operations in the Third World, on the grounds that there is not very much that is new about it and that it relies on an empirical base that is far too limited (see, for example, Cohen, 1987, ch.7; Jenkins, 1984; Gordon, 1988). Much of this criticism appears quite justified. Nevertheless, the activities of TNCs, wherever they are and in whatever industry, are increasingly being integrated into global processes of supply, production and marketing and the theorists of the new international division of labour have rendered great service by highlighting these phenomena even if they have done so in a rather one-sided manner. By concentrating too much on the TNCs' search for cheap labour, the NIDL fails to connect economic with political and cultural-ideological transnational practices. It is true that most foreign investment is for the domestic markets of host countries, and that the 'export processing' industries that are at the centre of the NIDL thesis account for only a small part of TNC foreign investment in the Third World but, as I have argued for the cases of Mexico and China (Sklair, 1989, forthcoming), the *symbolic* significance of export oriented development strategies is extremely important in the contemporary global system. To this extent, the neo-Marxist, world systems and NIDL theorists are in general agreement.

Modes of production theory

There are, however, many who call themselves Marxists, who appear to have rejected entirely the whole problematic of dependency. They argue that the reasons for underdevelopment in any given Third World country lie mainly within the country itself rather than in the position of the country within any particular part of the global capitalist system. More specifically, the prospects for revolution can be deduced from the *mode of production* within a particular social formation (society) and the class forces that are struggling for power. The mode of production concept has been theoretically developed by a group of French structuralists (see Taylor, 1979). So while dependency theorists argue for general delinking from the world capitalist system, some mode of production theorists argue that capitalist industrialization is the only reliable path to development and, eventually, socialist revolution in the Third World (Warren, 1980). Edwards (1985, ch.5) usefully characterizes these as 'destructive' and 'regenerating' views of capitalism, respectively. On this theory, global capitalism provides the necessary impetus for revolution in the countries where TNCs are most active. So, where neo-Marxists argue that the revolutionary forces in the Third World need not wait for Western-style capitalism in order to produce successful communist revolution, mode of production theorists maintain the orthodox Marxist thesis that communism can only come about when the organized working class, the proletariat, destroys the class power of the bourgeoisie through an anti-capitalist revolution. Marx himself even suggested that this need not necessarily be a violent revolution, but might be achieved by democratic means in advanced societies (see Kagarlitsky, 1989, pp.101–2).

Mode of production theorists may have more in common with the *dependentistas* than they seem to realize. Their arguments suggest that the lack of development in the Third World is due to obstacles, both internal and externally-imposed, to capitalist industrialization. This is really not very different from what dependency theories argue. The mode of production approach produces a type of *dependency reversal* theory in its insistence that capitalist industrialization can succeed in the Third World. In this they agree with the advocates of the TNCs who continually proclaim that they are the only reliable vehicles for development though, of course, there is a serious disagreement about the nature and likely outcome of the process. The disagreement revolves around the role of the class struggle in the Third World, and it is not only with representatives of the transnational capitalist class, but also with dependency theorists. Marxists criticize neo-Marxists for concentrating too much on questions of international exchange and terms of trade (exploitation by the First World of the Third World) and too little on questions of production and ownership (capital accumulation and class struggle). The argument begins to move from economics to politics.

The politics of development

How do dominant and subordinate classes deal with the problems of development within the global system? All these actors have *development strategies*, articulated and most actively propagated by 'modernizing elites' of one type or another (see Gereffi and Wyman, 1987; Lewis and Kallab, 1986). As the government and the ruling class and its allies are almost always the main actors in the pursuit of development strategies, much of the research in this area has been focused on the political centre.

The basic problem of any government in any society is to secure its own power, with or against 'modernizing' and 'traditional' elites, both in terms of the monopoly of force and the creation of legitimacy. While conventional theories of 'modernization' have identified TNCs as carriers of democratic values and practices to the Third World, such views have been powerfully criticized from many quarters. The theory of *bureaucratic authoritarianism* (BA) elaborated by O'Donnell (1979) is one of the strongest and most influential challenges to the idea that the TNCs have exerted a benevolent influence on economic and political development, particularly in Latin America. BA refers to the tendency of ruling classes in Third World societies to turn to authoritarian solutions in order to implement their development strategies, particularly the project of export led industrialization, which requires rather more social discipline than other strategies.

The argument suggests that the participation of the TNCs in Third World countries can only be assured when they have an 'acceptable' business climate in which to operate, and that BA regimes are more likely to provide such a climate. Therefore, whether or not TNCs actually intervene in the internal politics of countries in which they invest (sometimes they do, and sometimes they do not), their very presence is said to predispose towards BA regimes. It is of great significance that most of the NICs are presently or have been in recent times one-party states, not necessarily totalitarian in the classic sense, but certainly lacking in most of the genuinely pluralistic institutions that characterize advanced industrial societies. This has led many people to argue that, under the conditions of the global capitalist system, industrialization is only possible for developing countries where bureaucratic authoritarian regimes can organize the production process, and particularly the labour force, to satisfy the demands of the transnational corporations and the world market. However, some argue that TNCs are indifferent to democracy rather than hostile to it (see Becker, 1987). Perhaps it would be more accurate to say that the TNCs are 'indifferent' to democracy in the Third World as long as the people do not elect left wing governments!

The idea that regimes in developing countries have institutionalized specific mechanisms for dealing with TNCs, and vice versa, has been conceptualized in terms of the 'triple' or 'tripartite' alliance between the host state, the TNCs and the outward oriented elements in the indigenous bourgeoisie. The studies by Evans (1979) on Brazil, Gillespie (1984) on Egypt and Ihonvbere and Shaw (1988) on Nigeria, all focus on the ways in which transnational triple alliances operate in the developing countries. The so-called 'comprador bourgeoisie', groups that orient themselves to the interests of foreigners in general and TNCs in particular, play a central role in these analyses of the triple alliance. The idea of the triple alliance gives a concrete class structure to dependency of various types and, as I shall go on to argue, it is the economic, political, and cultural-ideological power of the triple alliance (expanded into a transnational capitalist class) that keeps any development that takes place 'dependent'.

The very idea of the 'comprador bourgeoisie,' central to the dependency approach, appears to have fallen into disuse in recent years and there have been various attempts to reconceptualize what it refers to. Sklar's (1987) *post-imperialism* theory identifies a new class, a *managerial bourgeoisie* This new class is said to have a local wing and a corporate international wing. Compradors have usually identified with the interests of the TNCs, whether they are directly employed by them or not, for both encourage the transformation of traditional patterns of consumption and behaviour in developing societies, though post-imperialism theory has yet to confront this particular issue.

This is an important part of what I intend by the *transnational capitalist class* (TCC), but with two important differences. First, the theoretical functions of the TCC and the *managerial bourgeoisie* are quite different. The managerial bourgeoisie is the key class in a post-imperialist world where the struggle between capital and labour, and probably capitalism and communism too, has become less important. This class, in the Sklar–Becker formulation, encapsulates the best interests, in a developmentalist sense, of the nation. It is engaged in a non-deadly, if not always exactly friendly, struggle for business with transnational capital abroad and a relatively consensual, if not always cooperative, project for national development at home. The concept of the TCC, on the contrary, is embedded in a theory of the capitalist global system, operating through the transnational practices of the TNCs, as they attempt to achieve a reformation of capitalist hegemony in the Third and the Second Worlds.

Second, Sklar's concept lacks a genuinely global dimension because it has no clear analysis of the cultural-ideological sphere, and in particular, it misses what I consider to be the fundamental significance of the culture-ideology of consumerism. This class, whatever we call it, cannot be properly understood and its historic role cannot be adequately explained, outside the necessity that produces the eternal contradiction of capitalist accumulation on a mass scale.

The central issue is whether or not a Third World bourgeoisie can become hegemonic in its own realm and drive towards 'real' development (as Becker asserts for Peru's 'New Bourgeoisie') or whether the only realistic option for Third World bourgeoisies, under the present system of global capitalist hegemony, is to throw their lot in with the TNCs, as Evans argues for the triple alliance in Brazil.[9] The logical extension of this argument is that some form of interdependence might be possible, where Third World actors could carve out niches for themselves in the crevices that the hegemon TNCs leave unattended. And this is precisely the conclusion that Evans reaches in his more recent work on the computer industries of Brazil and South Korea (Evans and Bastos Tigre, 1989).[10] Of course, Evans is not alone in this opinion, for it is a short step from the interdependence thesis to a full-blown 'production sharing' conception of the global system, the positive capitalistic version of international division of labour theory (discussed in Sklair, 1989, ch.1).

This is not only the case for the capitalist class, but also for the working class and other subordinate classes. Where the TNCs are active in Third World direct investment, in the form of factory production, they naturally augment (and sometimes almost create) an industrial proletariat. Very often the jobs in TNC factories are among the best paid and most highly valued in developing countries. This has led to a new lease of life for the old concept of 'labour aristocracy' and it has been attached to the workers who have these jobs, in comparison with the workers in the informal or the indigenous sectors (see Lloyd, 1982; Boyd *et al.*, 1987).

Particular attention has recently been paid to the position of women in TNC factories (Lim, 1985; Elson and Pearson, 1989), and this will be examined in Chapter 4. In addition, many other categories of workers in the formal and informal sectors in all three worlds have been progressively drawn in to the global capitalist system by the simple expedient of severely restricting and in more and more cases absolutely destroying their prospects for self-sufficiency in the provision of food, shelter and other 'necessities' of life. While barter-based natural economies can coexist with monetized market economies, the latter relentlessly marginalize the former. In this process the TNCs have played a key role, particularly in the privatization of consumption.

These theories of development and their implicit or explicit approaches to the analysis of the global system all remain quite controversial, each with its own adherents and detractors, and each guiding substantive research in a variety of problem areas. The inability of critics to kill off previous theories entirely, and of theories to defend themselves against their critics to the satisfaction of all concerned, have led several writers to conclude that development theory is in crisis (see Booth, 1985; Mouzelis, 1988; Sklair, 1988a). The way out of the crisis, in my view, is to refocus our attention away from state-centrist ideas of First World countries exploiting Third World countries, to the analysis of the global system. In order to do this it is necessary to show how transnational practices have been monopolized by key institutions in the capitalist global system. This entails a conception of the economic, the political and the cultural-ideological spheres.

Economy, polity, culture-ideology

The bearers of transnational practices within the global system stand in determinate relationships to all other categories of actors. Groups may be included or excluded from participation in the system. One of the most important historic tasks of transnational capitalism has been to include various previously excluded groups within its realm of influence. This inclusion is, however, partial and it is not the same within the economic, the political and the cultural-ideological spheres.

In the economic sphere, the global capitalist system offers a more or less circumscribed place to the wage-earning majorities in most countries. The workers, the direct producers of goods and services, have occupational choices that are generally free within the range offered by national capitalisms, but they do change over time and place. For example, the reduction in manufacturing jobs over the last decades in some high wage countries has forced workers to seek jobs in other less well paid and less secure sectors or, as has happened particularly in the United States and the United Kingdom, forced older workers displaced from traditional industries (like mining and steel-making) into permanent unemployment. The other side of the coin is that some of the manufacturing jobs lost in high wage countries have turned up in low wage countries. This has, undoubtedly, over the last few decades, brought many rural people in the Third World into the towns and cities, whether forced off their lands by hunger or predatory landlords, or as willing migrants in search of a better life. As Brydon and Chant show (1989, ch.5), there is an important gender dimension to this.

Transnational migration, by no means a novel phenomenon, is also a prominent feature of many communities. In the twentieth century, large numbers of people have migrated from poor countries to richer countries in search of work, from Europe to the Americas, from black to white-ruled Southern Africa, from Mexico and Central America and the Caribbean to North America, from the Caribbean and the Indian subcontinent to Britain and from southern to northern Europe. The rapid increase in such migration since the 1950s has prompted one commentator to speak of the 'New Helots' (Cohen, 1987).

The inclusion of the subordinate classes in the political sphere is very partial. To put it crudely, the global capitalist system has very little need of the subordinate classes in this sphere. In the parliamentary democracies the parties must be able to mobilize the masses to vote every so often, but very few countries make voting compulsory. In most parliamentary democracies voter turnout tends to be around half to three-quarters of the electorate. While political organization is usually unfettered, the structural obstacles to genuine opposition to the capitalist system are such that there are rarely any serious challenges to it. Where serious challenges do emerge, for example in the case of the election of the socialist, Salvador Allende, as president of Chile in 1970, the threat is removed by violent overthrow of the constitutional power by the capitalist class through the army and the police, with the support of other key sectors of the establishment. In the Chilean case, as is well known, this was done with the active collaboration of the US government and TNCs.[11] In one-party states, spontaneous political participation by the masses is actively discouraged and realistic threats to the prevailing order tend to be focused on changing the people at the top, *coup d'etat*, rather than on changing the conditions under which global capitalism operates.

The cultural-ideological sphere is, however, entirely different. Here, the aim of the global capitalist system is total inclusion of all classes, and especially the subordinate classes in so far as the bourgeoisie can be considered already included. The cultural-ideological project of global capitalism is to persuade people to consume above their own perceived needs in order to perpetuate the accumulation of capital for private profit, in other words, to ensure that the global capitalist system goes on for ever. The culture-ideology of consumerism proclaims, literally, that the meaning of life is to be found in the things that we possess. To consume, therefore, is to be fully alive, and to remain fully alive we must continuously consume. The notions of men and women as economic beings, or political beings, are discarded by global capitalism, quite logically, as the system does not even pretend to satisfy everyone in the economic or the political spheres. Men and women are consumers. The point of economic activity for 'ordinary members' of the system is simply to provide the resources to be consumers, and the point of political activity is to ensure, usually through inactivity, that the conditions for consuming are maintained. This system has been evolving for centuries, first for bourgeoisies all over the world, then spreading to the working classes in the First World, and slowly but surely penetrating to all those with disposable income everywhere.

This is why I have persisted in using the label *cultural-ideological*, risking the sin of inelegance for the possibility of clarity. Culture *always* has an ideological function for consumerism in the capitalist global system, so all cultural transnational practices in this sphere are at the same time ideological practices, thus cultural-ideological. This is not an empirical assertion, for if it was it would no doubt sometimes be false and usually impossible to prove one way or the other. The idea of cultural-ideological transnational practices and, in particular the idea of the culture-ideology of consumerism in the global system, are conceptual tools in the theory of the global system. Global capitalism does not permit cultural neutrality. Those cultural practices that cannot be incorporated into the culture-ideology of consumerism become oppositional counter-hegemonic forces, to be harnessed or marginalized, and if that fails, destroyed physically. Ordinary so-called 'counter-cultures' are regularly incorporated and commercialized and pose no threat, indeed through the process of differentiation (illusory variety and choice), are a source of great strength to the global capitalist system. For example, the celebrations of the twentieth anniversary of the revolts of 1968 became a media event in Europe, less so in the Americas, and were relentlessly commercially exploited, with the willing and presumably lucrative participation of many of those who had then been (and still are) dedicated to the overthrow of the capitalist system. Consumerist appropriations of the bicentennial of the French Revolution are another interesting example. We shall have to wait for the year 2017 to see what the culture-ideology of consumerism makes of the Bolshevik revolution!

The culture-ideology of consumerism is, as it were, the fuel that powers the motor of global capitalism. The driver is the transnational capitalist class. But the vehicle itself is the mighty transnational corporation.

History and theory of the transnational corporation (TNC)

As D.K. Fieldhouse (1986) remarks in his critique of the concept, the term *multinational corporation* was first coined by David Lilienthal, the head of the great US public utility the Tennessee Valley Authority, in 1960, long after its reality had made itself felt. Notwithstanding its apparent novelty, the multinational (or, here-after, transnational) corporation dates back to at least 1867. Until the 1940s it was predominantly a European phenomenon, and 'is neither homogeneous in function nor consistent in character' (Fieldhouse, 1986, p.24).

Despite Fieldhouse's erudite attempt to consign the concept to the dustbin of history, most observers agree that it is both suffi-ciently homogeneous in function and consistent in character to be useful. While TNCs are certainly to be found in a wide variety of economic sectors they share the same basic function of capital accumulation on a global scale, and the same consistent character of having to work out global strategies to ensure their continued growth. However, Fieldhouse does have a point. TNCs are not all of a piece. Take the question of size.

In the mid-1970s, only eight oil companies shared 30 per cent of the market, seven copper companies shared 25 per cent, six baux-ite companies shared 58 per cent, seven iron ore companies shared 50 per cent, and a few tea, coffee, banana and tobacco companies shared 60 per cent or more of their markets (see Dunning, 1981, ch.1). This left thousands of other, smaller TNCs scrambling for tiny market shares in most branches of production. Thus, the first major distinction to be made is between the major TNCs, the *Fortune* 500 type of corporations and the rest[12]. The rest is, of course, made up of many different types of TNCs. For example, a relatively small company in terms of employees, sales or assets, may still hold a dominant place in the global distribution of a crucial commodity, usually by virtue of its technological superi-ority over its competitors.

Research on the TNCs

Research on the transnational corporations relies on no single methodology but borrows from comparative and cross-cultural research, for which there are long and varying traditions in the social sciences. Concretely, the main types of inquiry can be categorized as follows:

Conceptual studies

This includes works where the substantive and theoretical consequences of the internationalization or globalization of capital rather than a particular industry or country are the focus. Though their interpretations differ widely, the theories of scholars like Hymer (1979) and Vernon (1971) (both conveniently excerpted along with other important contributions in Modelski, 1979), Barnet and Müller (1974), Bornschier and Chase-Dunn (1985), Moran (1985) and Dunning (1981), agree on the centrality of the TNC in the analysis of the global system. By explicitly identifying categories of corporations like the *Fortune* 500, they also convey the impression that a qualitatively new force is at work in the global system.

Sectoral case studies

In these studies TNCs in specific industries are investigated globally. Sectors are often split into manufacturing, service and natural resource based industries. Within these broad categories further subdivisions are common. Examples include Gereffi (1983) on pharmaceuticals and Henderson (1989) on electronics; Gorostiaga (1984) on financial TNCs, Anderson (1984) on transnational advertising agencies and Price and Blair (1989) on the service sector in general; Tullis and Hollist (1986) on food and Nwoke (1987) on minerals.

Country and/or regional case studies

The focus here is on the impact of the TNCs as a whole on one country or region. There are now few areas in the world where the impact of the TNCs has not been researched by someone and good examples of this type of study are Kowaleski (1982) on the Caribbean, Onimode *et al.* (1983) on Nigeria, Wang (1984) on China and Jenkins (1984) and Newfarmer (1985) on Latin America.

Gender-based studies

The spread of the TNCs has brought significant changes to the sexual division of labour in both the First and the Third World. Several industries in which TNCs are active, like electronics and apparel, employ many more women than men, whether they are located in poor or rich countries. Good examples of such studies are Nash and Fernandez-Kelly (1983), Lim (1985) and Elson and Pearson (1989).

Promotional literature

Global business publications are full of material whose main aim is to further the interests of the TNCs. Much of it is clearly apologist, particularly that produced directly by TNCs or by public relations firms on their behalf (for which see the analysis of Stauffer, 1979). However, some is based on serious research, like Micou (1985) on TNCs in the Third World, and Mertz (1984). There are also many volumes in which academics join forces with TNC executives to state 'the case for the multinationals' (see Madden, 1977).

TNCs and foreign direct investment

The history of the TNC is, of course, bound up with the history of foreign direct investment (FDI). Although FDI had been substantial from the beginning of the twentieth century, it really took off in the 1950s, as a result of the flow of funds from the United States into Europe after the Second World War. US firms already had considerable sums invested in European subsidiaries between the two wars, and post-1945 FDI served both to rebuild what had been destroyed and to extend it. A political motive was clearly bound up with this economic activity. US foreign policy was based on the necessity of stopping the worldwide advance of communism in Europe and elsewhere through the economic development of areas under 'threat'. US firms did not meekly follow the foreign policy line of their government against their own interests. There were large profits to be made from investing in a whole host of European industries.

In the 1950s and the 1960s many US firms grew so large so fast that Europeans began to speak of the 'American takeover' of their economies. The widely read and influential book of the French politician and columnist, Servan-Schreiber, translated as *The American Challenge* (1968), summed up these fears about the loss of economic independence, and recommended that European industry and commerce should learn from the methods of the Americans and try to beat them at their own game.

American economic activity in the international arena (or American economic imperialism, as it was increasingly being labelled) began to be identified as a problem in urgent need of resolution, and to be conceptualised in terms of the multinational or transnational corporation. In the 1970s, almost all the major international agencies in the economic and trade fields produced recommendations on how to regulate the activities of the TNCs, in the recognition that even more than the rich countries in which the bulk of FDI was located, the poorer countries needed protection (see Tharp, 1976; Grosse, 1982). Transnational corporation investments might appear minor relative to the total GNP of most countries, but they were extremely important in the context of particular branches of the economies of poor and some richer but small countries. The UN Department of Economic and Social Affairs took a special interest in these issues and a series of intensively-researched reports in the 1970s led to the creation of a Commission on Transnational Corporations and a research centre. This eventually became institutionalized as the UN Centre on Transnational Corporations, which now has the difficult task of trying to reconcile the interests of the TNCs and the communities eager for their investments (see Caplan, 1989).

Activity at the quasi-governmental level, like the UN and OECD, has been more than paralleled by a plethora of unofficial pressure groups that monitor the activities of the TNCs, wherever they may be. The Transnationals Information Exchange (TIE), for one, is a particularly active global network which has developed counter-strategies to combat the overwhelming resources that the TNCs can muster when they are attacked. These strategies are based on research to identify the interests behind the target companies 'to such an extent that their image, reputation and credibility are jeopardized by continued support of corporate denial of justice' (TIE, 1985, p.33). Some of the campaigns in which TIE has been involved have lasted many years, for example the Nestlé Infant Formula boycott (to be discussed in detail in Chapter 5), the campaign to force corporations to divest in South Africa, the struggles on behalf of Coca Cola workers in Guatemala and Control Data workers in Korea, as well as several campaigns against TNC policies in the United States.

Church and consumer groups, mostly in North America and Europe, campaign frequently against perceived abuses of TNC power. CIE, the US-based Interfaith Center on Corporate Responsibility, and the International Organization of Consumer Unions, have all collaborated on many projects, and there are literally hundreds, perhaps thousands of transnational networks now monitoring the TNCs all over the world. Many of these organizations have regular newsletters, for example the Interfaith Center has *The Corporate Examiner* and the flood of environmentalist and consumer-advice literature that began in the 1980s often contains material critical of the TNCs.

The TNCs' own views can be found in a variety of sources, for example in their 'public interest' advocacy advertising in the world's mass media (see Sethi, 1977), and in countless US-government sponsored settings (for example, US Congress 1973). The contest between the TNCs and their critics is, however, very unequal. For the United States, Mander (1978, pp.19–20) notes, in all seriousness: 'During the early 1970s, all environmental groups together spent about $500,000 per year in advertising in order to offset an average of about $3 billion in corporate expenditures on the same subjects. This ratio was relatively small, only 6,000 to 1, which may help explain the early success of the environmental movement.'[13]

These struggles pit the small people against the might of the transnational corporations, some of whom are richer than most countries. Nevertheless, even the poorest or smallest countries can, theoretically at least, frustrate the expansion plans of any one of these TNC giants by the simple, if often costly, expedients of refusing permission to trade or manufacture within that country's territory or by nationalizing (expropriating) the property of a TNC already in business there. There is a large amount of literature on this question.[14]

TNCs and Third World governments

The experience of expropriating countries, especially in the Third World, is very mixed. While there do seem to be systematic differences between extractive industries like petroleum and metal ore mining, and manufacturing industries like consumer goods, the general conclusion is that where the TNCs are patient and persistent they usually at least recover the value of their seized assets. Either they have a sufficient leverage over processing and marketing, for example in the extractive industries, as shown in Moran's book (1974) on the copper industry in Chile, or they have sufficient control over intra-firm transfers, particularly transfer pricing.[15] As Sigmund (1980) demonstrates for Latin America, when compensation is finally paid, it often overstates the value of the assets. Here the foreign and the domestic elements of the transnational capitalist class are clearly seen working through the agency of the home-country state in defence of their interests. The most thoroughly studied case is 'indigenization' in Nigeria, and I shall discuss this in detail in Chapter 4.

Most of this research, as is immediately obvious, is posed within the logic of state-centrism. There have, however, been some attempts to go beyond this and to develop conceptions of TNCs not as representatives of the power of the state, as tends to happen within state-centrist analyses, but as independent of and even, on occasion, opponents of the state. While all TNCs are domiciled, for legal purposes if no other, in particular countries, many people have argued that some TNCs are actually more powerful than most nation-states. Such notions as Barnet and Müller's (1974) 'global reach' of the TNCs, and Vernon's (1971) 'sovereignty at bay' thesis reflecting the increasingly powerful positions of TNCs in their dealings with governments, though emanating from totally different perspectives, illustrate just how widespread such ideas were (and still are).

In some respects these ideas are clearly quite realistic. Many of the largest TNCs have assets and annual sales far in excess of the GNP of about half of the countries of the world. In 1986, according to the World Bank, 64 out of 120 countries had a GDP (gross domestic product) of less than $10 billion. United Nations data for 1985–6 show that 68 TNCs in mining and manufacturing had annual sales in excess of ten billion dollars, while all the top 50 banks, the top 20 securities firms, and all but one of the top 30 insurance companies had net assets in excess of ten billion. The McDonald's fast food corporation (total sales of $12.4 billion), Japanese and West German Railways (total revenues $16 and $12.5 billion, though both actually lost money in that year), and 12 retailing and supermarket chains (sales ranging from the US-based Sears Roebuck's $44 billion to the Japanese Daiei chain's $10 billion) were also members of what could be called the '10 billion dollar club' (see UNCTC, 1988, annex tables).

The dependency perspective focused attention on this unequal relationship between, on the one hand, mighty TNCs and the powerful home countries that looked after their interests all over the globe and, on the other, the relatively weak and powerless Third World countries in which they were involved. Norman Girvan's (1976) study of mining TNCs in the Caribbean evocatively labels this relationship 'Corporate Imperialism'. However, many have argued that the dependency perspective failed to explain how the practices of the TNCs and those who act as their agents in the Third World actually operated to produce underdevelopment, particularly where something like the kinds of development that are taken for granted in the First World have occurred regionally or in particular industries in some Third World countries.

The principal methodological difficulty of the attempt to specify the developmental effects of TNCs in the global system is to isolate their effects and differentiate them from the general effects of the processes of 'modernization' (a concept abandoned by most researchers but which lives on regardless). The complexity of this issue lies in the fact that the TNCs are themselves directly and explicitly responsible for the ways in which such processes work out in most societies, but they are also often indirectly and implicitly responsible in ways that are hidden from view. Modern techniques of communication have intensified the demonstration effect whereby the practices and beliefs of one society are introduced to other societies and have increased the speed with which consumption patterns common to one socio-cultural grouping spread to all corners of the world. Few will wonder why the products and lifestyles of the industrialized world seem desirable and relatively accessible to many in the developing countries. However, the extent to which this is due to the deliberate efforts of TNCs to sell their products and services is often difficult to determine. It is for this reason that it may be useful to begin to analyze these processes, not with the nation-state or with the transnational corporation, but with the idea of transnational practices.

Notes

1. See Owen and Sutcliffe (1972), with a useful annotated bibliography; and the more recent survey by Brewer (1980).
2. This is a very bare summary. For a comprehensive, balanced and very clear account of modernization theory and its main critics, see the textbook by Harrison (1988).
3. The best single source for these views is the book of readings edited by Eisenstadt (1970). Harrison (1988) updates the references, but the central issues are the same.
4. Corbridge (1986) is an excellent guide to this literature. Frank (1984) has a large bibliography, for and against.
5. See the various and eclectic contributions to the volume edited by Doran *et al.* (1983).
6. See, in general, *United Nations Secretariat* (1984); Mikesell and Whitney (1987). I look in more detail at the bauxite-aluminium industry in Chapter 4. My own research attempts to establish criteria for evaluating positive and negative developmental effects of TNC manufacturing investment in the Third World.
7. In addition to Wallerstein's own works, see Bergesen (1980), Chase-Dunn (1989) and, of course, *Review*.
8. See Bergesen's (1982) attempt to introduce 'globology' and 'world class relations' as props for world systems theory. The whole issue of *International Social Science Journal*, vol. 34, no. 1 (1982), 'Images of World Society' is interesting in this respect.
9. For some illuminating discussions of similar questions in the context of African bourgeoisies see Lubeck (1987); and for South East Asia, see Higgott and Robison (1985). I shall return to this issue in Chapter 4.
10. The centrality of the electronics and computer industries makes them particularly important for questions of Third World development. See, for example, Henderson (1989); and Negandhi and Palia (in Kaynak and Lee, 1989).
11. Exhaustively documented by Kaufman (1988, pp.4-37) under the euphemistic heading 'Direct constraints of official and non-official U.S. origin'. See also, US Senate (in Modelski, 1979, ch. 14).
12. The US business magazine, *Fortune*, publishes annual lists of the biggest corporations in the United States and around the world, ranked on a variety of indicators. Other sources do the same, but the label of a '*Fortune* 500 company' has stuck.

13. Mander (1978) argues for the total elimination of television, and contains much material that is of relevance for my critique of the culture-ideology of consumerism.
14. Sigmund (1980) analyzes nationalizations in Latin America, while Kobrin (1980) and Jodice (1980) evaluate theories of expropriation and test different views on a large sample of expropriations in several industries. For the more general issue of physical attacks on TNCs, see Gladwin and Walter (1980).
15. For argument and data on this question see Long (1981) and Murray (1981).

3

Corporations, classes and consumerism

The conceptual space for transnational practices (TNP)

The concept of transnational practices refers to the effects of what people do when they are acting within specific institutional contexts. It focuses attention on observable phenomena, some of which may even be measurable, instead of highly abstract and often very vague relations between conceptual entities. It is not only *impossible* to theorize fruitfully on the basis of abstract relations which are nothing but abstract relations, but it is *only possible* to theorize fruitfully on the basis of abstract relations that refer directly to observable phenomena in material reality. Transnational practices are, of course, abstract concepts, but they refer directly to the practices of agents and derive meaning from the institutional settings in which they occur, and because of which they have determinate effects. TNPs do not, themselves, constitute a theory. They do, however, provide a conceptual framework within which a theory may be constructed. At this point, I shall briefly sketch out the theory of the global system based on the three spheres, the economic, political and cultural-ideological transnational practices.

The global system is most fruitfully conceptualized as a system that operates at three levels, knowledge about which can be organized in three spheres, namely the economic, the political and the cultural-ideological. Each sphere is typically characterized by a representative institution, cohesive structures of practices, organized and patterned, which can only be properly understood in terms of their transnational effects. The global system, at the end of the twentieth century, is not synonymous with the global capitalist system, but the driving forces behind global capitalism are the dominant though not the only driving forces behind the global system. Thus, the primary agent and institutional focus of economic transnational practices is the transnational corporation.

However, there are others. The World Bank, the IMF, commodity exchanges and so on are mostly driven by the interests of the TNCs. The underlying goal of keeping global capitalism on course is in constant tension with the selfish and destabilizing actions of those who cannot resist system-threatening opportunities to get rich quick or to cut their losses. It is, however, the direct producers, not the capitalist class who usually suffer most when this occurs as, for example, the tin miners of Bolivia and the rest of the world found out when the London Metal Exchange terminated its tin contract in 1985 (Crabtree, 1987).

The primary agents of the political and cultural-ideological TNPs may be somewhat more contentious. The theory of the global system being developed in this book proposes that the primary agent in the political sphere is a still-evolving *transnational capitalist class*. The institutions of the *culture-ideology of consumerism*, as expressed through the transnational mass media, are the primary agents in the cultural-ideological sphere.

It may be helpful to explain this in terms of what each of these three primary agents typically produces, the results of its practices. TNCs produce commodities and the services necessary to manufacture and sell them. The transnational capitalist class produces the political environment within which the products of one country can be successfully marketed in another. The culture-ideology of consumerism produces the values and attitudes that create and sustain the need for the products. These are analytical rather than empirical distinctions. In the real world they are inextricably mixed. TNCs get involved in host country politics, and the culture-ideology of consumerism is largely promulgated through the transnational corporations involved in mass media and advertising. Members of the transnational capitalist class often work directly for TNCs, and their life styles are a major exemplar for the spread of consumerism. Nevertheless, it is useful to make these analytical distinctions, particularly where the apparent and real empirical contradictions threaten to swamp the theory.

This theory of the global system, then, revolves around the perceived necessity for global capitalism to continually increase production and international trade, to guarantee the political conditions for this to occur uninterruptedly all over the world, and to create in people the need to want to consume all the products that are available, on a permanent basis. There are, of course, other forces at work in the global system, and in some respects global capitalism has had to come to terms with these, particularly when they become opposing forces. This can be illustrated by looking more closely at the economic, political and cultural-ideological spheres.

Economic transnational practices

Economic transnational practices are economic practices that transcend national boundaries. These may be entirely contained within the borders of a single country even though their effects are transnational. For example, there may within one country be a consumer demand for a product which is unavailable from domestic supply. The retailer places an order with a supplier who fills the order from a foreign source. Neither the retailer nor the consumer needs to know or care where the product comes from, though some countries now have 'country of origin' rules making mandatory the display of this information. There may be a parallel situation in the supplier country. Local producers may simply sell their products to a domestic marketing board or wholesaler and neither know nor care who the final consumers will be. The transnational corporation enters the scene when sellers, intermediaries and buyers are parts of the same global organization.

One important consequence of the expansion of the capitalist world economy has been that individual economic actors (like workers and entrepreneurs) and collective economic actors (like trade unions and TNCs) have become much more conscious of the transnationality of their practices and have striven to extend their global influence. Over recent years imports and exports have been vested with great political and cultural-ideological significance, and it is very likely that increasing numbers of consumers now register the country of origin of what they are buying, and producers now register the destination of what they are producing, and this knowledge may affect their actions. The volume of economic transnational practices has increased phenomenally since the 1950s, as evidenced by the tremendous growth of foreign trade,[1] and this means that even some quite poor people in some poor countries can now distinguish many consumer goods in terms of their origins and the status-conferring advantages that some origins have over others.

Jobs

The most obvious and tangible effect of economic TNPs is the creation of jobs when a foreign corporation opens a factory or an office abroad. These jobs are usually seen as benefits, certainly by the workers who flock to take them up, and by the governments that have established incentive programmes to attract them in the first place. In addition to jobs, the measurable benefits of economic TNPs include the exports due to foreign firms, and the backward linkages that they set up in the host economy, that is the locally produced goods and services they purchase, either from existing firms or from firms established primarily to supply the TNCs. Backward linkages also create jobs.

But all these jobs have costs. In the first place, governments all over the world offer fiscal incentives to attract foreign firms to open factories. For example, in 1958 the Irish Republic decreed that profits from exports by Shannon Industrial Estate companies would be exempt from tax for 25 years, and profit tax remission for firms outside Shannon was to be 100 per cent for a period of 10 years. This was extended subsequently several times (Sklair, 1988b). This is quite common in Second and Third World countries too. Further costs are the bureaucracies set up to woo and service foreign manufacturers; and the imported goods that the foreign firms use in the production process.

It is difficult to know whether FDI would take place without incentives and to work out the actual cost to the people of the tax remissions and infrastructural investments made by the host governments of the countries where TNCs enjoy these privileges. The relentless drive to attract more and more foreign investment (high tech by preference, but practically any would do) that characterized the 1980s continues and there are now very few countries anywhere in the world that do not have some incentives to attract FDI. This is a measure of the potency of economic transnational practices in the global system.

A seemingly simple and straightforward phenomenon like a TNC opening a factory or an office 'offshore' (in a foreign country) has very wide ramifications. It is clearly a central economic transnational practice.[2] Let us pursue this further.

Much of the expansion in manufacturing employment in the global system since the 1950s has come from relatively few industries, such as automobiles, electronics, textiles, household goods, and toys. In some countries which have tried to promote export led industrialization, the most dynamic parts of their economies have tended to be those with heavy foreign involvement. Cases of this can be found in southern Europe, Latin America and in Asia. But the growth of new industry jobs in many countries has hardly kept pace with the loss of jobs in traditional indigenous industries, and TNCs have directly caused the loss of at least some of these indigenous jobs by forcing domestic competitors out of business. For example, foreign electronics firms have pre-empted the creation of a domestically-owned electronics industry in all but a few countries. However, a domestic, if not entirely domestically-controlled, electronics industry can survive as a result of the stimulus given by foreign firms, as Grieco (1984) illustrates in the case of India's struggle with IBM.

There are two issues to be considered: first, the desirability of incentives for foreign firms, and second, which incentives are most liable to be effective. While it might seem simple common sense to argue that, for example, tax relief on profits must be an important factor in the decision of a manufacturer to produce offshore, this is not always relevant. For most foreign investors involved in export processing in low wage locations, foreign plants are cost centres, rather than profit centres. Where profits are declared, tax relief tends to represent an extra bonus rather than a necessary incentive to foreign investors.

Host countries are interested not only in how many jobs are created for how long at what cost, but also what kinds of jobs are created. One of the main criticisms levelled at US and

European transnational corporations in Asia, Africa and Latin America is that their operations are predominantly of the export processing variety, employing low wage workers (mainly 'nimble-fingered' young women) in monotonous and often physically debilitating labour, the products of which constitute a small proportion of the value-added of the final commodity. In such enterprises top managers and technicians tend to be expatriates and little if any advanced training is offered to the local workers. In the extreme cases, this type of foreign investment will not upgrade the host economy in any meaningful sense. This is not the case in all countries, however, and the composition of the labour force in a particular export-oriented industry or zone may change over time. As most of these zones are in Third World countries, these issues will be taken up in the next chapter.

The size and character of the domestic market and the types of foreign companies that investment agencies set out to attract, bear heavily on the nature and effects of economic TNPs. Foreign-owned industry tends to outperform domestically-owned industry in exporting in most Third World and indeed in some sectors in First World countries. However, many exporters import the materials and components used in their exported goods rather than buy them locally. This reduces the magnitude of local value added, a key measure of the benefit of foreign investment. What the TNCs spend locally can be broken down into three components, namely wages and salaries, utility and service costs, and material linkages.

Jobs created by FDI in the Second and Third Worlds have added significance to those created in the First World. One difference is in the nature of the foreign currency involved. Few countries outside the First World have transferable currencies. The hard currencies of the First World, especially US dollars, Japanese yen, and the major European currencies, can be used freely in international trade, while the soft currencies of the rest of the world's countries are generally not acceptable for the settlement of international accounts. If a soft-currency country wants to import something it must earn or borrow one of the hard currencies to pay for it. Usually, the hard currency exchanged by foreign investors to pay wages, salaries and utility and other costs, has a significance in Second and Third World countries that it does not have in First World countries.

Linkages

The purchase of materials and components, *backward linkages*, is usually in foreign currency, but linkages also have a more general industrial significance in all three Worlds alike. Linkages may be either backward, when the purchasing firm, which need be neither foreign nor an exporter, buys what it needs locally, or forward, when the seller firm supplies a local firm with what it needs to produce something else. The ideal state of affairs from the point of view of host countries is where foreign firms actually stimulate the creation and growth of the suppliers of their needs, particularly those materials and components that have a high value-added quality, within the local economy, and where the output of these foreign firms goes into the local economy for further processing. These are what Hirschman calls 'input-provision, derived demand, or backward linkage effects' and 'output-utilization or forward linkage effects' (Hirschman, 1958, ch.6). These linkages constitute the first criterion of what I have labelled a 'successful development effect' (Sklair, 1989, ch.9).[3]

This is one of the key issues involved in the transformation of economic growth into general development. Suffice it to say, at this point, that even in the midwest region of Ireland, widely regarded as the most successful free zone in the world, whose agencies have an unsurpassed international reputation, the impact on the Irish economy of the foreign-owned sector in terms of linkages is uninspiring. Repeated official and unofficial enquiries have suggested that the foreign exporting sector buys very little that is of Irish manufacture, and even when it does buy locally it tends to buy low value-added goods, like packaging materials and industrial consumables. As my own research shows, local purchases in the export-oriented zones in Egypt, Mexico and China are very much less than in Ireland, perhaps in the region of 1 or 2 per cent (Sklair, 1988c, 1989, pp.197–202, forthcoming).

It is important to look behind the aggregate figures of local sourcing to try to identify where linkage effects could realistically be expected to result from the transnational practices of established and potential TNCs, and what the host authorities could realistically hope to do about it in terms of their transnational practices. In Ireland, three separate initiatives were established in the midwest region to tackle this problem. The Shannon Development Company had a 'Matchmaker' service to match up the capacities of local suppliers with the needs of industrial purchasers, the Irish Development Authority 'Project Identification Unit' supplied local firms with information on the purchasing requirements of the multinationals, and the Irish Goods Council did the same thing. These activities are mirrored in many countries all over the world where TNCs are seen as potential purchasers of local goods.

The effort to create backward linkages reveals some important economic transnational practices. The logic of transnational production either forbids, permits, or encourages backward linkages. Where a product is entirely integrated within the TNC or its captive suppliers' networks, or where the intermediate components or materials used are of such a specialized nature that there are simply no available suppliers outside the existing TNC network, then backward linkages are literally *forbidden* by the logic of global production.

For TNCs involved in more traditional and non-state-of-the-art product lines, where materials and components are more readily available, on the surface at least, the logic of TNC production appears to *permit* backward linkages. This is seen, correctly, as potentially very rewarding for the domestic industry, and in some First World non-hegemon countries and in the NICs the supply of materials and components, for example to the automobile TNCs, has certainly been economically rewarding. In most Second and Third World countries this has not generally happened. The reasons are that local production is not of the quality required by the world market, prices are too high and delivery is unreliable.

No one familiar with the performance of domestic industry in most countries outside and some inside the First World would be surprised by this but, even so, one might wonder why the figures for local sourcing are quite so low when local materials and components are available. The logic of global production is again operating, but through transfer pricing and the use of captive suppliers. By the very nature of the case, the demands of commercial secrecy, this is difficult to research. Only when Second and Third World factories actually begin to produce what TNCs need at competitive price, quality and delivery, will host country governments be in a position to challenge the TNCs on linkages. Where this has already happened, particularly in the case of automobile parts, it tends to be connected with local content requirements. TNCs tend to get round this by buying up or establishing their own local suppliers (see Bennett and Sharp, 1985). However, in such cases, TNCs can occasionally be seen actually to *encourage* backward linkages.

The job creation and job destruction effects of TNCs have very wide ramifications and they are sociologically the most important economic transnational practices. This will be illustrated further in the next chapter, with particular reference to the developmental effects of TNC practices, and the sexual division of labour they have created.

Political transnational practices

In a paper entitled 'Transnationalism and the New Tribe', James Field Jr describes the historical occurrence of what he labels 'transnational individuals' and the growth of the tendency towards 'purposeful transnational philanthropy' in the United States (Field, 1973, pp.11–12). In Field's view, by the late nineteenth century the organizational revolution had transformed transnationalism from an individual to a company affair, and two levels of culture emerged, global and local, with a New Tribe of those imbued with transnational global culture. This is a good first approximation of the concept of the *transnational capitalist class* that I want to develop.

What is missing from Field's account is the connection between political transnational practices and the global capitalist system. The reason for this is that Field's New Tribe is imbued with the rather vague mission of transmitting 'Western techniques' to traditional societies and although this opens the door to many fascinating details about the structures of culture contact, it is at a rather high level of generality for explanatory purposes and it seriously underplays the role of the classes responsible for capitalist expansionism.

Nevertheless, there is a considerable degree of interest in transnational political practice at this level. The *Yearbook of International Organizations* (Union of International Associations, 1988–9) lists thousands of bodies classified as: federations of international organizations, universal membership organizations, inter-continental membership organizations, regionally defined membership organizations, organizations emanating from places, persons and other bodies, and organizations having a special form, including foundations and funds. The subject guide traverses the spectrum from 'abattoir' to 'zymurgy' (the art of fermentation); a sample page from the universal membership organizations section details the International Association of Legal Science, World Alliance of Reformed Churches, Association of Geoscientists for International Development and Amnesty International.

Most of these are what Willetts (1982) labels 'Pressure Groups as Transnational Actors'. Willetts identifies two main categories, namely *sectional* groups (including TNCs, trade unions, professional associations and recreational clubs), and *promotional* groups (welfare agencies, religious organizations, communal groups, political parties and specific-issue groups). Any such classification is bound to be somewhat arbitrary and, as Willett acknowledges, many groups can be placed in more than one category. Research emphasis is usually on the relationships between governments and non-governmental organizations (NGOs). A large number of these are attached to the ultimate NGO, the United Nations Organization, and over 1,200 NGOs were instrumental in the creation of the UN.

It is difficult to assess the importance of such organizations. Clearly, within particular realms of human experience they may play crucial roles in assisting individuals and groups to achieve their ends. However, in the terms of the theory of the capitalist global system elaborated here, apart from those directly or indirectly responsive to the interests of the TNCs as expressed by the transnational capitalist class, their transnational practices are distinctly marginal. Another way of putting this is that where their activities are not marginal, they tend to be very responsive to the TNCs. Therefore, in the following discussion, the emphasis will be on the political practices of the transnational capitalist class (TCC) and the groups or classes with which it has its most significant contacts. A terminological point is in order here. The term *transnational capitalist class* is used interchangeably in the singular and the plural. This is to signify that its national and its global membership may be distinguished for the sake of convenience, but that the concept of the TCC entails global interests. There are, of course, cases where the interests of the class as a whole, to promote global capitalism, are transcended by other interests for individual members, where Jews refuse to do business with Germans, or Arabs with Jews, or North Americans with communists, for example. The strength and unity of the *transnational* capitalist class are, therefore, always open to empirical questions.[4] The weight of the evidence is that it is growing stronger and more united and, as I shall go on to argue, this can be best explained within the context of the culture-ideology of consumerism.

The transnational capitalist class

The transnational capitalist class is not made up of capitalists in the traditional Marxist sense. Direct ownership or control of the means of production is no longer the exclusive criterion for serving the interests of capital, particularly not the global interests of capital. The *international managerial bourgeoisie*, of which I made some conceptual criticisms above, is defined as: 'a socially comprehensive category, encompassing the entrepreneurial elite, managers of firms, senior state functionaries, leading politicians, members of the learned professions, and persons of similar standing in all spheres of society' (Becker and Sklar, 1987, p.7). This is a very useful formulation, all the more so because it echoes another one, developed quite independently from a case study of the Mexico–US border. The membership of the 'political cliques' that assisted the entrepreneurs in running the Mexican Border Industrialization Programme in its first decade is described as:

> a local government official, lawyer, accountant, banker, customs broker, labor contractor and in most cases the owner of factory land and buildings. US businessmen from industrial development committees and chambers of commerce from nearby US cities also usually form part of this clique. (Baird and McCaughan, 1975, p.9)

The most important elements specifically missing from both of these formulations are the professional purveyors of the culture-ideology of consumerism, the mass media and promotional personnel whose task it is to sell the consumerist goals of the global capitalist system to the masses. These goals have to be sold to producers, citizens and consumers.

The political practices of the transnational capitalist class will be analyzed in terms of two issues. First, how the TCC operates to change the nature of the political struggle between capital and labour. This can be measured in terms of its domestic and transnational political organization, direct and indirect TNC interference in host country politics and the extent to which these constrain and are constrained by the domestic and/or transnational labour movement. Second, the transnational capitalist class aims to downgrade certain domestic practices by comparison with new and more glamorous transnational practices and to create a 'comprador' mentality. This can be measured by the local and in some cases international brain drain from domestic to transnational enterprises, mainly but not exclusively TNCs. The people who make up this brain drain are the backbone of the transnational capitalist class, the class whose political role is to persuade co-nationals that their interests are identical with, or at least best served by, those of the TNCs.

Labour and capital

Neither the global capitalist class nor the global working class operates to any great extent through transnational political parties or trade unions. However, such groupings do exist and they do have some effects on, and are affected by, the political practices of the TCC in most countries.

There are no genuine transnational political parties, though there appears to be a growing interest in international associations of parties, which are sometimes mistaken for transnational parties. The post-Comintern Communist Movement, the Socialist International, international Fascist organizations, and the Green movement (about which more will be said below) provide the only models we have for such organizations, and none of these can be currently regarded as successful in global terms. Building on the rather flimsy basis of European Community elections where there is some evidence of multi-state party platforms, Goldman (1983) argues that the prospects for transnational political parties are increasing. Few would agree with even this modest claim.

There are various transnational political organizations through which fractions of the TCC operate, for example, the Rotary Club and its offshoots and the network of American Chambers of Commerce that straddles the globe. Prominent among these organizations is the Trilateral Commission, made up of the great and good from the United States, Europe and Japan, whose business is 'Elite Planning for World Management' (see Holly Sklar, 1980). There are few major cities in any First or Third World country which do not have members of or connections with one or more of these organizations. They vary in strength from the sophisticated First World centres, through important Third World cities, like Cairo and Mexico City, to nominal presences in some of the poorer African and Asian countries. They are backed up to a greater or lesser extent by many powerful bodies, such as the foreign trade agencies of the major hegemon powers, and (in parts of the Third World) specialized bodies like the World Bank and the US Agency for International Development (USAID).

Labour is represented by some genuinely transnational trade unions.[5] The World Federation of Trade Unions (WFTU) was founded in 1945, with 350 delegates representing 67 million workers in 56 countries. This immediately postwar show of labour unity included members from the United States (the CIO, but not the AFL), Britain, the Soviet Union, China and India. WFTU split under the pressure of the Cold War in 1949, when the British TUC and the CIO from the United States (followed by the AFL) set up in opposition the International Confederation of Free Trade Unions (ICFTU). ICFTU followed a strict international and national 'no contact' policy with the WFTU, which it saw as entirely Soviet dominated. In the 1980s, the WFTU had over 200 million members in 70 countries (most of Eastern Europe and communist unions in Western Europe and Japan), though the Italian communist trade union had withdrawn and the French began to distance themselves from WFTU in the mid-1970s, ostensibly to improve the climate for domestic solidarity. ICFTU has about 90 million members (in 92 countries, including Western Europe, the Americas and most of the Third World). The World Council of Labour, a Christian oriented movement, has about 15 million members.

In addition, there are some industrially based transnational union organizations, for example the International Metalworkers Federation, and the International Union of Food and Allied Workers' Associations, and these have been involved in genuine transnational labour struggles, and have gained some short term victories. However, they face substantial difficulties in their struggles against organized capital, domestically and transnationally (see Rowan *et al.*, 1980) and they must be considered as marginal most of the time in the global system.

While they would not disagree entirely with this judgement, there are some researchers who see rather more positive future prospects for a transnational labour movement, or a 'new labour internationalism' as it is called. In part a response to the new international division of labour, a new international labour-oriented labour studies is rapidly emerging (see the bibliography by Waterman and Klatter in Boyd *et al.*, 1987). However, the interest and acuity of these studies cannot obscure the fact that the labour internationalism they set out to document and analyze has occurred only fleetingly. These scholars know the reasons why, and they do not hide them. The level of unionization to be found in TNC-owned industry in different countries varies a great deal. The question cannot be realistically discussed, however, unless there is some measure of the genuine independence of the union. We must distinguish at least three cases: first, where unions are prohibited or repressed; second, where official government or company unions are permitted; third, where genuinely independent unions actually operate.[6] While most TNCs in most countries will follow the local rules regarding the unions, host governments, particularly in export processing industries (not always under pressure from foreign investors), have suspended national labour legislation. Some cases will be discussed in the next chapter.

Downgrading of domestic practices

Even the most casual observer of the Second and Third Worlds, and even some non-hegemon members of the First World, cannot but be struck by the widespread belief that indigenous practices are often unfavourably compared with foreign practices. The downgrading of domestic industry, for example, is a subtle and circular process, in which the newcomer has all the advantages and the incumbent all the handicaps. The necessity for and the presence of the foreign company are constant reminders of the deficiencies of the domestic economy; new methods are defined as more efficient (if not necessarily more desirable) than the traditional methods of production current in the host economy; and where entirely new products enter, this only underlines the inadequacies of the host. These can all have a depressing effect on local industry. Although academic researchers have questioned the notion of 'dualism' (the division of socio-economic structures into 'traditional' and 'modern' sectors), as rather too clearcut and simplistic, there may be an element of the self-fulfilling prophecy at work here. The more powerful the belief that domestic industry is inferior and unreliable, the more likely is it actually to become so.

It is useful to distinguish between economic and political practices here. In terms of economic logic, a traditional enterprise may be fulfilling the needs of the local consumers through efficient use of domestic inputs, while in terms of political (transnational) logic the traditional enterprise is perceived as quite inefficient because of its lack of international competitiveness. In more dramatic terms, the downgrading of domestic industries reflects the success of the transnational capitalist class in dragging them into the global economy and thereby transforming them, even in a rather minimal sense, into transnational industries.

The presence of expatriate managers and technicians in foreign firms in even the most industrially advanced countries, serves to intensify the distinction between foreign new and domestic old industry. Recruitment of top management appears to be through two circuits, but with a predominantly one-way flow. Transnational companies, particularly those with international reputations, have less difficulty in recruiting the available staff, either from indigenous firms or from other foreign companies. Indeed, there is some evidence of a transnational staff circuit as random conversations in airports and more systematic interviews with TNC executives confirm. The larger transnationals commonly train key staff at headquarters (usually US and European) and for some, a job in the factory of such a parent is the first step in a global career. There is a good deal of evidence to suggest that managerial and technical talent flows from the domestic sector to the transnational companies rather than vice versa, particularly but not exclusively in the Third World (see Gershenberg, 1987, on Kenya; Okada, 1983, on Indonesia). The local economy may derive benefits from this brain drain, even sufficient to offset the costs, if there is seen to be fair competition between the TNCs and the indigenous firms for trained managerial, technical and craft personnel. The optimum situation would be a policy that would force the TNCs to train young people rather than entice away those already trained and working in the domestic sector. These young people are, of course, those from whom tomorrow's transnational capitalist class will be recruited.

The downgrading of domestic industry may be compensated for by the more progressive business environment that foreign, and particularly high technology US, European or Japanese companies promote. Transnational corporations can give a competitive stimulation to existing domestic companies by demonstrating the business potential of new lines or products, and they can also directly influence the creation of new indigenous firms. In general, higher expectations of transnational firms for business services and a better-educated workforce may provoke the state into public spending that might otherwise not have taken place. For example, some governments would probably not have spent as much on telecommunications as they have done without the stimulus of a foreign-dominated export sector that produces hard-currency earnings, and the expectation that such facilities, however expensive, would attract even more companies. The management and workers of those domestic firms which join the TCC may well benefit from this in the long run, as well as the foreign-controlled sector. It must be noted, however, that the managers and workers of those domestic firms that go under will not see this as an undiluted benefit.

There can also be a knock-on effect of the higher and more innovative technology that some foreign firms employ, all through society. This generates a climate for the technological upgrading of industry as a commercial proposition, and it also ensures that hardware and software are conveniently available, at a price, for those who wish to take advantage of them in any sphere. Contact with famous name international firms undoubtedly encourages local manufacturers, impressed by the demonstration effect of the success of prestigious foreign firms, to consider seriously the uses they could make of the new technologies.

The price that the state will pay to sustain the costs of the TNCs will depend largely on the power of the transnational capitalist class and its domestic members. Whatever the price happens to be at a given time, and this can vary dramatically, it will be a price worth paying for some and not for others. What accounts for the complexity of the problem of evaluation is not only the economic and social costs involved themselves, but the interests, conflicting or in harmony, of those who pay the costs and those who reap the benefits. It may be an over-simplification to conceptualize all the different interests in terms of class struggle, particularly as some of the interest groups involved and some of the alliances of interests forged may defy analysis in conventional Marxist terms. Nevertheless, there are class interests involved even though they may not always conveniently reduce to one labouring class versus one capitalist class.

The transnational capitalist class, fractions of the labour force, and other support strata that the TNCs have created, will all increasingly identify their own interests with those of the capitalist global system and, if necessary, against the interests of their 'own' societies as the transnational practices of the system penetrate ever deeper into the areas that most heavily impact on their daily lives. The specific function of the agents of transnational political practices is to create and sustain the organizational forms within which this penetration takes place and to connect them organically with those domestic practices that can be incorporated and mobilized in the interests of the global capitalist system. In order to do this the transnational capitalist class must promote, outside the First World heartlands of capitalism, a 'comprador' mentality throughout society.

'Comprador' mentality

A comprador mentality is the attitude that the best practices are invariably connected with the global capitalist system. Comprador mentality is either a 'cost' or a 'benefit' and whichever way we look at it we are bound to beg a very important question. This is the point at issue in the ideological struggle between those who believe that TNCs will inevitably damage Third World development prospects in the long run, as against those who believe that there will be no development prospects without the TNCs. This struggle revolves around opposing material interests of competing classes and groups in all countries.

There are those who see the destiny of the Third World as bound up with the adoption of all that is 'modern', often embodied in the products and practices of the TNCs. On the other hand, there are those who are deeply suspicious of the modernization represented by the TNCs, particularly where this is perceived as Western or US dominance in culture, industry, warfare, science and technology. This is a field riddled with dilemmas. Modern warfare and the modern economy, for example, require increasingly higher levels of technology and this cannot be avoided if any state wishes to participate, or if threatened, survive in the contemporary world.

A battery of concepts, some of which have migrated from social science jargon to the mass media, identify those on either side of the divide. The academically discredited distinction between *traditional* and *modern* is now common currency, while the notions of *inward-oriented* and *outward-oriented* describe those who look for guidance and sustenance to the resources of their own groups as opposed to those who look outside, usually to the West. Much the same idea is expressed by the distinction between *local* and *cosmopolitan* orientation. As it is, more or less by definition, an extra-First World phenomenon, the question of the comprador mentality will be resumed in the next chapter.

It is difficult to think productively about 'modernization' for many reasons, not least the problem of what is *appropriate* in the adoption of innovation. The proper approach to development lies, no doubt, somewhere between a slavish attachment to all things foreign and an atavistic distaste for any type of change. An illustration of how appropriate choices for the different groups and classes in the capitalist global system can and do change is provided by the analysis of counter movements to the global capitalist project. These are movements that aim to undermine the power of the TNCs, and the transnational capitalist class, and to force people to think critically about the ways in which the system as a whole promotes the culture-ideology of consumerism.

Counter movements

Although the agents of global capitalism are firmly in control and the TNCs are clearly the dominant institutional force, there are, as we approach the millennium, two counter movements that could represent real threats to the global capitalist system. The first, rich country protectionism, comes from within global capitalism, but in the form of national as opposed to systemic interests. The second, the Green movement, is a very widely based and variegated collection of individuals and groups that includes those on the fringes of the global capitalist system as well as some who are fundamentally opposed to it, mainly from the libertarian left but also from the authoritarian right.

Protectionism

Protectionism is, of course, not a new phenomenon. Indeed, the most potent argument against it may be that we know only too well how protectionism contributed to the great depression of the 1930s. Nevertheless, as the World Bank and other august proponents of the perpetual increase of global trade never tired of reminding us throughout the 1980s, many First World countries began to step up protectionist measures in that decade. The free entry of goods (particularly consumer goods) from abroad has never been a feature of global trade. Restrictive measures have been directed at Third World manufacturers whose electronic and electrical products, garments, shoes, toys, sporting and household goods were said to be unfairly flooding vulnerable First World markets. The interesting twist to this issue is that it was Japan, clearly now a First World country, and in the opinion of many now the most dynamic economic power, that was often identified in the United States and in Europe, as the worst offender, with the four East Asian NICs not far behind.

The tendency to protectionism is increased by the belief that a substantial part of TNC manufacturing industry is 'footloose'. Transnational corporation production tends to be globally integrated into vertically organized production processes. Offshore plants tend to be financially controlled from abroad, they tend to be rented rather than owned, and their managers tend to have cosmopolitan rather than local perspectives. All of these factors weaken the ties that such businesses have with the communities in which they are located and make it less difficult for them to close down and/or relocate if and when business conditions deteriorate in one country relative to other countries. This happens in the First World as well as in the Third World. For example, Hood and

Young (1982) document the closure of several old established US firms in Scotland to seek cheaper production sites elsewhere. The mobility of the TNCs, the job losses that usually follow, and the identification of 'cheap imports' with goods previously produced at home, increase protectionist pressures among labour and small domestic capitalists alike.

While protectionism as a transnational political force appears to have little likelihood of success in the forseeable future, the threat of it is ever present as a reminder that the orderly progress of global trade in the interests of the TNCs has to be maintained and those who transgress will be punished. This works both ways. First World markets are open to Third and Second World goods only as long as their markets are also open to First World goods and, increasingly, services.[7]

Protectionism is not a serious counter movement to global capitalism because if it was successful it could do great damage to the system and, ultimately, destroy it. All parties realize this, and so protectionism acts as a bargaining counter for the rich, and a bluff for the poor, and mainly comes to life in its use as a rhetorical device to satisfy domestic constituencies. For example, desperate politicians tend to fall back on it to appease working class voters in the United States and the United Kingdom. The Green movement is much more serious, actually and potentially.

The Green movement

With the sole exception of the global communist movement, the Green or environmentalist movement presents the greatest contemporary challenge to the global capitalist system.[8] This is paradoxically confirmed by the fact that both capitalist and socialist economists, politicians and ideologues are increasingly trying to jump on to the Green bandwaggon and to appropriate its policies for themselves. This is not surprising, because although capitalists and socialists are usually reluctant to spell out their plans for global domination, Green politics are largely based on a straightforward conception of planet earth and what needs to de done at the global level to sustain human life on it.

The key threat that Green politics poses to the capitalist global system is in the matter of the consumption of non-renewable resources. While Green politics are based on the belief that the resources of the planet are finite and have to be carefully tended, global capitalist politics are based on the belief that the resources of the planet are virtually infinite, due to the scientific and technological ingenuity released by the capitalist system that will ensure unlimited replacement or substitution of resources as they are used up.

Green politics are closely connected with the emergence of a critical consumer movement. The idea of *consumerism* has experienced an important dialectical inversion in recent years. It is commonly used in two senses. In this book I use it to denote an uncritical obsession with consumption. It is, however, also commonly used in an opposite sense, as in the consumer movement's version of consumerism, to denote suspicion of consumer goods, a wish to know more about how they are produced and who produces them. This version of consumerism can lead to a radical critique of consumption. To minimize confusion, I shall use *consumerism* where I mean the first, and the *consumer movement* to denote the second.[9]

Kaynak (1985, p.15) defines the consumer movement 'as a movement seeking to increase the rights and powers of buyers in relation to sellers' and presents a useful historical account from the first cooperative society, founded in Scotland in 1769, to the present. He connects the rise of consumer movements in different countries with the position of the country in the world market, but from a marketing rather than a political economy point of view. His discussion of consumer movements in the Third World, however, does confuse the two meanings of consumerism. Food riots in North Africa, he writes, 'are examples of what LDC consumers are concerned with – the right to consume' (p.20). But this misses the real distinction between diametrically opposed beliefs based on entirely different conceptions of the satisfaction of human needs. Thus, it is to the culture-ideology of consumerism, and how it is broadcast in the global capitalist system through a variety of transnational practices, that we must now turn.

Cultural-ideological transnational practices

There are many who argue that the key to hegemonic control in any societal system lies not in the economic nor in the political sphere, but in the realm of culture and ideology. Those for whom this idea is a novelty may be surprised to learn that it was the writings and political practice of a Marxist, and a communist militant at that, which were largely responsible for the present currency of this view among radical thinkers. Antonio Gramsci, who spent most of his adult life in one of Mussolini's prisons, elaborated on Marx's insight that the ruling ideas of an epoch are the ideas of its ruling class, to create a theory of hegemony and a theory of classes of intellectuals whose function it is in any literate society to propagate or to challenge these leading ideas. Gramsci's *Prison Notebooks* represent not only a stirring monument to the human spirit under adversity, but a significant turning-point in the history of Marxist ideas and their relevance for the twentieth century. This is partly because in the sphere of culture and ideology the material conditions have changed to such an extent that what Gramsci was arguing about hegemonic processes in the 1930s has become more, not less, relevant today than it was then. To put the point graphically, while Marx and his nineteenth-century comrades would have no great difficulty in recognizing the economic and the political spheres today, despite the major changes that have undoubtedly taken place in the last hundred years, in the cultural-ideological sphere the opportunities for hegemonic control on a global scale have changed out of all recognition.

In one of the first quantitative studies of what he terms the communication explosion, Cherry (1978) argues that global telecommunications are based on a 'tripod skeleton' of three main circuits, transatlantic/Europe, Far East/Europe, and North/South America. Shipping, air transport, telephone and telegraph generally follow these routes. The Pacific satellite system, just emerging when he was writing in the 1970s, turns the tripod into a quadripod. This is, of course, not an analysis of the technical possibilities, for modern telecommunications and transportation of goods and people can go virtually anywhere by any route. It is an analysis of the actual communications practices in the global system in terms of traffic.

Under the umbrella of the United Nations, dozens of agencies are involved in the organization of global communications. The Rome Plan of 1963, revised in the Mexico City Plan of 1967, divided the world into thirty-four communications zones. The fact that Europe was split into ten zones reflects the politics of the global system rather than its technology, and suggests that 'the world is not shrinking everywhere like a deflated balloon, but very irregularly, more like a dried apple, furrowed and distorted' (Cherry, 1978, p.135).

The 1980s witnessed an unprecedented increase in the scale and scope of the electronic media of communication, as well as genuine innovations in their nature. Technological advances, international competition and consequent relative price reductions in producer and consumer electronics have led the US, European and Japanese TNCs, that for the most part control the electronic media, to develop global strategies for the establishment and aggrandisement of their various hegemonic practices that would have been technically impossible, and in some cases even unthinkable a few decades ago (see Schiller, 1981; McPhail, 1987). This gives the potential for distribution of messages on a scale never before achieved. The claim that it is a qualitatively new stage in the global history of communications is quite justified. The fact that this is happening within and as a result of the capitalist global system suggests to me that a qualitatively new relationship between culture and ideology is being forged.

All those who argue that it is the medium not the message that characterizes this revolution are, in my view, entirely wrong. The fact that a greater variety of messages may be broadcast on a vastly greater scale does not alter the fact that the central messages are still and more powerfully those of the capitalist global system. McLuhan's famous 'the medium is the message' is true to the extent that corporations, increasingly transnational corporations, control the media to propagate *their* message, as McLuhan himself occasionally acknowledges. An excellent indicator of this is the phenomenal increase in the 1980s in commercial sponsorship of what used to be considered purely cultural events, such as operas, museum exhibits and sports.[10] The commercialization of the Olympic Games by some of the world's largest TNCs is a paradigm case (see Tomlinson and Whannel, 1984).[11]

The recognition that the transnational practices in the culture-ideology sphere were seriously asymmetrical had to be addressed in a way that was not necessary for economic and political TNPs. The reason for this is the peculiar status of culture-ideology in the reproduction of global capitalism. Here it is useful to distinguish between private and public media. The main difference between them is that private media are used mainly to transmit commercial data and documents, often under conditions of extreme security, while public (mass) media are used mainly to broadcast 'entertainment', always under conditions of the greatest visibility to the paying public. Both forms were revolutionized in the 1980s by the development and dissemination of new information and communication technologies, such as cable and satellite television, video and the institutionalization of the capacity for total packaging of cultural products.

Bagdikian (1989) characterizes those who control this system as 'the lords of the global village'. They purvey their product (a relatively undifferentiated mass of news, information, ideas, entertainment and popular culture) to a rapidly expanding public, eventually the whole world. Bagdikian argues that national boundaries are growing increasingly meaningless as the main actors (five groups at the time he was writing) strive for total control in the production, delivery, and marketing of what we can call the cultural-ideological goods of the global capitalist system. Their goal is to create a 'buying mood' for the benefit of the global troika of media, advertising and consumer goods manufacturers. 'Nothing in human experience has prepared men, women and children for the modern television techniques of fixing human attention and creating the uncritical mood required to sell goods, many of which are marginal at best to human needs' (Bagdikian, 1989, p.819). Two random facts: by the age of 16, the average North American youth has been exposed to more than 300,000 television commercials; and the Soviet Union is now selling advertising slots on cosmonaut suits and space ships! In order to connect and explain these facts, we need to generate a new framework, namely the culture-ideology of consumerism.

The culture-ideology of consumerism

The mass media perform many functions for global capitalism. They speed up the circulation of material goods through advertising, which reduces the time between production and consumption. They begin to inculcate the dominant ideology from an early age, in the words of Esteinou Madrid, 'creating the political/cultural demand for the survival of capitalism' (1986, p.119). The systematic blurring of the lines between information, entertainment, and promotion of products lies at the heart of this practice. This has not in itself created a culture and ideology of consumerism, for these have been in place for at least the last century and perhaps longer in the First World and among comprador classes elsewhere.[12] What it has created is a reformulation of consumerism that transforms all the public mass media and their contents into opportunities to sell ideas, values, products, in short, a consumerist worldview. The medium *is* the message because the message, the culture and ideology of consumerism, has engulfed the medium. The problem, therefore, is not *Understanding Media* (the title of McLuhan's great if somewhat misconceived book) but *Understanding Global Capitalism*, the system that produces and reproduces both the message and the media that incessantly transmit it.

The connections between global capitalism and the culture-ideology of consumerism must be laid bare. In an attempt to do this, Featherstone, for example, develops a useful composite picture of contemporary consumer culture. He writes:

1. Goods are framed and displayed to entice the customer, and shopping becomes an overtly symbolic event.
2. Images play a central part, constantly created and circulated by the mass media.
3. Acquisition of goods leads to a 'greater aestheticisation of reality. (Featherstone, 1987, p.21)

The end result of these processes is a new concept of *lifestyle*, enhanced self-image. This 'glosses over the real distinctions in the capacity to consume and ignores the low paid, the unemployed, the old' (p.22), though the ubiquity of the culture-ideology of consumerism actually does include everyone (or, at least, all urban dwellers) however poor, because no one can escape its images. And, it must be added, very few people would choose to escape its images and what they represent in terms of the good, or better, life. This is the central dilemma of any critique of consumerism (and also of the politics of the consumer movement).

Many scholars (pre-eminently Ewen, 1978) point up the distinctive role of the United States in the campaign to make consumer culture universal. Through Hollywood, and the globalization of the movies, via Madison Avenue, from where Ewen's 'captains of consciousness' created the modern advertising industry, to the more geographically diffuse but ideologically monolithic television networking conceptualizers, the transnational capitalist class in the United States has assumed leadership of the culture-ideology of consumerism in the interests of global capitalism in the twentieth century.[13]

A good illustration of this is in the origin of the soap opera, one of the most highly developed media forms through which mass consumerism is projected. It began in the 1920s when Glen Sample, an American advertising agent, had the idea of adapting a newspaper serial for the radio, a medium already dominated by commercial interests. The programme, 'Betty and Bob', was sponsored by a flour manufacturer, and Sample used the same idea to promote Oxydol washing powder for Proctor and Gamble, under seige from Unilever's Rinso in the US market. Oxydol won out, and the so-called soap opera that was used to sell it gave its name to a genre, massively reinforced by its wholesale adoption by television all over the world since the 1950s.[14]

The universal availability of the mass media has been rapidly achieved through relatively cheap transistor radios, cassette recorders and televisions, which now totally penetrate the First World, almost totally penetrate the urban Second and Third Worlds, and are beginning to penetrate deeply into the countryside in every country. Thus, the potential of global exposure to global communication, the dream of every merchant in history, has arrived. The socialization process by which people learn what to want, which used to occur mainly in the home and the school, is increasingly taking place through the media of the global communications industries.

Informatics and consumerism

There is general agreement that on all key measures there has been an enormous growth not only in the availability but also in the use of the mass media in the developed world over the last few decades. Even in many poor developing societies substantial growth has been achieved. The motor of this growth has been the rapid spread of corporate computerization (and also personal computers among the better off) and personal receivers, the relative prices of which have been reduced substantially over time. This development parallels (not accidentally) the enormous growth of the TNCs themselves since the 1950s, both in scope and geographical spread. There is now hardly a country in the world where the TNCs are not active in some form or another. TNCs (like national businesses) are dependent on accurate and rapid information. Logistical problems of corporations operating outside their home countries increase this dependence. Electronic communications, and especially computer to computer links, not only give the possibility of extra-efficient operations to TNCs within the network, but also give increasing competitive advantage over those outside. This is where size, generally, and globalization, in particular, become conditions of survival in some fields.

The systematic study of information technology (informatics) is in its infancy and although there is general agreement that its potential for human progress is enormous, there is a good deal of pessimism as to the probability that those who control it will actively seek this end over their own private interests (see Schiller, 1989; *Journal of Communication*, 1989). Through advanced informatics, for example, many agencies have been analyzing, disseminating and predicting information about the likelihood of famine in Africa. Whether all this activity actually reduces the suffering in the region is very doubtful.

Control over data processing and telecommunications is, unsurprisingly, dominated by US, Japanese and European TNCs. While manufacturing capacity is more evenly spread, overall, the dominance of US-based TNCs is clear. TNCs from the United States were said to control over three-quarters of the total volume of transborder data flows, including transmission, storage and processing in the early 1980s (see Mowlana, 1985, ch.5). The contribution of the non-hegemon countries is mainly restricted to assembly and fabrication, usually on contract or as quasi-captive suppliers to a TNC.

Nevertheless, control does not entail *specific* effects in the economic, political and cultural-ideological spheres. In order to demonstrate a connection and to begin to document specific effects it is first necessary to show how the structural conditions of the global system are inherent in the ways in which the communications TNCs operate. Hamelink makes what appears to be the useful distinction between the information-independent and the information-dependent countries. He points to the increase in 'global cultural synchronization' through which information-dependent countries are made more similar in commercially-relevant areas to the information-independent countries from which most of the messages they receive about the world emanate.

> Global use of data flows – particularly through transnational corporations – is thus likely to have an impact on the synchronization of techniques (e.g. via the standardization of equipment), symbols (e.g. through the use of the universal computer language) and social relations (e.g. through the organisation of industrial production and job patterns). (Hamelink, 1984, p.72).

From the 1970s on there has been a considerable surge of scholarly and public interest in the private media and, latterly, in their role in the Third World. UNESCO-sponsored research, particularly associated with the International Commission for the Study of Communication Problems, led to the publication of *Many Voices, One World* (MacBride Commission, 1980), which set the agenda for the 1980s and provided a spur to the creation of World Communications Year (1983), continuing World Conferences on Strategies and Policies for Informatics, and other initiatives. Three inter-connected themes informed these activities, namely the continued control of cultural industries by a small group of immensely powerful TNCs; the effects of this control on those countries too poor to have much of an independent presence in these industries; and the opportunities that the new technologies offer for the development of the Third World. Given the disparities between the information capacities of developed and developing countries, and the technical nature of these disparities, 'a vital question becomes, do transnational data flows increase the informational advantage and social impact of transnational corporations?' (Hamelink, 1984, p.14).

These all look like important questions but, once again, the methodology of state-centrism serves to blur rather than clarify the issues. The national origin of the agents of media control is not the point. Many TNCs in and of the Third World, and even some in and of the Second World, have entirely independent systems of communication and, of course, more or less all sovereign states run their own mass media. The issue is not whether nationals or foreigners control the media, but whether the interests of those who do control the media, nationals or foreigners, are those of the capitalist global system. It is the culture-ideology of consumerism, not the nationality of the lords and stewards of the global village, that is at issue. These questions will be further analyzed through a discussion of what has been labelled cultural, and more specifically, media imperialism, in Chapter 5.

Hamelink sums up the impact of informatics in the developed countries in a manner that suggests a gloomy future for Third World countries caught in the TNC-woven web of private and public communications. Despite its state-centrism, it is worth quoting at length as it catches some key specifics of the practices of the communications industries' project for global consumerism.

> In developed countries it can be observed that the widespread utilization of informatics:
>   – offers some new job opportunities but on balance creates more unemployment;
>   – offers some decentralization in social decision-making, but on balance reinforces centralized administration and tends to erode democracy;
>   – offers potentially to enhance citizen participation in local government, to inform citizens of their rights and duties, and to provide new information-services to citizens, but on balance it reinforces local dominant coalitions, makes local government more expensive to run, makes it less responsive to the general public, and tends to exclude many interests;
>   – offers potentially more security for data processing and transmission, but on balance threatens privacy in unprecedented ways;
>   – offers the suggestion of more social equity, but on balance adds to existing social disparities the phenomenon of information inequality. (Hamelink, 1984, p.89)

The stirrings of a global debate on the creation of new consumption needs provides a complex set of tests for these hypotheses. Consumption tends to be more class-specific in poor societies than in rich societies. In poor societies not many people have much discretionary income left after they have satisfied their basic needs of food and shelter, if indeed they can satisfy these at all. In rich societies, on the other hand, most people do have enough discretionary income left (or have easy access to credit) after they have paid for their food and shelter, though the numbers who do not appear to be growing at an alarming rate in some rich countries (as the growth of homelessness in the United States and the United Kingdom seems to suggest). Thus, different strata in such societies may spend their money on rather different things.

The creation of needs depends on multi-layered structures and dynamics connecting individual characteristics of the consumer with processes operating at the societal level. The global capitalist system propagates an integrated culture and ideology of consumerism through the manipulation of existing consumption needs and the creation of new ones. The creation of these new consumption needs by TNCs tends to be neither random nor arbitrary, but structured in terms of a hegemonic world view. In one interesting analysis of this issue, Sauvant and Mennis (1980) argue that the TNCs act as transmission belts along which the contents of what they label the TNC 'business culture' are carried from the rich countries to the poor countries of the world. This results in 'inappropriate sociocultural patterns' which impede independent development.

This provocative thesis, very much connected with the questions of the transnational capitalist class discussed above, and their influence over the popular masses in developing countries, lies at the centre of the debate over the economic, political and cultural-ideological TNPs in developing countries. It is precisely the 'business culture' introduced and propagated by the TNCs that is considered by many to be the *sine qua non* for 'modernization' (as opposed to 'dependency reversal' or radical 'development') in the Third World. The struggle to create a new 'modernist' concept and practice of consumerism in the Third World is one of the crucial conjunctures of economic, political and cultural-ideological transnational practices.

The theory of the global system: a summary

The theory of the global system can be summarized, graphically, as follows. The global system is made up of economic transnational practices and at the highest level of abstraction these are the building blocks of the system. The political practices are the principles of organization of the system. They have to work with the materials on hand, but by manipulating the design of the system they can build variations into it. The cultural-ideological practices are the nuts and bolts and the glue that hold the system together. Without them, parts of the system would drift off into space.

In order to work properly the dominant forces in each of the three spheres have to monopolize the key resources for which there is great competition. The transnational corporations strive to control global capital and material resources, the transnational capitalist classes strive to control global power, and the transnational agents and institutions of the culture-ideology of consumerism strive to control the realm of ideas.[15] Effective TNC control of global capital and resources is almost complete. There are few important national resources that are entirely exempt from economic transnational practices. Transnational capitalist classes rule directly, through national capitalist political parties or social democratic parties that cannot fundamentally threaten the global capitalist project, or they exert authority indirectly to a greater or lesser extent as the price levied on non-capitalist states as a sort of entrance fee into the global capitalist system. In the last resort, it is the global control of capital and labour that is the decisive factor for those who do not wish to be excluded from the system.

The control of ideas in the interests of consumerism is almost total. The ideas that are antagonistic to the global capitalist project can be reduced to one central counter-hegemonic idea, the rejection of the culture-ideology of consumerism itself. Without consumerism, the rationale for continuous capitalist accumulation dissolves. It is the capacity to commercialize and commodify all ideas and the material products in which they adhere, television images, advertisements, newsprint, books, tapes, films and so on, not the ideas themselves, that global capitalism strives to appropriate.

Notes

1. According to World Bank data global exports rose from $94 billion in 1965, to $1,365 billion in 1986 (*World Development Report*, 1988, Table 14).

2. Job creation is, of course, not the only important economic TNP, though it is probably the most important from a sociological point of view. For perspectives from political science, see Blake and Walters (1987); from international relations, Modelski (1979); from interna-

tional finance, Grou (1985); from geography, Taylor and Thrift (1986); from history, Teichova *et al.* (1986); from law, Horn (1980); from anthropology, Idris-Soven *et al.* (1978); and, of course, various types of economic perspectives, for which see Dunning (1981) and Rugman (1982). These economists pursue what they term the *eclectic* theory, and in view of the overlap between the various perspectives this does make some sense. My theory of the global system is intended to be the basis of a sociological perspective on the TNCs.

3. This is not to argue that all linkages are necessarily beneficial to the host economy. It is also important to note that linkages in extractive and manufacturing industries may have different characteristics (see, for example, Radetzki, 1977).

4. For an example of a very critical test case, the experience of US TNCs in Iran in the 1980s, see Bassiry and Dekmejian (1985).

5. For a clear brief guide to international trade unionism, see Press and Thomson (1989, chs.1 and 2).

6. These are very complex questions. For a stimulating discussion on the influence of foreign interests in the development of Nigerian unions see Otobo (1987).

7. The literature on protectionism is enormous. A useful study that airs the key First–Third World issues is Yoffie (1983). See also World Bank (1987, ch.8).

8. Although there are certainly differences between national Green movements, as there are within them, for my purposes here the differences are far less important than the common ground. On the growing importance of the Greens in the Soviet Union, see Gorst (1989) and 'Russia's Greens' (*The Economist* 4 Nov. 1989, pp.27–8, 34). The idea of *ecoglasnost* is apparently gaining ground in Eastern Europe.

9. The inversion is nicely illustrated by Editors of *Fortune* (1972), a critique of the consumer movement on behalf of the prime ideologues of consumerism. See also Sinclair (1987, p.65). Ewen (1988, ch.10) notes the same inversion for 'environmentalism'.

10. One very interesting example of this is the sponsorship by various US transnationals, like American Express and Kodak, of historical monuments, not only in North America, where we might expect it, but in China's tourist sites!

11. The American television networks paid over $600 million for the Winter and Summer games of 1988; Coca-Cola and Visa paid $22 and $15 million respectively for exclusive use of the five-ring symbol (as reported in *The Independent* [London], 15 September 1988).

12. The history and theory of consumerism are, at last, being seriously researched. In addition to the references in the text, see Boorstin (1968); McKendrick *et al.* (1982) on the development of consumerism in eighteenth-century England, and in particular the role of Josiah Wedgwood; Belk (1988b) and Webster (1987) for a useful review of some recent American works.

13. The creation of 'consumer engineering' in the United States (see Sheldon and Arens, 1932), discussed by Ewen (1976), confirms that this phenomenon long predates the golden age of the 1950s.
14. See Mattelart (1986, ch.1), where she illuminates the crucial role of the media in creating the housewife as consumer. See also Flora and Flora (1978) on *fotonovelas*.
15. These *very roughly* correspond to what Barnet and Müller (1974) refer to as Global Factory, World Managers and Global Shopping Center.

4

Transnational practices in the Third World

There is a strong tendency in some quarters to assume that all transnational practices (TNPs) in the Third World are unwelcome and malign, just as there is a strong tendency in other quarters to assume that they are all welcome and benign. Transnational corporations, transnational capitalist classes and the culture-ideology of consumerism are all seen as evil attempts to undermine the freedom and cultural autonomy of weak and poor victims, or the only true paths to development and the only reliable vehicles for releasing the poor from their misery.

These are very significant differences. Nevertheless, there is one point on which both interpretations tend to agree, namely the general unstoppability of the spread of TNPs in the global system, and particularly in the poorer and hence more vulnerable parts of it. This is a very central issue for any sociology of the global system in so far as it makes the difference between a dismal chronicle of inevitability, which is absolutely not my intention, and an attempt to illuminate what is happening by a theory of what makes it happen and, by implication, what could make other things happen in other ways.

The ultimate strength of capitalist global hegemony is that it continually works, and works very hard, to *persuade* people that the system is natural, fair and fundamentally better than any realistic alternative. Global capitalism is successful to the extent that it does persuade people. Where the capitalist state has to use force, the army or the police, then this is clearly a failure of hegemony, though where people are persuaded that the use of force is legitimate, this may actually increase hegemony.

Most Third World countries are one-party states of one type or another and many are ruled through the routine exercise of physical force by the army and the police. This is not in the long term interests of global capitalism, and TNCs through their governments have been known to put pressure on dictators for the purpose of creating or restoring pluralist political systems. Capitalism depends on both the reality and the illusion of choice, but people are not fools and the global capitalist system offers many genuine choices. This creates many contradictions and paradoxes. In the previous chapter some general contradictions and paradoxes of economic, political and cultural-ideological TNPs were discussed. In this chapter the focus will be on the economic TNPs of transnational corporations, and the political TNPs of transnational capitalist classes in the Third World. The culture-ideology of consumerism in the Third World will be the subject of Chapter 5.

Economic TNPs in the Third World

The analysis of economic TNPs, and particularly the role of the transnational corporations, begins with a paradox. Historically, what has come to be known as the Third World has attracted only a tiny proportion of all the foreign investment that has taken place, while the economies of many poor countries, and even some rich ones, are commonly said to be dominated by foreign capital and/or foreign firms. All of the *Fortune* 500 corporations do not have the same economic impact on the United States, for example, as a few copper TNCs have had on Chile, or fruit companies on Central America or mining corporations on Southern Africa.

Up to the early years of the twentieth century, the typical pattern of foreign investment was of the portfolio type, where private capitalists individually, or through financial organizations, would invest funds in such foreign enterprises such as railways or mines or trading companies, and simply collect the dividends as they came in. Naturally, some of these investors, particularly those who were speculating in the more unpredictable ventures, lost money, but by and large the European and American 'coupon clippers' as they were sometimes called, did very well out of their overseas investments.

Portfolio investment had low visibility in the sense that it was very difficult for the general population to discover who actually owned how much of the resources and enterprises in their countries. There was often very little foreign involvement in the day-to-day running of the enterprises. Nevertheless, some large firms were directly active overseas in the nineteenth century, the names and identities of which were (and in some cases still are) well known. These included the great British trading companies in West Africa, in which are to be found the origins of Unilever, the North American fruit companies in Central America, whose activities gave rise to the expression 'banana republic', and the East India Company which was to provide the basis for British colonial administration in India. This type of investment, which involves the establishment of an enterprise over which the parent company exercises decisive management control, is termed foreign direct investment (FDI), and it is this type of foreign investment with which this chapter is mainly concerned.

A serious contradiction lies at the heart of much of the critical research on TNCs in the Third World. The rhetoric of most Third World governments and radical researchers on the damage done by FDI in general and specific TNCs in particular, seems at odds with the almost universal scramble of these same Third World governments advised by (in some cases) the same radical researchers to create policies to attract more and more FDI into their countries. The best way to approach this contradiction is to see it as a genuine clash of radical theory and pragmatic experience. The theory is that development for a Third World country is not possible within the orbit of capitalist imperialism, a dependency theory of the type discussed in Chapter 2; while the experience is that FDI has often led to some 'development', apparently for the benefit of all. This is particularly the case where TNCs become involved in the creation of much-needed infrastructural resources. A good example of the complexities involved is the Volta Dam project in Ghana.

The Volta Dam and linkages

Ghana is fortunate in having large accessible bauxite and hydro-electric potential, both of which have been at the centre of the country's development planning. When Ghana became independent in 1957 the US aluminium corporations, Kaiser and Reynolds, outbid British interests to develop the bauxite industry. The plan was that foreign capital would build a dam on the Volta river to generate power, and that the private sector would own the smelter.[1] The original idea that Ghana should take a 40 per cent stake in the project vanished early on. As the magazine *West Africa* put it:

> By stripping the Volta scheme of all the ancillary facilities which could have stimulated a Ghanaian industrial revolution, Kaiser and Reynolds succeeded in creating the conditions for one of the most prosperous aluminium smelters in the world . . . at what was then the lowest power rate in the world. (*West Africa*, 1980, p.523)

The companies set up the Volta Aluminium Company (VALCO) in 1959. Girvan isolates four main aspects of this type of project:

1. *Resource accessibility.* Ghana agreed to provide cheap power, but the Ghanaians never expected the smelter to take as much as 65 per cent of the dam's power. Many other industrial projects never got off the ground due to energy shortages, and Ghana has been forced to import power from the Ivory Coast.
2. *Bauxite supply.* VALCO got the monopoly rights over ore which they did not exploit for marketing reasons; and the company operated as an enclave industry.
3. *Payment stream.* VALCO became 'the most spectacular beneficiary of the tax regime in Ghana devised to attract foreign investment'. Revenues from the bauxite are used to service the debt incurred to build the dam which provides the TNCs with the cut price power to smelt the ore.
4. *Status of the Master Agreement.* The agreement was geared to the details on the prevention of nationalization and left little room for re-negotiation (cited in *West Africa*, 1980, p.573).

By 1974 Kaiser operated in twenty-five countries and was running:

> a crazy shipping system which sends Ghanaian bauxite to Scotland, Guinean alumina to the US, Jamaican alumina to Ghana and Ghanaian aluminium all round the world. Such policies only make sense to the corporate investors and stem from the perceived need to avoid integrating the industry in any but the core capitalist countries. (*West Africa*, 1980, p.612)

Despite the cheap Volta power (and water supply) that permits expansion on smelting, the TNCs refused to build an alumina plant to process local bauxite. Eventually, Ghana was forced to build one itself (Tsikata, 1986, ch.1). Over the years, the British taxpayer has paid hundreds of millions of pounds to provide electricity below cost for British Aluminium to smelt Ghanaian bauxite in Scotland. The Kaiser Corporation has a similar deal in New Zealand.

The real developmental loss for Ghana is that most of the power from the Volta goes to VALCO, so there is little left for local use. In 1980, only 5 per cent of Ghana's people had access to electricity. So while it would be difficult to argue that there were no benefits for Ghana, or for other Third World countries in similar projects, it is quite clear that the interests of the TNCs in obtaining cheap power in Ghana as part of their global industrial strategy run counter to the interests of Ghanaian development. How, then, can a poor country maximize its benefits from such projects? Vernon's theory of the product cycle and its 'obsolescing bargain' is an attempt to answer this question.

Vernon (1971) argues that over a period of time, and particularly as a new technology matures, host countries are more able to drive harder bargains with the TNCs that wish to invest in them. This may be the case in some industries, or for some products but as, for example, both Moran's study of the Chilean copper industry (1974) and Girvan's of the Caribbean bauxite industry (1976) demonstrate in rather different ways, the control that globally integrated corporations can exert on distribution and marketing may nullify what appears on the ground to be a better bargain for the host.

The concrete form in which the host may benefit is, as noted in the previous chapter, the creation of linkages. Both backward linkages, when a TNC buys local materials and goods and adds value to them, and forward linkages, when domestic companies buy intermediate goods that the TNCs produce and add value to them, can have substantial financial, employment and technical effects. Lim and Pang (1982) in a study of three export-oriented electronics TNCs in Singapore show that productive local linkages are possible, but both the firms and the location are atypical. Hill (1982), in a study on the Philippines, illustrates a more typical pattern, where local linkages are created by assemblers who establish joint ventures with licensees or foreign firms. However, in these cases, what is labelled 'local sourcing' often conceals import content through assembly kits for various products. Lall's study of the Indian truck industry (1985, ch.5) is more encouraging, but India until quite recently has treated the TNCs relatively strictly (Stoever, 1989).

My own studies of export oriented zones in China (Sklair, forthcoming), Egypt (1988c), Mexico (1989), and Ireland (1988b), suggest that backward and forward linkages tend to be very meagre, and these cases may be rather more typical of the Third World as a whole than the relatively highly developed enclave, Singapore. The developmental effects of TNC investment must be judged on a case by case basis and cannot be judged in isolation from the development goals of the countries concerned. The six criteria of positive development that I use in my own research (linkages, retained foreign currency earnings, genuine technology transfer, upgrading of personnel, conditions of work and equitable distribution) are one way to tackle this problem.

It must be immediately obvious that such arguments will be somewhat confused unless a definition of development can be agreed. This realization has led to a great deal of debate and, although it cannot be said that a general consensus has been reached on how best to define development, a good deal of light has been shed on the processes involved in different types of development. For my part, it seems clear that a viable distinction can be made between economic growth (measured on such criteria as GNP per capita, proportion of the labour force engaged in industry, and the proportion of manufactured goods in total exports) and development, which has somewhat wider social and political implications. The crucial difference between economic growth and development, as I am using the term here, is that development may include everything that is already included in economic growth plus criteria of distribution of the social product and democratic politics. It is not possible to be much more precise than this without becoming hopelessly entangled in a series of impossible dilemmas. This approximate definition, not unlike others in hotly contested areas of inquiry, is also a guide to further research.

The world system as a system of nation-states and state-centrism as an explanatory framework, obviously do have a place in the analysis of these problems, as was illustrated in Chapter 1. The theory being propounded here sees the global system as primarily a capitalist global system and the main forces in it as the transnational corporations, transnational capitalist classes and the culture-ideology of consumerism. In order to lay bare the workings of the global system we must focus on the TNC. As the analysis of the Volta Dam project suggests, economic transnational practices in the Third World are largely what the TNCs are doing in the economic, the political and the cultural-ideological spheres.

Transnational corporations in the Third World

Transnational corporations, like all businesses, are not charitable organizations but organizations devoted to the pursuit of profit. It is irrelevant to criticize TNCs operating in the Third World because they are out to make profits. However, the means by which TNCs make profits in the Third World are a legitimate area of interest. Radical critics argue that TNCs in the Third World make their profits by exploiting cheap labour to produce goods that people often do not really need.

The logic of transnational production and marketing is at least partly based on standardization. Naturally, there are many TNCs that run specific production lines to serve specific markets (see Hill and Still, 1984a, b), but it is usually the case that a TNC will prefer to enter a new market with a standard product rather than incur the costs of retooling, redesign and perhaps restructuring of distribution. Therefore, it follows logically that it will normally be in the interests of the TNCs to try to create the market for their standard products in new locations irrespective of the perceived social needs of the indigenous populations, as Levitt (1983) persuasively argues.

TNC production and trade create new consumption needs in developing countries. Armstrong and McGee (1985), for example, show how cities in Asia and Latin America play a crucial role in the dissemination of 'Western' cultural values, particularly the philosophy of consumerism, and the central functions of the TNCs in this. These processes are not universally welcomed. A typical criticism is:

> The presence of transnational corporations in the manufacturing sectors of developing countries facilitates the transmission of their

'business culture,' their management concepts and operational
techniques, to Third World partners and to local entrepreneurs . . . .
Their sales campaigns have resulted, for example, in increasing
consumption of white bread, confections and soft drinks among the
poorest people in the world by convincing people that status,
convenience, and sweet taste are more important than nutrition.
(Jefkins and Ugboajah, 1986, pp.170–1)

This charge is illustrated with many telling examples from advertisements on Nigerian radio and television. Hamelink (1988, pp.2–
3), among others, extends the geographical scope.

A study of laundry cleaning products (detergents and soaps) in
Barbados (James, 1983), shows in detail how TNCs go about transforming consumption needs and capturing Third World markets.
In the early 1970s the local firm that had been producing soap since
1943 was closed down by the action of its major shareholder, who
also owned an import agency. For the previous few years the soap
factory had been losing business because of imports of synthetic
detergents, mainly through Lever Bros, the local branch of Unilever.[2] The importer had decided to clear the way for a more
profitable relationship with Lever Bros by eliminating the local
laundry soap competition entirely. The consequence of this was
that by the end of the decade the Unilever detergent and one other
brand had captured 90 per cent of the market in Barbados. Both
brands had heavy advertising expenditure and James demonstrates
empirically that consumers ranked the brands according to the
claims of the advertisers (soil and stain removal etc.), despite the
fact that independent tests showed very little actual difference
between the brands. The Unilever product cost twice as much per
ounce in Barbados as it did in England, and by driving out cheaper
local alternatives the end result for the lower income consumer in
Barbados was a product that was too expensive, too well-packaged
and often surplus to requirements. It is difficult to disagree with
James when he argues:

it is the existence of Lever Bros which itself sets a limit to the extent
of the trade-offs by ensuring the dominance of the type of products in
which multinational companies in general, and Lever Bros in
particular, have a comparative advantage, namely, brand
differentiated goods which are intensively promoted. That is to say,
the barriers to entry to the industry are such as to ensure the

dominance of the highly priced and expensively packaged products. Those involved in packaging and distributing the unbranded varieties wrapped in plastic are small-scale operators lacking both the necessary resources and marketing skills to capture a larger share of the detergent market. One of them expressed the fear that Lever's would cut off his sources of supply if his share of the market expanded sizeably. As far as competing local production is concerned, a number of industrialists interviewed said that they had considered the possibility but stressed the superior marketing skills of Lever Bros, diseconomies of small scale production and consumer preference for imported goods as the major disincentives. (James, 1983, p.148)

It is most unlikely that this is a special case, either in terms of product (detergents are a typical branded and highly competitive consumer product) or location (Barbados has no exceptional rules to encourage or discourage TNC products or advertising).

There is no straightforward way to deal with the question of appropriate products. The TNCs will naturally and in many cases justifiably argue that what their critics consider to be the creation of new needs in developing countries in order to boost profits is, in fact, a response to changing consumer needs that arise in societies that are in the process of urbanization and industrialization. I shall discuss in detail the underlying issue of the culture-ideology of consumerism and the role of the TNCs in it, in the next chapter.

However we may criticize the practices of the TNCs in the Third World, for most people whatever they do will be secondary to the major benefit they bring, namely the creation of employment.

TNC employment

As the discussion in the previous chapter indicated, the central sociological effect of economic transnational practices revolves around the impact of the TNCs on employment. There are some TNCs that have been operating in Latin America, Africa and Asia for decades and have won enviable reputations as model employers. At the other extreme there are others, for example in export processing zones, in which minimum wages are suspended, unions are forbidden and benefits, job security and conditions of work are very poor by any standards.

Vaitsos some years ago made the important point that:

> In the same product lines where foreign investors generally specialize, national firms do not necessarily behave differently and in some cases they might promote the direct use of less labor. In such cases the issue is not the foreignness of the ownership of the firm but the foreignness of the product and its technology to the conditions characterizing the producing country. (Vaitsos, 1974, p.345)

For most TNCs, plant size and branch of industry are more important determinants of their employment practices than the bare fact of foreign ownership. The biggest, the *Fortune* 500 corporations, often take the question of corporate identity very seriously and, although the wages they offer are not necessarily any better than those of other companies, their facilities and non-wage benefits do tend to be superior.[3] Such firms strive, though not always successfully, to inculcate feelings of membership of a global family among their mainly female employees through company magazines, competitions related to work and non-work activities, and widespread use of company logos on small gifts and prizes (see Fuentes and Ehrenreich, 1984).

TNCs have been responsible for the introduction of new industries and thus new categories of manufacturing (and also some non-manufacturing) employment into many developing countries over recent decades (see Grunwald and Flamm, 1985). There are several industries in which TNC Third World employment is significant. In consumer electronics, toys, apparel, automobile parts and sports goods, a major part of global production is carried out in the assembly plants of TNCs. This has repercussions all through the labour force. Operatives who have never previously held factory jobs need to be trained, expatriates are replaced with indigenous managerial and technical personnel, and indigenous capacity springs up in unfamiliar and/or high technology industries. Almost all of what was said about this in Chapter 3 is relevant wherever TNCs create jobs, but there are some additional factors to be considered where this occurs in the Third World.

We may distinguish the following cases:

1. The introduction by TNCs of industries where there were previously none at all. Export processing zones (EPZ) are often established in industrially virgin territory, for example, the Special Economic Zone at Shenzhen in China, some of the

maquila towns along Mexico's border with the United States and the Bataan EPZ in the Philippines.

2. The introduction by TNCs of new types of production into developing countries that are already industrializing in a substantial way. The technological upgrading of manufacturing and services in many of the Newly Industrializing Countries for which the TNCs are responsible is one example.
3. The direct or indirect intervention of TNCs in the structure of Third World industries through the processes of acquisition of indigenous companies, predatory pricing and restrictive practices to destroy local competition and enticements designed to attract key personnel from domestic to TNC employment.
4. There may also be differences between TNC employment in wholly-owned subsidiaries and in joint ventures, licensing agreements and other forms of foreign investment.

While TNC investment in the developing countries levelled off somewhat in the 1980s (UNCTC, 1988), the growth of export-oriented employment, mainly due to increased TNC activity in export processing (often referred to as 'production sharing' in the business press) continued to be rapid. In many of the lower-wage countries the growth of this type of employment has been the only real employment growth. This comment in a recent ILO/UNCTC study of EPZs in the Caribbean is very typical:'In spite of the small number of jobs generated so far, the rate at which EPZs create employment is, however, so high that they rank as the most dynamic agents for job creation compared with other sources of national employment' (Long, 1986, p.60). The point to note here is that it is the lower-wage countries for which this is the case and the crucial impact of the TNCs has been to create intense pressure to keep down labour costs in order to attract foreign investment. It is, therefore, not surprising to discover that in some, though not all, export oriented zones (EOZs)[4] the rights of workers to organize is curtailed, either formally or in practice, and that trade unions are either suppressed or manipulated through government–TNC collaboration (see Edgren, 1982).

There is a good deal of controversy over this issue. Fröbel and his colleagues, who developed the idea of the new international division of labour (1980), used the export processing zones and the 'world market factories' in them, to illustrate their thesis that the

NIDL was basically an extremely exploitative system. The main characteristics of this system they identified as disposable cheap labour, minimal skill transmission due to the fragmentation of work and maximum locational flexibility (footloose factories). In similar vein, the International Confederation of Free Trade Unions, the non-communist bloc transnational labour movement, issued a pessimistic report on export processing zones in 1983, focusing on the 'suppression of trade union rights'. ICFTU listed the problems of EPZs as a disappointing level of job creation, an extremely unbalanced structure of employment, low wages and poor working conditions, minimal job security, long hours and high intensity of production, minimal social services, poor living conditions, health and safety risks, special labour legislation and suppression of unions, and cases of non-ratification of ILO Conventions (ICFTU, 1983). Similarly, among researchers (with the partial exception of some free-market economists), it is rare to find a good word about EPZs. This is particularly true of feminist research on the TNCs.

The sexual division of labour

The spread of the transnational corporations has brought significant changes to the sexual division of labour in the Third World. It is well known, for example, that in many export oriented zones around the world most of the employees are women, often in the 16 to 24 years old, unmarried group. From the *maquilas* along the Mexico–US border to the electronics and garment factories of South East Asia, reports of 75 per cent of jobs being taken by young females in the foreign-owned sector are common.[5] The entrance of women into the manufacturing workforce, particularly into its most modern sectors, is clearly having important consequences in many Third World countries (see Tiano, 1988). This state of affairs produces a dilemma. In most countries women are glad to have jobs in factories and to earn cash, however tedious the work and however low their earnings are relative to male wages (but not to previous or alternative female pay). The geographical distribution of foreign direct investment (FDI) in many developing countries has meant job openings for women not only in the cities but also in small country towns and rural areas. Foreign direct investment in some countries of the Third World has resulted in a predominantly male state sector industrial labour force being augmented by many more women in private, especially foreign-owned, industry. The entry of the TNCs, therefore, has had effects on the sexual division of labour as well as on the division of labour in general (see Brydon and Chant, 1989, ch.7).

The impact of modern industry TNCs on patriarchal social relations in the developing countries has stimulated a great deal of interesting research in the 1980s (see, for example, Lim, 1985; Nash and Fernandez-Kelly, 1983; Garnsey and Paukert, 1987). There are three analytically separate (but empirically inter-twined) dimensions to be considered. These are as follows:

1. The sex composition of the TNC shopfloor labour force in the developing countries.
2. The opportunities for women to be upwardly mobile within TNCs compared with domestically-owned industries.
3. The impact of both of these on the position of women outside the sphere of employment in Third World countries.

1. The sex composition of the TNC shopfloor labour force, particularly in EOZs, has to be seen in the context of a substantial body of evidence to suggest that, in general, urban employers in the Third World tend to prefer men over women (Anker and Hein, 1986). Garnsey and Paukert (1987, pp.12–24) suggest that there are relatively more women working in industry in Asia than in Africa and Latin America. However, the TNC-dominated export industries tend to employ more women than men. The reasons for this have stimulated a great deal of argument and it is not always possible to generalize cross-culturally. For example, in Mauritius women have a legislated lower minimum wage than men (Hein, in Anker and Hein, 1986, ch.7), whereas in Mexico there is no legal difference, though men do tend to monopolize the higher-paying jobs (Sklair, 1989, ch.8). So while differential wage rates might explain the preponderance of women in the Mauritius EPZ, they do not explain it in the Mexican *maquilas* (in-bond factories). However, as is widely attested, irrespective of minimum wages, women do tend to earn less than men in the First as well as the Third World.[6]

A more convincing explanation is that the industries that are most common in the EPZs, apparel and electronics assembly, are industries that employ many more women than men wherever they are (see Nash and Fernandez-Kelly, 1983, Part IV; Mitter, 1986). Why do these industries employ mostly women? The answer to this question is usually in terms of the boring, monotonous and repetitive nature of the work and the widespread belief that women make a more docile, patient (long-suffering?) labour force, less likely to join unions and/or organize to improve their conditions. Despite some evidence to the contrary of Third World women in EOZs organizing fierce resistance to exploitation, of a sexual as well as a general nature, the overwhelming weight of evidence supports the view that most women workers in EOZs, while not necessarily enthralled by their jobs, are glad to have them and much prefer them to the alternatives on offer. This issue will be resumed in (3) below.

2. While TNCs are not universally renowned for their commitment to feminist principles, there is a sense in which the generally more egalitarian employment practices of the United States and Europe spill over into developing countries through TNC direct investment. The increasing though still very minimal participation of women in managerial, technical and higher professional occupations within the corporation has already attracted a good deal of attention, but there is little research specifically on the phenomenon of the female salariat in TNCs in the Third World (see Garnsey and Paukert, 1987, pp.57–67). My own research in Mexico suggests that female managers tend to be found in those departments that are concerned with interpersonal relations within the plant (personnel, public relations, training) and that women who start off in these areas and succeed are occasionally promoted to higher levels of management. There is also a route through from secretarial and personal assistant positions to higher levels.

Cultural attributes (English language skills, style of life, adoption of US or European rather than local 'attitudes and values') appear to be just as important as more formal job skills in the promotion of women as well as men in the TNCs in developing countries. In the absence of systematic research on these questions one can only speculate on the likely consequences of changes in employment practices. There is little evidence that a woman's chance of advancement is any worse in the TNCs than in domestic industry. More research in this area is needed. It is difficult to know whether the increasing participation of Third World women in managerial, technical and professional employment in TNCs in the Third World is simply part of the 'indigenization' process of replacing expatriate with local personnel, or whether it is a qualitatively different phenomenon in its own right.

3. One entirely unresolved issue revolves around the question of the balance of costs and benefits for women due to the entry of the TNCs in the Third World. Some have argued that the TNCs have disrupted traditional family life where they have hired more women than men, for example along Mexico's northern border (see Fernandez-Kelly, in Nash and Fernandez-Kelly, 1983). As Susan Tiano has shown, this view might imply some contradictory sexist assumptions (in Ruiz and Tiano, 1987, ch.4). Work on TNC investment in Asia has similarly brought to the surface some of the problems and contradictions of the analysis of patriarchal societies from a progressive feminist perspective. There is clearly a connection between the preference of TNCs to hire women over men in EPZs in order to procure a more docile labour force (regularly cloaked in the rationale that 'nimble-fingered girls' are more suited for assembly work), and the cruder forms of patriarchy in some Third World countries.

However, as Lim and Foo (1987) argue, it is difficult to generalize on the impact of TNC employment on different groups of women even within the same society. Their research on Malaysian and Singaporean women export-industry workers (a category that mostly includes TNC workers) shows that ethnicity and the availability of alternative employment can be key factors in the social and moral evaluation of women workers, and that there are substantial variations in the conceptions of factory work for women (whether in TNCs or not) across different communities. This does not necessarily disprove the contention that TNCs exploit women workers in particular in the Third World, though it does modify the thesis to the extent that in some developing countries TNCs do provide some good jobs for women that help them to fulfil relatively freely chosen cultural needs.

The point, however, is not whether exploitation of women or men occurs in TNC factories, for they are capitalist institutions predicated on the exploitation of all the factors of production. The point is, to what extent is the abuse of women and men as workers over and above *capitalist exploitation in a particular society* more characteristic inside than outside of TNCs? Are they guilty of more abuse than domestic companies? The International Labour Organization (ILO), the Asian Regional Team for Employment Promotion (ARTEP) and others have conducted worthwhile research on these issues. The ILO's 'Multinational Enterprises Project' has produced a series of reports on the employment effects of the TNCs, mostly in Third World countries and, although some abuses are documented, the general conclusions of Fröbel *et al.* Fernandez-Kelly, ICFTU, and other leftist-populist critics are not entirely supported.

For example, in an ARTEP study of export zones in Sri Lanka, South Korea, the Philippines, Malaysia and India, Maex (1983) demonstrates that poor wages and conditions are explained better by the characteristics of the workforce in zone industries (mainly young women), than by their location or the ownership of the plants. Young women are not poorly paid because they work for TNCs in export zones, they are poorly paid wherever they work, but TNCs may well employ young women in the zones because they are cheaper to employ than older men in some countries.

Dror points out that: 'With few exceptions, the incentive package does not include easily identifiable features pertaining directly to labour, such as suspension of labour laws, prohibition of trade union activity or lower (minimum) wage' (1984, p.706). His four case studies, of Mauritius, Pakistan, Philippines and Sri Lanka, however, reveal a variety of repressive labour practices. In Pakistan: 'The wholesale exemption of EPZ enterprises from the provisions of so many labour laws leaves many issues to the mercy of the individual contract of employment' (p.709), while in the Philippines: 'The Bataan administrator said that some EPZ employees were paying 75 per cent of the minimum wage for six months, then dismissing the workers and hiring others at the 75 per cent rate' (p.711). Similar practices can be found elsewhere, for example in the Mexican *maquila* industry and in China's Special Economic Zones.

The trade unions have been particularly strong in the Bataan EPZ, but this is unusual in export zones (see Mitter, 1986, pp.74–9). It is not surprising that the typical EPZ worker does not join a union because most unions are male-dominated and tend to be completely unresponsive to the needs of women workers. The absence of strong unions has been connected with the alleged propensity of TNCs to hop from one cheap labour zone to another

(Fröbel *et al.*, 1980), though Dror finds little evidence of 'footloose' industries. Despite some notorious examples of TNCs abandoning their Third World (and sometimes First World) workers without legal compensation, there is no evidence to suggest that TNC plants inside or outside of zones are statistically any more likely to close down than domestic companies. To add to the complexity, Maex finds that wages in Asian EPZs tend to be somewhat lower than national averages (Maex, 1983, p.53), while Dror suggests that 'in most EPZs remuneration is often somewhat higher than in comparable occupations in the same country' (1984, p.715). My own research in Mexico (Sklair, 1989, ch.7–9) similarly shows the impact of gender and ownership on wages to be very complex.

We are, therefore, forced to conclude that it is impossible to generalize about TNC employment practices in export zones *per se*, though we can generalize about the effects of TNC employment practices on particular industries and particular workforces. To recall Vaitsos' point, it is not the foreignness of the firm that makes the difference but the foreignness of the product and its technology, what can be called its *transnationality* within the global capitalist system.

Transnational pressures on TNCs

Many TNCs embark on offshore production to escape from their domestic unions, particularly in the United States. This is another area of considerable controversy.While some argue that the anti-labour nature of many of the governments in such low-wage countries makes the task of the TNCs even easier, others argue that the TNCs tend to bring a more progressive atmosphere into labour relations than had previously been the case in such countries. It must be said, however, that it is not only the obviously authoritarian Third World regimes, desperate for FDI, that have sometimes been prepared to sacrifice the interests of their workers in order to insure the jobs created by the TNCs.

And this, of course, has always been the central dilemma and one that the critics of TNC practices in the Third World cannot escape. The problematic global economic situation of the 1980s sharpened the horns of this dilemma for both TNCs and Third World governments and workers. While there is no convincing evidence that the TNCs can bring salvation to the Third World, in many poor countries the TNCs are seen as responsible for the only bright spots in the economy and society. This is why the strategy of 'export led industrialization fuelled by foreign investment and technology' (ELIFFIT) has been so powerful.[7] The most visible aspect of this is the jobs that the TNCs have created. Irrespective of the fact that many, perhaps most of these jobs are low paid, dirty (even the gleaming electronics industry is on the defensive against charges of health and safety problems for its workforce) and monotonous, they are very widely sought after and they carry high prestige. It is not only the numbers of TNC jobs but their specific character in Third World contexts that imbues them with prestige. At the lowest level in the TNC hierarchy, the operatives, there is clearly a reputational element at work, in so far as working for a company that has an international name appears to mean something positive for most people. Further, the huge resources of the larger TNCs always promise skill enhancement and local promotion. The evidence on this question is sketchy (Enderwick, 1985). Transnational corporations are sensitive to home country criticisms that they are exporting jobs and, the less menial the jobs, the more vulnerable the TNCs.

Transnational corporations label this process 'production sharing'. The argument is that the First World will contribute the high-value technology and components for the production process, while the Third World will contribute the low-value low skill labour. Any upgrading of skills in Third World TNC production is liable to be challenged by home-country constituencies, at the same time as it is welcomed by those in the host country. This is a zero-sum game (particularly in the United States) in that each occurrence of technical upgrading of a TNC plant in a developing country is at the same time proudly announced for host-country consumption by the TNC, and seized upon in the home country as evidence of job destruction. Technological developments, in particular computer aided design and manufacturing (CAD/CAM), introduce further complexities.

An example of this process is in the fashion garment industry. Here, information on current consumer preferences can be transmitted by computer almost instantaneously from the marketplace to the factory, wherever it might be, and even design modifications or completely new designs can be electronically fed into CAD/

CAM equipment in the factory for instant production. This has led to some repatriation of the apparel industry from the Third World back to the First. For the small producer, subcontracting to a TNC, the system is prohibitively expensive and the expertise required to run it is considerable, so it tends to be controlled by TNCs, or by the gargantuan retailers that they supply. This means that garment workers in the Third World who benefited from the search for cheap labour by the TNCs in the past, can no longer assume that their jobs will always be safe from relocation back to the First World (Elson, in Elson and Pearson, 1989). However, it is too soon to say with any degree of certainty to what extent computerization spells the end of TNC jobs in the Third, or in the First World (Caulkin, 1989).

The case of the Mexican *maquila* industry illustrates this well. The *maquila* (in-bond) industry was introduced along Mexico's northern border in the mid-1960s and was extended to the rest of the country in 1972. The Mexican government set up the *maquila* programme to create jobs, earn dollars and introduce technology. For the US firms, including many *Fortune* 500 corporations, the main point was that labour was much cheaper in Mexico. From very small beginnings, by 1990 about 1,500 plants employed almost half a million workers producing a great variety of goods. The *maquilas* have been accused of causing job losses in the United States due to companies moving to Mexico. United States proponents of the *maquilas* argue that these jobs are bound to go anyway and that the advantage of the *maquila* industry on the border is that it has always used a high proportion of US materials, components and services. They have claimed that far from destroying jobs the *maquilas* may actually create new jobs in the United States. It may be difficult to persuade a television assembly worker whose plant in the United States has closed and relocated to Mexico that the *maquila* industry creates jobs in the United States, but it is not so difficult to persuade a worker who makes television components in a US factory that supplies an assembly plant in Mexico, that the *maquila* industry protects US jobs.

Maquila proponents have also had to persuade successive Mexican governments that the *maquilas* are good for Mexico. Many US-owned *maquilas* claim to be in the market for locally produced materials and components, backward linkages. As I explained in the previous chapter, there is no export zone anywhere that has a good record on linkages, but few have a worse record than the *maquila* industry. The inability of Mexico to produce (or to sell) these materials and components is a fact that Mexican and US *maquila* facilitators tend to obscure when presenting their case in Mexico! Clearly, both sides cannot win. Either the *maquilas* continue to buy from the United States and protect the jobs of US suppliers, or the *maquilas* buy in Mexico, and these jobs are lost.

Another supposed benefit for Mexico is the replacement of US managers, technicians and highly trained personnel in the *maquilas* by Mexicans. This has happened to an appreciable extent. United States-owned *maquilas* have, of course, great incentives to employ Mexican managers and technicians. They speak Spanish, they are familiar with local conditions and they are much cheaper than equivalent US personnel. Technology transfer has also taken place to some extent and there are a few highly advanced *maquilas*. But, again, any gain for Mexico will usually mean a loss for the United States.

Every case has its special characteristics. For Mexico, the shared border with the United States and the dramatic devaluations of the peso explain the rapid growth in the 1980s, but other features, for example, the changing positions of indigenous managers and technicians, are quite typical of the spread of economic transnational practices in employment and other areas.

Gradually, TNCs appear to have seen the benefits of (or in some countries accepted the inevitability of) employing host-country managers and technicians to run their plants.[8] It is likely that the chief executive of a TNC plant in a Third World country will still be from the home country, but it is now quite common to see host-country nationals occupying salaried positions at all levels. Studies show that up to 40 per cent of expatriate US executives fail on foreign assignments, and have to be sent home, and that expatriate managers are increasingly considered by the TNCs to be a source of avoidable trouble and expense (Harvey, 1985). The rise of the international business schools over the last decades and the substantial increase in the numbers of Third World students in the universities and technical institutes of the First World have provided an ever-increasing pool of potential local employees for the TNCs, and recruitment is brisk. The business schools also provide recruits for domestic industry, and in many Third World countries the government gives young graduates from such institutions posts

with high degrees of responsibility in national development agencies where they can make substantial contributions to the welfare
of their nations.

Training and technology

The role of the TNCs in training is quite controversial. Not everyone accepts the 'received knowledge' that TNCs are good at training managers, and that these managers spread their know-how
throughout Third World host societies. For example, in the case of
Kenya, Gershenberg (1987) found that publically-owned firms,
and to a lesser extent TNCs in equity joint ventures with the
Kenyan government, are more likely to foster local management
training and dissemination of know-how than private firms. Although there is an important ethnic factor in this research, namely
the predominance of Asian over African managers in the sample,
the finding is still significant.

  Another study, on Indonesia, has suggested that the TNCs are
more liable to attract managers from local firms than to do their
own training (Okada, 1983). Much more research is needed on the
differences between TNC, joint venture and domestic firms, in the
private and public domains, in this context, particularly as it is
likely that more Third World governments will insist on joint venture and similar agreements as a condition for the continued presence of the TNCs.

  From the point of view of the TNC, the main point of managerial and technical recruitment is often posed in terms of the
need to transfer technology to the host society. There is a large
literature on technology transfer, though not much of it is from the
perspective of the developing countries. There are, however, a few
exceptions. Adikibi (1983) analyzes how the TNCs that controlled
the modern tyre sector in Nigeria produced to global standards
and did so with a good complement of indigenous managers and
technicians. There was no doubt that these people could produce
tyres, but when the TNCs withdrew from Nigeria during the
Biafran war, production ceased in the factories because of the
ways in which the TNCs had organized the division of labour on
the shop floor. The indigenous personnel, while they were fully
trained in the specific features of their own parts of the process,

were excluded from positions that gave access to the whole of the production process. Thus, the TNCs protected their monopoly in technique while appearing to transfer the technology to local people.

This is neither uncommon (see, for example, Sano, 1983) nor surprising (Stewart, 1978, ch.5), in light of the technological dependence of most Third World industries, and the analogous technological dominance of the TNCs. For many TNCs, protection of technology is a matter of corporate life and death. Exposure to hostile action by host governments might be substantially increased if the host governments believed that their nationals could run the plants. Therefore, many TNCs might feel that there were risks inherent in training local technicians and managers too well. Such considerations are relevant for the ways in which TNCs set out to create 'comprador bourgeoisies' (and 'comprador proletariats' in some cases) as specific elements in the transnational capitalist class in their Third World operations.

Nevertheless, TNCs do introduce much useable technology into the Third World, and while it may not lead to the conquest of global markets it may still have a very positive effect on industry and employment in particular countries. The ILO 'Multinational Enterprises' programme, noted above in connection with export processing zones, also sponsored a series of studies on the employment generation effects of technology choice by TNCs in the Third World. Studies in Singapore, Nigeria, Brazil, India and Kenya uncovered a very wide range of technologies in use and if indirect employment is taken into account, a considerable job creation effect is visible. Though technological change does tend to lead to more capital intensive than labour intensive development, there can be substantial employment created indirectly through backward and forward linkages. An example from the Kenya study is where employees left a TNC car assembly plant to set up their own roadside workshops (ILO, 1984, ch.III).

In the case of joint ventures (and similar arrangements) there are different issues at stake. Here, the transfer of technology is often the main point of the exercise. In a study of thirty-three European chemical and pharmaceutical joint ventures in Indonesia, Thailand, Philippines, Singapore and Malaysia, Lasserre (1982) discovered that home-country technicians were not trained to train in specific socio-cultural settings. Training, in any case, was very limited, local staff visits to home-country plants were not very involving, and on-the-job training tended to consist of little more than watching expatriates at work. Thus, 'although on paper there is a training effort, the results are far from satisfactory' (Lasserre, 1982, p.57).

This is not very surprising when we consider that most joint ventures appear not to be entirely voluntary. One study, based on sixty-six Third World firms (and the evidence from other studies), found three main reasons for setting up joint ventures: host-government pressure, the need for the partner's skills and the need for other attributes or assets. In addition, the creation of joint ventures was often due to non-tariff barriers threatening the market position of the TNC (see Beamish, 1985).

The difference between such joint ventures and *indigenization* (forcing domestic ownership on a foreign company) may be narrow. Where developing countries restrict the numbers of expatriates that are permitted to remain in TNC employment in the host country or the level of ownership that the TNC retains, the power of the TNC appears to be undermined. But there is little evidence to suggest that where a TNC has actually *survived* indigenization, its effective control has been very much affected. The TNCs are extraordinarily adept at creating and managing the transnational managerial and corporate bourgeoisies. Indigenization can in some cases be seen as a force strengthening the TNC by disarming its opponents, as studies of Indonesia (Okada, 1983) and of Nigeria suggest. I shall look at the case of Nigeria in more detail below, in the section on the transnational capitalist class.

Transnational corporations and Third World food

In many Third World countries food industries constitute the bulk of the industrial sector. Food products account for about 30 per cent of Third World manufacturing output and more of employment (Fath, 1985). This is not surprising, for one would suppose that every country has to satisfy the basic needs of its people for food as a first priority. As many developing countries are slowly but surely moving from economies based predominantly on agriculture into manufacturing and service industries, and as Third World populations are moving in great numbers from rural to urban areas, there are concomitant changes in the structures of food provision in these countries (Abbott, 1987). Briefly put, all these changes in employment and residence mean that fewer and fewer people in the developing countries are able or willing to procure their own food directly from the land and so they are becoming more and more dependent on bought and processed food and drink. This has, of course, been the case in the advanced industrial societies for a very long time, but with the difference that the food and beverage industry today is concentrated in the hands of a relatively small number of TNCs (see Clairmonte and Cavanagh, 1988). This has introduced a qualitatively new circumstance that was not operating when today's First World countries were making their transitions to industrialization and urbanization (see Leopold, 1985).

Women and food production

It is impossible to analyze food production in the Third World in isolation from the relationship between the sexual division of labour and the sources of economic power. In land-scarce societies, like many Latin American countries, men will tend to monopolize the land, both through male peasant appropriation of family plots and the big landlord system of production. In sub-Saharan Africa, where land hunger is more rare, women tend to be left alone to cultivate and market their produce. However, where agriculture starts to become mechanized, usually under the auspices of the colonial powers and/or foreign investors, men begin to take more interest and to appropriate the economic gains for themselves (see Boserup, 1970; Brydon and Chant, 1989, ch.3).

Patrilocal residence, where women join the households of their husbands rather than vice versa, and the continued strength of the system of domestic production, where families consume most of what they produce rather than buy and sell in the market, have always been seen as obstacles to capitalist development in the Third World and as strong reinforcements for the maintenance of feudal–patriarchal relations. Ever since the earliest days of colonialism, however, capitalism has developed long-standing mechanisms to integrate such recalcitrant social formations into the global system of production and distribution. Third World rural economies were brought into the global system by making it more difficult for their populations to live outside the market, thus forcing them to produce crops that could be sold, as opposed to producing crops that they themselves consumed. The global commodity system was largely based on persuading the peoples of the non-industrial countries to produce the food and industrial raw materials that were necessary for the continuous growth of capitalism and industrialization in the First World.

In order to achieve this the colonial authorities had to engineer a switch from subsistence production of basic food crops to the production of cash crops for the international market and to replace what is often termed the 'natural' economy of non-industrial societies with the 'money' economy of industrial societies. This has undoubtedly led to the enrichment of specific rural and urban groups in the Third World, those who have successfully adapted to the changing demands of the global marketplace, but it has also resulted in many Third World countries losing their original self-sufficiency in food and becoming highly dependent on food imports from the First World. Such economic transformations tend to undermine both the national independence of Third World countries, and the autonomy of women where this is based on some degree of control over land.

Historically, this is a surprising and a disturbing conclusion. In the nineteenth century, the effects of economic development, colonialism and capitalism were widely thought to be wholly favourable to women. The assumption that modernization would help to liberate women from the semi-servitude of 'primitive' patriarchal societies was deeply embedded in the consciousness of charitable institutions and individuals in the West, not least the Christian missionaries who flocked to save souls, introduce underwear and establish proper moral codes in the empires of the colonial powers. However, these optimistic hopes, while not entirely misconceived, appear to have ignored the many formidable traditional obstacles to the emancipation of women that still remain in most Third World societies, as well as new obstacles created by the so-called 'modernization' processes themselves. Thus, women's work in domestic food production has remained largely invisible (see Boserup, 1970; Petritsch, 1985), while the role of the TNCs is broadcast from television, radio, newsprint and billboards all over the Third World. Agribusiness is global!

Agribusiness

According to United Nations studies (see Fath, 1985), in the 1970s less than one-third of the food consumed in the Third World was processed. Affiliates of TNCs accounted for about one-eighth of the Third World food processing industry, and about 90 per cent of this was in the branded goods and the export sector. TNCs tend to be active in wheat and corn milling, animal feed, poultry, processed dairy products, canned fruit and vegetables, breakfast cereals, margarine and table oils, confectionery, soft drink concentrates, beer, coffee and cocoa products. In the export sector, TNCs are still central in bananas, fish, canned fruit and tea; quite important in vegetable oils, cocoa, coffee and flowers; but no longer central in sugar and beef products.

In no single developing country will the TNCs entirely dominate the production and marketing of food and, indeed, compared with some industries, the role of the TNCs in food looks quite minor. TNCs tend to dominate specific product markets rather than whole industries. In Mexico in 1970, for example, there were no foreign dairy bottlers and only one ice-creamer, but ten out of twelve canned milk producers were foreign. The primary interest of the TNCs in Mexico, as everywhere else in the Third World, is in the urban middle-class market. For example, Nestlé refused to develop a cheap infant milk for the Mexican government low-cost food agency, and Nabisco refused to develop a soy-based breakfast cereal for government distribution. 'Rather than investing in research and development of new products for the poor, foreign firms invest in advertising existing products for the well-to-do' (Whiting, 1985, p.370). While Mexico exports food, but not processed foods, foreign food processors are net importers, and where TNCs use local raw materials the contracting arrangements tend to drive the poorer peasants off the land.

The relationship between cash crops, particularly those for export, and subsistence crops for local consumption, has occasioned an intense and sometimes bitter debate that has been going on for decades, if not centuries, and goes to the very heart of the global capitalist system and its transnational contradictions. In the 1980s the debate revolved round what has been labelled the World Bank 'complementarity thesis'. Bassett's (1988) case study of Ivory Coast cotton is a good example. Four parts of the thesis are distinguished. First, the trickle-down fertilizer hypothesis predicts that local food crops will benefit from increased fertilizer use on the cash crop. In the study area what actually happened was that food crops were displaced from the head to the end of the fertilizer rotation in more than half the cases. The second hypothesis is that cash cropping increases the general mechanization of agriculture. What actually happened was that mechanization was concentrated on land clearing incentives, representing an 'extraordinary subsidy to the relatively wealthy progressive farmer' (Bassett, 1988, p.52). The third prediction is that cash crops will create regional food markets. The rice that the peasants in the research area bought came from Burma, Thailand and China, not from the Ivory Coast or its neighbours. Finally, the complementarity thesis predicts that services and subsidies for export crops will also benefit food crops. They did not, for the obvious reason that the cash crop companies have no interest in developing food crops.

In this case, subsistence requirements could still be met from cotton income, but as there appears to be no clearly demonstrated link between cash crop promotion and improvements in food crops to make up for the shortfall in the cropping area that results from giving over the land to cash crops, the issue of food security must be raised. Between 1970 and 1986 the Ivory Coast, often regarded as one of Africa's success stories, more than tripled its cereals imports, its external debt rose more than thirty-fold, and food production per capita barely kept up with population growth (World Bank, 1988, Tables). Like other Third World countries its quest for World Bank-induced export earnings through cash crops has been purchased at a high price with no apparent significant complementarity in food crops.[9]

Not everyone, however, fully accepts that TNC involvement in Third World agriculture always does lead to food insecurity. Scott (1985) argues that the criticisms of TNCs in food processing export industries in the Third World often fail to distinguish between *national* and *personal* food security. Foreign investment, Scott claims, may reduce food insecurity in a variety of ways, for example by increasing export diversification. But what is possible in theory, does not always happen in practice, and there are many Third World countries that were recently more or less self-sufficient in basic foodstuffs, that are now increasingly dependent on imports. This is not entirely explained by huge increases in population, as is widely propagated by the mass media and widely believed. Many very poor countries, and even some that have suffered famines in the 1980s, like Ethiopia, have actually turned over land to cash crops for export. In Egypt, the growing reliance on huge imports of cheap grain from the United States has made it uneconomical for local farmers to grow grain, and large tracts of land that once grew food for local consumption now grow strawberries, luxury vegetables and other cash crops for export (see Steif, 1989).

In different circumstances this might be a great success story, after all, the world's largest food grain importer is Japan. However, Egypt's grain imports more than doubled between 1970 and 1986, from under 4 million to almost 9 million tonnes (about 180 kg per head), foreign debt increased twenty-five fold, to over $22 billion, and when the IMF forced the government to increase the price of bread, there were riots in the streets.[10] Transnational involvement in the Egyptian food system can by no stretch of the imagination be said to have improved Egypt's long-term food security. How, we may ask, can a country like Egypt, by no means the poorest or most vulnerable in the Third World, find itself in this position?

There are, of course, many answers to this question at many levels. The role of the TNCs in solving or intensifying the problems of hunger in the Third World is extremely controversial. The range of views put forward in a small sample of recent works on the subject (see Abbott, 1987; Berardi, 1985; George, 1985; Tullis and Hollist, 1986), illustrates well the complexities of the issues and the difficulty of solving them. For example, the TNCs that control the world grain trade are criticized if they do not sell grain to the Third World, and they are criticized if they do. Everyone agrees, however, that a few TNCs control the global trade in grain, as well as the trade in other basic commodities. Andrae and Beckman (1985), in a provocative study of Nigeria, label the global grain system, a 'wheat trap'. Burbach and Flynn (1980) suggest that similar problems in Latin America have similar explanations.

Let us focus our attention on where Third World grain imports come from and how they happen to be available in such massive quantities. For this, we need to look at the history of the United States Public Law 480 (PL 480). *Foreign Agriculture*, a US Department of Commerce magazine, under the unequivocal title 'U.S. Food Aid Builds Cash Markets in Developing Countries' (February 1984, pp.20–1) provides an account of PL 480, in celebration of its thirtieth anniversary. 'PL 480 was enacted as a means of exporting surplus U.S. commodities to dollar-short nations' and 'has become an important vehicle for developing commercial export markets, for meeting humanitarian food needs, and for spurring economic and agricultural growth in the developing world' (p.20). Since 1954, over 300 million tonnes of agricultural products valued at $33 billion have been sent to more than 100 countries under the programme. Over 70 per cent has moved under Title I, concessional sales, of which 80 per cent has gone to the Third World, representing almost one-third of total US direct aid to them. The main recipients have been India ($6 billion), Egypt ($2.7 billion), South Korea ($1.9 billion) and Indonesia ($1.7 billion). 'Aid often is a springboard to trade . . . PL 480 has established itself as one of the United States' most successful market development tools' (p.20). Korea, Taiwan and Mexico now buy significant amounts of US produce, and Egypt, Indonesia, the Dominican Republic, Morocco, Tunisia and Peru are beginning to do so. About half of US grain exports go under PL 480.[11]

All the expertise of a fully computerized trade and product information service is available for US exporters and no corner of the global marketplace is left un-intelligenced. The United States spends hundreds of millions of dollars on a Targeted Export Assistance Program (TEA) under the interestingly labelled Food Security Act of 1985, to help US producers disadvantaged by unfair competition from abroad. The 'Country Briefs' section of *Foreign Agriculture* for September 1986 lists the following:

> *Jamaica's* programme for local milk production is an 'excellent opportunity to export high-quality U.S. dairy cattle' (p.20).
>
> *Egypt's* growing demand for protein meals for animal feed is welcomed as the United States is the largest supplier of feeds. A new floating elevator at Abu Keer near Alexandria (built with USAID funds) will facilitate bulk shipments.
>
> *Korea's* growing rapeseed imports are causing anxiety, as they could cut into US soybeans sales.
>
> *Taiwan's* cattle industry is expanding, opening the door for US alfalfa sales.

Foreign Agriculture is full of evidence to suggest what the cynical reader must have already suspected, and what the open-minded reader may well be beginning to suspect. Is the global food strategy of the United States designed to undermine the capacity of Third World countries to feed themselves, and render them dependent on cash crop earnings to buy food from ever-bulging US silos supplied by fully mechanized US farms? When anything is being grown in the Third World, the United States seems to stand ready to supply all the technical inputs required. This is an understandable conclusion, but it is flawed in one essential respect, namely its state-centrism. The US government as such has no interest in rendering the Third World unable to feed itself. Apart from the assumed humanitarian philosophies of most US politicians and citizens, nothing is better designed to drive poor countries into the arms of the communists than shortages of food. It is quite absurd to suggest that the US government, or any other food surplus government, plans such things.

It is not absurd, however, to suggest that, implicitly, TNCs might see their best interests served in such a strategy.[12] Transnational corporations in the grain business, financing its production, transporting it around the world, building handling facilities, processing it, breeding fine seeds, might well consider that the inhibition of Third World grain production will maximize their profits. They might also, and in a perverse way, quite sensibly believe that if US farmers can produce grain 'cheaper' than farmers in the Third World then it will also be in the interests of the Third World to participate in such a global food system. In this they will find enthusiastic allies within the Third World in the political sphere, in the bureaucracy and in business circles, who might prefer cash crops (see Burnell, 1986, ch.3). As Tullis and Hollist (1986) point out in the introduction to their book on the international political economy of food:

> Urban-biased policy makers frequently have fostered an increase in exports in order to earn foreign exchange without much regard for impacts on rural employment, nutrition, migration, or domestic food security. Until now, fostering economic growth through export expansion has been the easiest and safest thing to do politically. (1986, p.viii)

We can be sure that this is true of most transnational capitalist classes.

Cash crop exports are politically 'safe' in the sense that hard currency earnings allow Third World governments to buy in cheap grain to feed their urban populations, and relieve them of the problems of ensuring adequate food supplies from what sometimes appears to be a permanently disgruntled peasantry. Cash crops can also, of course, be commercially very lucrative, but only when they are acceptable on the world market. This is rarely under the control of the producer country, even less the actual direct producer, the farmer, but is increasingly coming under the control of the TNC conglomerates that manage the global food system. The case study by Sanderson (1985) on the emergence of the 'World Steer' is a good illustration of this process.

The world steer, like the world car, has emerged over the last decades through an international standardization of producer technology and a specific set of social relations. These are transnational in scope (combining US feedlot technology, European antibiotics and the Japanese market for boxed beef); and based on international standards for consumption and trade. This is not synonymous with foreign domination, for national firms in Brazil, Mexico and Argentina are also into the world steer.

> The homogenization of tastes for certain products (and the productive processes they imply) shows that there is little difference in the creation of a luxury commodity for foreign consumers and its creation for domestic elites at the expense of the rural poor. (Sanderson, 1986, p.127)

There are two very important points here. First, the global standardization of taste is global only in a class sense. Capitalism has yet to make high quality beefsteak available on a regular basis for all the inhabitants of the rich countries, let alone those in the poor countries. Second, the system tends to work for more affluent foreign consumers and domestic elites by making life more difficult for the rural poor. For example, as Mexico exports more and more live cattle for processing in the United States, the hides and by-products traditionally used by poor Mexican consumers and artisans are now being re-imported for sale at much higher prices.[13] This raises two questions. Why should the TNCs produce what the poor need? Who is to determine what the poor in the Third World really do need?

Mindful of questions such as these, many Third World governments have tried to establish food policies in order to ensure an acceptable level of food security over the medium and long term.

With few exceptions, they have turned to the TNCs for help in this daunting task. Consequently, some transnational economic practices have increased the capacity of Third World countries to feed themselves. But even in such cases, there are those who argue that it is the interests of the global capitalist system that are being primarily served, even if some of these interests happen to be those of the transnational capitalist class within a Third World country, and benefits eventually filter down.

Sano's book on food in Nigeria demonstrates how a government's attempt to cut its food imports by stimulating domestic production led to an increasing dependency on imports of farm inputs, especially fertilizer and machinery. The TNCs control research and production of new seed varieties and, as many studies have argued, the so-called Green Revolution was managed in large part through the TNCs and ended up benefiting the rich farmer and merchant classes, and increasing the poverty of the rural masses.[14] Even some apparently successful agricultural projects are suspect:

> though they might be instrumental in reducing the level of food imports in the course of the next five to ten years, they will increase Nigerian dependency on foreign-manufactured commodities and know-how . . . imports like fertilizers, pesticides and agricultural machinery. (Sano, 1983, p.66)

In this case, dependency moves from the primary level of food imports, to a secondary level of technical inputs, and then to a tertiary level of import substitution plants run by the TNCs. As with import substitution in Latin America and parts of Asia, the heavy costs of imports sustained by these projects seriously reduced their economic benefits for Nigeria. State government claims that

> contracts for machinery and equipment were primarily awarded to foreign firms at overvalued prices, even when the items were available in Nigeria, and that the training of the Nigerian staff in the project was insufficient to enable it to take over the project (p.71)

are all too familiar.

Criticisms like this of TNCs, based on their foreignness, are often confused with those based on transnational practices, which domestic firms may share. The choice in the Third World is not between foreign exploitative private capitalism and domestic altruistic communitarian enterprise, in the food or in any other industry. The choice is more likely to be between more or less efficient foreign exploitative transnational corporations and highly protected and perhaps corrupt local state, parastatal or private firms. The point at issue is not whether a corporation and its practices are foreign, but to what extent they are transnational. This raises the question of political practices and the transnational capitalist class, to which I now turn.

The transnational capitalist class in the Third World

The term *comprador*, from the Portuguese 'to buy', has its origins in the employment of the domestic servants of white colonialists in India and China. These people would handle the household accounts of their employers and act as go-betweens with the local population. In China, the European trading houses began to employ local Chinese to act as their agents from the middle of the nineteenth century, and the term began to be attached to those who would serve the interests of the foreigner before the interests of their co-nationals.[15] In many Third World countries, therefore, *comprador* is a term of abuse and, as a consequence has lost most of the little value it ever had for analysis. This is why I much prefer the term *transnational capitalist class* or *classes* (TCC), for it has fewer of the pejorative connotations that have bedevilled the comprador class. Transnational capitalist classes do not identify with any foreign country in particular, or even necessarily with the First World, or the white world, or the Western world. They identify with the global capitalist system, reconceptualize their several national interests in terms of the global system, and take on the political project of reconceptualizing the national interests of their co-nationals in terms of the global capitalist system. What I referred to previously as the *comprador mentality*, the slavish attachment to things foreign, is not a necessary component of the ideology of the TCC, but it does occur (see Chan, 1987, ch.18).

Although the comprador class in one form or another has existed for centuries, the transnational capitalist class is a relatively new phenomenon. The basic difference between the two is that, whereas the compradors are entirely beholden to TNCs and foreign interests, the transnational capitalist class can develop into a class that may, under certain circumstances, begin to dictate its own terms to the TNCs and foreign interests. That this is rarely understood is a direct consequence of the combined influence of the state-centrist idea and the dependency thesis, both of which consistently confuse the power of the First World with the power of the TNCs, and the weakness of the Third World with the presumed weakness of its economic institutions. Of course, most TNCs are domiciled for legal purposes in the First World, and most Third World economic institutions are weak, but the number of exceptions to both rules is growing rapidly. The numbers of TNCs based in Third World countries, particularly the NICs, has grown rapidly in recent years, and some Third World TNCs are extremely large and wield considerable influence (Lall, 1983).

So, it is not the country of domicile of economic institutions or the classes that dominate them that is the primary consideration in explaining how the global system works, but rather the structural locations of institutions and classes in the global capitalist system. Frank and Wallerstein's versions of the international division of labour may have been accurate for some countries during some periods, but the re-formation of capitalism on a global scale in the latter part of the twentieth century has rendered it increasingly less so. This has been obscured because the connection between accumulation in the national context and the growth of the transnational capitalist class has been rather different in the First and the Third (and also now the Second) Worlds for a variety of reasons, of which corruption is one.

The transnational capitalist class in the Third World will undoubtedly be connected with foreign TNCs, though its members will not necessarily work for them. They may work through their own TNCs, which may be in a position to challenge other TNCs anywhere in the world, or as officials, or as independent professionals. In so far as these people share the interests of and are engaged in the practices of the global capitalist system they are members of the transnational capitalist class. So the idea of the transnational capitalist class includes fractions of both the old *indigenous bourgeoisie* and the *comprador bourgeoisie*.

How do these groups work in the interests of global capitalism? In one interesting project, Geyikdagi (1984), examined the attitudes of political elites in the Middle East to the TNCs. He found two types, the highly suspicious and the willing business partners. Regimes of the latter type, it appears, tend to be very susceptible to coups. Since the 1960s Third World governments have become better disposed to TNCs 'as they have experienced the benefits derived from foreign investment' (Geyikdagi, 1984, p.15).[16] It is not clear whether personal benefits or benefits to the development of the host country, or both, are meant. Whatever the case, it is not only governments in the Middle East that appear to be more pragmatic now than in the recent past and although anti-TNC rhetoric is still common for public consumption, the line is substantially moderated in regulations for and negotiations with the TNCs.[17] Despite the political problems that basically anti-Western regimes have in dealing with the TNCs, the Arab desire for Western, particularly US, technology is the crucial test, as Bassiry and Dekmejian (1985) illustrate in the case of the TNCs and the Iranian revolution.

This is only possible where there is a transnational capitalist class willing to deal with the TNCs when, for example, the comprador role may be too dangerous or has actually been abolished. They can thus be isolated from particular transnational corporations identified with particular imperialist powers. Such is the efficacy of propaganda for the global capitalist system that it is rarely capitalism itself that is targetted in such cases, but the symbols of American or European national power. The transnational capitalist class can exact a much higher price for its services than the comprador class ever could, for two reasons. First, the stakes are bigger than ever before, due to the expansion of *global* capitalism and its Third World interests. Second, Third World transnational capitalists have more choice in who to deal with than before. This does not necessarily put the country of origin of the individual capitalist in a better position, for most of the benefits of this changing situation may accrue to the Swiss banking industry, or the real estate markets in California and New York and the Côte d'Azur, as well as the purveyors of super-luxury consumer goods. Let us take some examples of Third World bourgeoisies and see to what extent they confirm or refute the emergence of a transnational capitalist class.

The African bourgeoisie

A useful place to start such a discussion is with some recent research on the African bourgeoisie. Lubeck, elaborating on de Janvry, contrasts the force of internal against external factors in explaining capital accumulation. The autonomy of indigenous accumulation is opposed to some form of dependency in terms of the economic rationality of the capitalist class in a poor society. It is in the interests of this class that the workers can afford to buy the types of products that it can realistically expect to sell them. Thus:

> the internally oriented bourgeoisie possesses an *objective* interest in wage-led rather than externally-determined demand for its products . . . *productivity increases* will extend workers' consumption into new commodities that were once considered luxury goods (motorcycles, housing materials, and small appliances), which in turn will provide new areas of investment for the indigenous bourgeoisie. It is a class alliance that creates an *objective* link between indigenous capital and labour and one that is also linked to the progressive features of capitalist development. (Lubeck, 1987, p.14)

This is a *sentiment* I strongly agree with, but as an *argument* it has three problems. First, the opposition between 'wage-led' and 'externally-determined' demand is more apparent than real. In all but the smallest countries export success, at least in manufactures, depends largely on a solid domestic market. The interests of the internally-oriented bourgeoisie may start with wage-led demand. But as the walls of protectionism tumble down in one Third World country after another, under the influence of the World Bank, GATT etc., externally-determined demand becomes more difficult to ignore. The only way around this is through some sort of arrangement with the TNCs.

Second, Nigeria, like most Third World countries, imports most of its motorcycles and motorcycle parts, non-traditional building materials and appliances. Import substitution or indigenous investment in these products is not unproblematic.

Third, although Lubeck does not actually say it, the implication of the argument is that 'progressive capitalist development' is an indigenous, national, project. The gist of my argument is that the global capitalist system leaves less and less space for exclusively national capitalist projects. It follows that members of the indigenous bourgeoisie who resist incorporation into the transnational capitalist class are, with few exceptions, going to be trapped in a spiral of declining markets, low technology and uncompetitiveness.

It is easy to ridicule such an argument by pushing it to absurd limits. To avoid this it is necessary to distinguish *foreign* and *transnational*, and also *autonomous development* and *national development*. Not all of the practices of the transnational capitalist class are transnational. There is still space for genuinely national economic, political and cultural-ideological practices, but the global capitalist system increasingly marginalizes such practices, making them commercially irrelevant. The transnational capitalist class is a bridge between the nation-state and the global system and the more assiduously it brings transnational practices into what were once the realm of the regional or the national, then the more faithfully it serves the interests of the system.

Kitching, in an otherwise excellent analysis of the problem of autonomous development, seems to confuse *autonomous* and *national* development when he argues that if there is no 'national capitalist development' then the bourgeoisie must be comprador in character (1987, ch.2). Confronting the problem of 'autocentric development' he argues that the 'progressiveness of capitalism' may produce 'genuinely transformatory capitalist development (. . . massively raising productivity and the general income level)' without a national bourgeoisie (p.50). But this reduces the distinction between the national and the comprador bourgeoisie to a quite arbitrary judgement on what constitutes *national* development.

This returns us to the notion of the 'objective' interests of the capitalist class. The objective interest of all capitalist classes, whether regional, indigenous, national, foreign or transnational, is the private accumulation of capital. How individual capitalists or groups of them choose to accumulate will have to be explained in terms of personality, entrepreneurial history and material opportunities. The argument presented here is that in the latter part of the twentieth century more and more capitalists have come to believe that their objective interests are best served through transnational practices, as evidenced by the phenomenal growth of the presence and influence of the TNCs outside the hegemon countries, and what I am describing as transnational capitalist classes.

Most of the scholars writing in Lubeck's book, while discussing African indigenous bourgeoisies, actually confirm this judgement.

Swainson concludes a detailed study of indigenous capitalism in Kenya and the export promotion strategy of the late 1970s as follows: 'At this stage, an indigenous bourgeoisie is unlikely to supplant foreign capital in any Third World country, whatever its level of development. A more likely picture is a varying degree of integration and interpenetration' (Swainson, 1987, p.160). Biersteker, on Nigeria, argues that: 'Indigenization thus encourages a *comprador* role for local business in a society already plagued by strong *comprador* tendencies' (1987b, p.272) and that 'foreign capital has not been seriously threatened by the indigenization exercise' (p.275). And Campbell (1987) demonstrates that indigenization in the Ivory Coast did not really challenge the dominance of foreign capital because to do so would have been to put the mode of accumulation at risk.

Indigenization is not the only test of the existence of a transnational capitalist class, but it is certainly a critical one. The case of Nigeria has attracted a good deal of scholarly attention in this respect and is worth looking at more closely.

Indigenization in Nigeria

We should distinguish here between *expropriation*, which suggests that little or no compensation is paid; *nationalization* and *forced divestment*, which leave the question open; and *indigenization*, which suggests that foreign personnel and control are changed to indigenous personnel and control. *Divestment* suggests that it is the TNC that is the prime mover.

Kobrin has studied no less than 511 acts of forced divestment involving 1,500 firms in 76 Third World countries from 1960 to 1976. His underlying hypothesis is that 'in the vast majority of countries where forced divestment is used selectively its being chosen vis-a-vis alternate regulatory or administrative policies is, inter alia, a function of firm and industry-specific characteristics' (Kobrin, 1980, p.69). His results refute the commonly expressed 'irrational economic nationalism' explanation of forced divestment in the countries of the Third World. Third World states tend to take over the foreign investments that they consider to be important for national development. Indigenization implies that there are locals, official or private, standing in the wings ready to take over the indigenized companies. Can it be demonstrated that what at first sight appears to be a paradigm case of indigenous, national forces dispossessing transnational corporations, is in fact a clear illustration of the emergence of the transnational capitalist class in Nigeria?

Nigeria is by no means an exceptional case though, like any country, it has its own peculiarities. One of these is the long history of incorporation into the global capitalist system by the TNCs (see Shenton and Freund, 1978). Oil-rich Nigeria, with a population of over 100 million, is by far the most populous and also one of the richest countries, on a per capita income basis, in Africa. The legacy of British colonialism and the lure of oil money are mixed blessings. Scholars have documented significant levels of TNC participation in agriculture (Oculi, 1987), the oil industry (Ihonvbere and Shaw, 1988), import substituting manufacturing industries (Biersteker, 1987a), and in the mining, service, financial and infrastructure sectors (in Onimode *et al.* 1983, *passim*).

The Nigerian case is illustrative of a common pattern. As a proportion of the total economy, TNC investment is small, but as a proportion in some industries, for example oil, machinery and financial services, it is substantial. In the advanced sectors, it is dominant. Nigerian scholars have pointed to major structural distortions in economy and society for which the TNCs are at least partly responsible. For example:

> Proposals for domestic production of iron and steel, petrochemicals, machine-tools and the like are typically discouraged or delayed by the mnc's in preference for quick profit-yielding manufacturing of semi-luxury consumer goods like lace, car assembly, beer, carpets, and so on. This is largely the result of a wooly acceptance of import-substitution industrialisation, which implies that import substitutes based on the imported semi-luxury consumption habits, rather than the basic needs of the mass-majority, would enjoy industrial priority. (Onimode *et al.* 1983, p.122)

Transnational corporations also exert influence by manipulating class contradictions through a compliant comprador bourgeoisie and a denationalised labour aristocracy. This encourages corruption and '*cultural degradation* . . . foreign intellectual domination, the imposition of imperialist values and the ossification of national culture' (*ibid*, p.125). These are the circumstances under which successive Nigerian governments have attempted to indigenize, in the hope of gaining control over their economic and ultimately their developmental destinies.

Indigenization occurred in Nigeria in three phases. The first decree was issued in 1972 by the military regime in alliance with the local bourgeoisie, who clearly expected to benefit from the initiative. This first wave of indigenization had few practical effects, and Nigeria's many TNCs managed to evade serious loss of control by enlisting members of the local bourgeoisie to 'front' for them, a universal practice where there are restrictions on foreigners engaging in certain economic activities.

The second decree, in 1977, represented a further attempt by the military government to wrest control from the TNCs, particularly to counter the defensive measures that the TNCs had developed to nullify the effects of the first decree. Because it appeared tougher, the second decree encouraged the TNCs to develop even more defences to protect their interests. Biersteker (1987a) lists the most important of them. In addition to fronting, TNCs resorted to public sale of shares to dilute ownership and retain effective control, technical agreements with Nigerian partners, negotiation of exemptions from the authorities, the two company strategy, changes in voting rules to disenfranchise local partners, dividing boards of directors, bringing in expatriate executives, bribery and simply ignoring the law. A further decree in 1982, this time initiated by a civilian government, reinforced state control of the banking and finance sectors and went a little way to encourage Nigerian capital to invest more in the manufacturing sector. However, the TNCs are still as strong as they ever were and the notion that the Nigerian government, let alone the average Nigerian, has any more control of the economy than before indigenization, is very doubtful.

All agree that the main beneficiaries of the indigenization process have been the state functionaries and those few Nigerians who now sit on the boards of TNCs (see Ake, 1985; Hoogvelt, 1979). The companies that were indigenized did not cease to be transnational, and did not cease to engage in transnational practices. Those who were running them were thus also engaging in transnational practices and were thus, potentially at least, members of the transnational capitalist class. Their new transnational roles would naturally increase the likelihood that they would identify their interests with the global capitalist system, objectively if not subjec-tively. This is a crucial point in the argument that links indigeniza-tion with the creation of the transnational capitalist class. Subjec-tively, patriotic Nigerians who have taken control of indigenized TNCs will see their own and Nigeria's best interests served by the success of their enterprises. They may be hostile to the global capitalist system and feel that they and Nigeria are victims of exploitation within it. But objectively, as participants in the system through their own transnational practices, they identify their inter-ests and those of their country with it. So indigenization can actu-ally create the conditions for a transnational capitalist class in what appears to be the most unfruitful soil.

Triple alliances and transnational capitalist classes

This argument can be criticized on the grounds that a state bureaucracy cannot be called a class. The Marxist definition of class in terms of private ownership of the means of production used to work well for most First World societies, but it always left much to be desired in the analysis of the Second and Third Worlds where the larger part of the means of production are owned and controlled not by private capitalists but by state or parastatal en-terprises. There is some justification for treating those who run these enterprises as capitalists if they manifest certain characteris-tics. The term 'state capitalist' has often been used to refer to those who run state enterprises in a manner that is virtually indis-tinguishable from private enterprises.

This group is often seen as part of what is termed the 'triple alliance' between TNCs, the local bourgeoisie, and the state bureaucracy. This has been documented in various Third World countries, notably Nigeria (see Ihonvbere and Shaw, 1988), Brazil (Evans, 1979) and Egypt (Gillespie, 1984), and my own research on class forces along the US–Mexican border (Sklair, 1989) and the Hong Kong–China border (Sklair, forthcoming) is cast in the same mould. The triple alliance is one form that the transnational capitalist class takes, particularly in those societies marked by export-oriented foreign investment. Alliances between foreign and local entrepreneurs in joint ventures, and between TNCs and para-statals in resource-based and infrastructural projects, are also common.

However, where we cannot identify a triple alliance, a society may still be dominated by a transnational capitalist class whose practices are genuinely transnational whether or not all three parties are represented. The TCC sees its interests bound up not with TNCs or foreign capital as such, but with the global capitalist system. It sees its mission as organizing the conditions under which the interests of the system can be furthered within the national context. While the comprador class may (but not necessarily) admit that its interests and those of the foreigners it serves are antagonistic to those of co-nationals, the transnational capitalist class conceives of its interests and the interests of the global capitalist system that it serves, as identical with those of national development. Indigenization such as has occurred in Nigeria has the function of transforming a comprador class formerly identified with foreign TNC interests, into a transnational capitalist class, increasingly identified with the interests of nominally or actually Nigerian transnational corporations. Ake (1985, p.175) puts this well when he suggests that indigenization may have 'reinforced the division of labour between the Nigerian bourgeoisie (as specialists in maintaining the political conditions of accumulation) and foreign capital (as specialists in production)'.

Evans (1979) argues that the countries of the capitalist core rely on political stability in the semi-periphery (the NICs), in order to assure the continuing accumulation of capital, and that the triple alliance delivers this, primarily through the 'state bourgeoisies' and the autocratic regimes that nurture them. On this thesis, state enterprise is the path to local accumulation, but it falls far short of meeting the needs of the masses. Purging this of its state-centrism, we must ask why the capitalist global system relies on stability in the Third World and how it uses the transnational capitalist class, whether in the form of the triple alliance or some other grouping, to deliver this. The answers to these questions will be found in the analysis of cultural-ideological transnational practices and, in particular, the culture-ideology of consumerism in the Third World, to which I turn in the next chapter.

Notes

1. This account is based on four unsigned articles in the publication

West Africa (1980); the collection edited by Tsikata (1986); and the book by Graham (1982).

2. For a highly critical account of Unilever's global operations, see the whole issue of *New Internationalist* (June 1987).

3. Not in all cases, however. For the chilling story of Coca-Cola in Guatemala see Gatehouse (1989). See also Street (1985).

4. The term 'export processing zones' is becoming increasingly dated as more of the zones are engaging in manufacturing as well as pure assembly activities, and more countries are granting access to their domestic markets for the products of these zones. In 1970 there were about 20 zones in 10 Third World countries; by the late 1980s there were more than 260 in more than 50 countries (see UNCTC, 1988, pp.169–72). I use EPZ and EOZ interchangeably.

5. See Lim (1985). Since the 1980s, the proportion of male workers in some of these zones has been on the increase, for example in Mexico and in East Asia. For an explanation of this trend, see Sklair (1989, ch.8)

6. Hirata (in Elson and Pearson, 1989) compares female and male workers in the French and Brazilian plants of an electronics TNC. See also Garnsey and Paukert (1987, p.29–44).

7. The ELIFFIT phenomenon is discussed in Sklair (1989). For a critical analysis of some of the problems that export orientation raises, see the papers in Kaplinsky (1984).

8. See Burnell (1986) on the growth of economic nationalism, and for the interesting case of Singapore, see Mirza (1986).

9. For a very instructive set of essays on the IMF and the World Bank in Africa, see Havnevik (1987). *Review of African Political Economy* regularly publishes relevant material.

10. As there were in many other countries in the 1970s and 1980s, documented in Walton's 'IMF riots' (1987).

11. For an interesting case study on food aid to Africa, see Vengroff (1982) and, more generally, H.O. Bergesen (1980). Maxwell and Singer (1979), though a little out of date, is still very useful.

12. The grain surplus has been a problem in the United States at least since the 1930s. See 'Consumer engineering the grain surplus' in Sheldon and Arens (1932). For a lively account of Cargill Inc., 'the largest grain trader in the world', see Burbach and Flynn (1980, ch.13)

13. Because of its proximity to the United States there has been much research on TNC export cash cropping in Mexico. See, for example, the case of 'strawberry imperialism' (Feder, 1978).

14. See the annotated bibliography on the Green Revolution by Karim (1986), and Tullis and Hollist (1986, esp. ch. 9 and 10) where the accuracy of this statement might be assessed.

15. Brown, in his absorbing book about Sino–Foreign Joint Ventures (1986, p.27), identifies one Tong King-sing as the first comprador to the Hong Kong firm of Jardines in 1863. Tong helped to establish the China Merchants Steam Navigation Company, which we shall en-

counter again in Chapter 6, in the discussion of the Shenzhen Special Economic Zone.

16. For further discussion of Third World–TNC relations see Akinsaya (1984), Bhatt and Jain (1984).

17. This is the case for regimes all over the Third, and increasingly the Second World. This is a central theme in my forthcoming book, provisionally entitled *The Re-formation of Capitalism*, where the related theories of crisis, breakdown and disorganization of capitalism will be tackled.

5

The culture-ideology of consumerism in the Third World

The dominant paradigm in the study of development in the 1950s and the 1960s was the *modernization* theory, based on the polar opposites of *traditional* and *modern*. Its underlying idea was that in order to develop, the countries of the Third and Second Worlds would have to become more like the countries of the First World in their economic, political and value systems. The first two requirements seemed theoretically unproblematic. Some form of free enterprise capitalist economy and some form of pluralist democracy were clearly called for. However, apart from some rather vague ideas about the need for individual achievement and entrepreneurial spirit, following the lead of Max Weber, the system of values necessary for development remained elusive. Many theorists put their faith in the virtue of innovation to transform the traditional into the modern, but the experience of the last decade with some innovative doctrines of religious fundamentalism has persuaded most of us that it is not innovation as such, but what is being innovated that is the issue.

Consumerism and producerism

It should be obvious from what has been argued above, that my own answer to this question of the value system appropriate for the successful transition to capitalist modernization is the culture-ideology of consumerism. Wells has suggested that the concept of 'modernization' needs to be analytically split and replaced by the concepts of 'consumerism' (defined as the increase in consumption of the material culture of the developed countries) and 'producerism' (increased mobilization of a society's population to work, and to work more productively in the non-consumerist sector of the economy). Thus it follows that 'development requires the maximization of producerism' (Wells, 1972, p.47), and that consumerism is 'basically antithetical to development' (p.48). He creates a useful typology (*ibid.*, p.195), distinguishing high producer-consumer societies (overdeveloped hedonistic), high consumer and low producer (declining parasitic), low producer-consumer (underdeveloped traditional) and high producer and low consumer (ascetic developmental).

It is not difficult to name names. High producer and consumer societies, like those of North America and Western Europe, as we saw in Chapter 3, are actually in the process of developing politically important movements that are challenging consumerism. Those societies that score low on both measures, particularly the African and Asian Fourth World, score low not because of conscious choice but because of lack of means of production and lack of spending power. Their elites, small as they are, consume prodigiously. The only type difficult to identify is the high consumer and low producer, the stagnant or declining parasitic societies. Some commentators, obsessed with enormous trade deficits and the loss of some traditional export markets, are beginning to affix these labels to the United States, but this is patent nonsense. Although Japan's productivity in the automobile industry, South Korea's in the steel industry and Hong Kong's in the apparel industry may be superior to that of the United States, the total value of production of the United States is more than three times as great as its nearest challenger (Japan), about as much as the rest of the First World combined and nearly double the amount of all the economies of the Third World!

The final type is where changes have been taking place in the last decade. Some communist and socialist societies, particularly China during the period of the Cultural Revolution (1966–76), well fit the description of ascetic developmentalism, where high producerism, especially the promotion of heavy industry and capital goods, is combined with low consumerism, the result of policies that hold down increases in the disposable income of the masses.

As we shall see in the next chapter, in the 1980s a substantial minority of China's urban and coastal populations lurched dramatically from a state of low to much higher consumerism while attempting, with difficulty, to sustain a high level of producerism. Writing before this eventuality, Wells argued that premature consumerism (an interesting if controversial concept), can never lead to development, even when promoted by an industrial policy based on import substitution. The conclusion that he draws is that those who genuinely want development should encourage coercive producerist elites. There are few today who would consider China's so-called Gang of Four to be a proper model for developmental leadership!

Wells' own substantive research, on the effects of television in Latin America, documents, not surprisingly, that the United States is a strong influence for consumerism and a very weak influence for producerism in Latin American television. Again, we must be careful not to fall into the trap of state-centrism. It is difficult to see how consumerism as opposed to producerism can be said to serve the national interests of the United States in the Third World. However, it is very easy to see how consumerism can be said to serve the interests of the global capitalist system, dominated as it has been for much of the twentieth century by TNCs domiciled in the United States. The dynamic of permanently increasing the consumption of the products of capitalist enterprise feeds through the profit maximizing practices of each individual unit to the system as a whole, irrespective of the consequences for the planet in which it happens to be located. The specific task of the global capitalist system in the Third World is to promote consumerism among people with no regard for their own ability to produce for themselves, and with only an indirect regard for their ability to pay for what they are consuming. In this sense, consumerism has nothing to do with satisfying people's biological needs, for people will seek to satisfy these needs without prompting from anyone else, but with creating what can be called *induced wants*.

Marcuse, in his now neglected classic *One Dimensional Man*, talks about *false needs* in a similar context (Marcuse, 1964). This seems to me to betray a Western intellectual arrogance stretching at least from Rousseau (forcing people to be free), which I probably share, but which must be avoided if the argument has to have any cross-cultural credibility. By *induced wants* I mean to suggest that after people's biological needs have been satisfied there is an almost limitless variety of wants that can be induced. Patterns of socialization either structure these wants in the interests of external interests, global capitalism and other-worldly religions being two examples, or encourage individuals and groups to follow their own more arbitrary tastes.

This implies that people in the Third World have to be taught how to consume, in the special sense of creating and satisfying induced wants (see Belk, 1988a). Advertising, the main (but not the only) channel through which the culture-ideology of consumerism is transmitted, has often projected itself as an educational, or at very least, an informational, practice (see Sinclair, 1987).[1] The study of the mass media in the Third World, and their relationship with advertising, is the obvious place to begin to search out the ways in which the culture-ideology of consumerism works. It is no accident that most of the research on this issue has been done within the framework of theories of cultural and media imperialism.

Cultural imperialism and media imperialism

In all the capitalist or quasi-capitalist societies, processed food, drink, tobacco, cars, personal and household products and leisure-related items, take up most advertising revenue. Though the patterns differ a little from country to country and between daily and periodical print media, radio, television and billboard advertising, the vast majority of goods and services advertised are consumer rather than producer goods and services. Most readers will probably react to this statement: so what? If this is indeed the case then it is a measure of the success of consumerism, not a comment on how obvious the statement actually is. Why is it more natural to advertise to persuade people to buy consumer products, particularly where what is being sold are minor differences (what the adpersons call the 'unique selling proposition') than to advertise to persuade manufacturers to buy goods and services that would improve their processes of production? Trade journals are full of the latter, but they are a tiny proportion of total advertising expenditures. So consumer advertising is not more *natural* than advertising producer goods, it only seems so within the culture-ideology of consumerism.

It appears to be even less *natural* that consumer advertising should so predominate over producer advertising in the Third World, because one would suppose that those most likely to be able to purchase goods would be the business community and the government, in the market for producer goods, and not the mass of the population. Nevertheless, consumer goods are just as heavily promoted in the urban areas of some Third World countries as in the First. This apparent paradox is often explained in terms of how *cultural imperialism* is reproduced through *media imperialism*. Both of these ideas are highly controversial.

The cultural imperialism thesis argues that the values and beliefs of powerful societies are imposed on weak societies in an exploitative fashion. In its neo-Marxist version, this usually means that First World capitalist societies impose their values and beliefs on poor Third World societies. Similar arguments have also been used to try to explain the consequences of the deleterious influence of the US media on rich countries, like Canada (Lee Chin-Chuan, 1980, ch.4), Australia (Sinclair, 1987) and the world in general (Tunstall, 1977). Kivikuru (1988), in an interesting analysis of Finland, suggests that such countries have developed relative autonomy through a process of 'modelling' on the United States.

Media imperialism follows logically from cultural imperialism. If US or Western control of culture is admitted, then it is clearly achieved through control of the mass media, which creates the conditions for conformity to the hegemon culture and limits the possibilities of effective resistance to it. These theories are strongly held (see, for example, Becker *et al.*, 1986; Mattelart, 1983; Schiller, 1981) and strongly disputed.[2]

There are four main types of criticisms of cultural and media imperialism theories. First, what is often identified as 'US cultural and media imperialism' is really just advanced professional practice. Second, there are quite different processes at work in different countries and national variations can be more important than global patterns. Third, all countries develop internal cultural and media forces which counteract the external influences of US cultural products. Fourth, US media flows may work for as well as against national autonomy.[3]

It will be immediately obvious that most of this debate is posed within the terms of the state-centrist paradigm and, as such, few could disagree that it is possible to challenge US hegemony successfully in a wide variety of ways. As in most industries, economies of scale tend to lead to the most efficient practices. (Let us not complicate matters at this stage by asking 'efficient for whom' or by noting that even this truism is being challenged by new flexible production methods in some science based industries.) The United States has the largest media industry by far and its practices are invariably taken to be state of the art. For example, in discussing the relationship between US and Third World media, Lee Chin-Chuan asserts that: 'coproduction has been largely limited to Anglo-American interests . . . . As a mockery to cultural diffusion, the coproduced products have been deliberately Americanized' (1980, p.82). He explains this in terms of the triumph of the US-driven commercialization of global television, one of whose consequences is 'a genuine pressure on local talents to conform to the arbitrary 'world standard' of technical excellence which may be at variance with native cultural needs' (p.102).

One can certainly find co-productions that are not particularly Americanized, some national media systems that vary significantly from others in being less Americanized, domestic elements that successfully resist Americanization attempts, and even cases where 'Americanization' does seem to promote cultural autonomy. Three interesting recent cases are the *glasnost*-inspired 'Americanization' of Soviet television (see Barnathan, 1989); the introduction of the VCR into Turkey (Ogan, 1988); and the purchase of a VCR system by the Kayapo people in Brazil to preserve their local culture, though some claim that it will actually destroy the culture, based as it is on oral tradition (reported in Ogan).

If we replace 'Americanization' with 'capitalist consumerism', we can see that there is a double process of cultural-ideological transformation going on here. Capitalist consumerism is mystified by reference to Americanization, while Americanization, the method of the most successfully productive society in human history, gives its imprimateur to capitalist consumerism. The centrality of the 'American dream' for the project of global capitalism was briefly discussed in Chapter 3. There the point was made that, contrary to expectations borne of the origins of capitalism in northwest Europe, the United States and not the European core became synonymous with capitalism in its global incarnation. The re-formation of capitalism, thus, is the Americanization of capitalism, the culture-ideology of consumerism its rationale. But to identify cultural and media imperialism with the United States, or even with US capitalism, is a profound and a profoundly mystifying error. It implies that if American influence could be excluded then cultural and media imperialism would end. This could only be true in a purely definitional sense. Americanization itself is a contingent form of a process that is necessary to global capitalism, the culture-ideology of consumerism.[4]

The link between Americanization and cultural dependence began with the Hollywood movie industry cartel in the 1920s and the 'star system' on which it was based. The way in which this was achieved is a paradigm case of the interrelationships between the economic, the political and the cultural-ideological spheres, structured by the economic interests of those who owned and controlled the industry and the channels through which its products were marketed and distributed (see King, 1984). The transnational practices that resulted from the Hollywood system are legion. Outside the United States, as Smith (1980, p.45) argues: 'advertising has been unable to manifest itself as a source of *independent* patronage of indigenous media because of American dominance in the advertising industry'. The theories of the media produced by Hollywood were based on a single mass market, as were later theories of global standardization of production. This entirely distorts the reality of the Third World, let alone the First and Second Worlds and so the theory has to produce practices that change the varying realities of separate societies to make its assumptions come true. According to Smith, in Asia in the 1970s there were more than 140 English language daily newspapers that soaked up most of the elite-oriented advertising revenue and set the standards of 'modernization' and 'Americanization' for everyone.[5]

This is nicely, though perhaps unwittingly, illustrated by a study of telenovelas, Latin American soap operas, by Rogers and Antola (1985). They show that in Latin America, hours of imported television programmes actually declined, on average, between 1972 and 1982. The Peruvian soap *Simplemente Maria* enjoyed a phenomenal success all over Latin America. *Maria* was tied in with the sales of Singer sewing machines, showing, according to Rogers and Antola, that large audiences and profits could be made 'while at the same time promoting an educational theme that contributes to national development' (1985, p.31). The 'educational theme' was that a slum girl who gets a job with a rich family can become an important fashion designer, but it is not clear exactly how this contributes to national development! Rogers and Antola also comment on the, largely Mexican, Spanish International Network (SIN), which has begun to reverse media imperialism by sending Spanish language programmes to US Chicano audiences. This conclusion is true only in the state-centrism sense inherent in the theory of cultural and media imperialism. What the success of *Maria* and SIN actually demonstrates is the triumph of consumerism, whether it is produced by North or South Americans.

This has been more widely understood by policymakers in the United States than elsewhere. A US Committee on Foreign Affairs report, *Winning the Cold War: the U.S. ideological offensive* (published in 1964) argues:

> In foreign affairs, certain objectives can be better achieved through direct contact with the people of foreign countries than with their governments. Through the intermediary of the techniques and instruments of communications, it is possible today to reach important and influential sectors of the population of other countries, to inform them, to influence their attitudes, and may be to succeed in motivating them to certain determined actions. These groups, in turn, are capable of exercising considerable pressure on their governments. (Cited in Mattelart, 1978, p.12)

The US conception of what it takes to win the Cold War is breathtakingly simple and cannot be dismissed out of hand. The ideology of free choice and consumer sovereignty may seem crude to the Western cynic but to the product-starved consumers in most of the Second and Third Worlds, as the history of the 1980s demonstrates beyond reasonable doubt, it is a potent force. The message of the 'American way' has indeed been transmitted over the heads of governments direct to the people, made possible by the technical innovations in communications that were discussed in the last chapter. This is nowhere more clearly to be seen than in the events that have been transforming East Europe and particularly the breaching of the Berlin Wall in 1989. The prime purpose of these transmissions has been to promote the culture-ideology of consumerism, even to those for whom the products were not yet available or who could not realistically be expected to be able to buy them.

Latin American research on the media

Since the 1970s, there has been a great flowering of research on these issues in Latin America, stimulated intellectually by the sympathetic critical response to dependency theory, and politically by the events in Chile during the period of the Popular Front government led by Salvador Allende and also media experiments in Cuba (see, for example, Kunzle, 1978; Hamelink, 1984, ch.2) and elsewhere. Roncagliolo, an active participant, has usefully summarized this research in a paper on 'Transnational communication and culture' (1986) and reference to this source will serve as an introduction to what is a complex and often physically inaccessible body of work.

Three central questions were posed by the researchers:

> What is the place of culture in the transnationalization process and of communication within cultural processes? What does the transnationalization of consumption consist of, if it signifies something more than the homogenization of demand at the international level? Is there such a thing as a 'transnational culture,' or are there simply internationalized patterns of behavior? (Roncagliolo, 1986, p.79)

In answering these questions several themes emerged, such as the study of international news flows (a critique of the 'mercantile concept of news' and the idea of 'information as a social good'); 'transnational culture' as universalization of culture promoted by transnationalization of media; new communications technology (how data processing and telecommunications have changed the ground rules for transnational communications) and the prospects for populist alternative communications.

Roncagliolo proposes a set of propositions that summarize the results of the research effort and at the same time represent an attempt to generate a theory of cultural and media imperialism that is neither state-centrist nor locked into the modernization framework. He starts with the rejection of 'communicationist' bias. It is the medium not the communication that is exchanged in the market, and so it is necessary to distinguish three types of merchandise, namely news, medium and public, and to recognise the predominance of the secondary market (advertising and publicity) over the primary market (messages). Therefore, it is not arbitrary that Latin American media pay more attention to the United

States than vice versa. This is not to be confused with the question of the free and balanced flow of information that obsesses some communications theorists.

This leads logically to a second proposition, that the 'transnationalization of messages is not a mechanical consequence of a supposed transnationalization of the media, but is a complex process accompanying the transnationalization of the economy and of politics' (p.82). The crucial paradox is that local media themselves remain relatively impermeable to transnationalization. Generally, TNCs produce the messages and locals distribute them, but the TNCs ultimately control the system through manipulation of the financial sphere, mainly advertising, which imposes a 'production-financing pincer' on local media systems, though it is always liable to a hostile reaction from nationalist and/or popular forces. The new communications technology accelerates the process of transnationalization but also permits new forms of alternative communications. These can only be defined in terms of the national/popular pole, against transnationalization. Defining them in terms of communications themselves (size, technique, politics) is a profound error, because they can rarely defeat the mass media at their own game. Finding the space for counterhegemonic communications is the real point.

Thus: 'the transnationalization process, far from being a strictly economic phenomenon involving the expansion of corporations, is defined in the political and cultural spheres – that is, in changes within political and civil society' (*ibid*, p.86). This transnational phase of capitalism is eroding the nation state and the transnationalization of communications that it produces is necessary for the creation of phenomena like the 'global supermarket' and the 'global village'. In this phase, the means of communication tend to become the dominant ideological apparatus and partially displace traditional socialization agencies. Echoing media theorists from all points of the ideological spectrum, Roncagliolo argues that 'the scope and intensity of the media presence have endowed the media with an unprecedented socializing efficiency' (p.87).

I have presented the ideas of Roncagliolo (and those he reports) at such length because they are unusually clear on two points that are at the core of my own argument, against most media research which sidesteps the issues. First, Roncagliolo avoids state-centrism and this permits the emergence of a more plausible theory of cultural and media imperialism based not on Americanization, which can easily be disproved, but on the culture-ideology of consumerism, for which the evidence is much stronger. Second, he problematizes the 'transnationalization of consumption' very fruitfully by distinguishing it from the 'homogenization' of international products. In this way he does what I have been trying to do, namely detaching consumerism from the products themselves and connecting it (and them) to the interests they serve in the global capitalist system.

South America is, of course, very heavily influenced by North America. One might argue that the culture-ideology of consumerism that I have portrayed here is specific to the American continent. Research from the Middle East (see Stauth and Zubaida, 1987) suggests that this is not the case. A study of a Cairo neighbourhood by Zayed illustrates the global dimensions of consumerism in an entirely different setting. He argues that:

> It is through consumerism that [traditional society] partly becomes westernized and 'modernized' . . . incursion of the capitalist system into the periphery entails two processes: growing intensification of market relations, accompanied by the intensification of consumerism and the diffusion of mass culture; the concentration and differentiation of production. (Zayed, 1987, p.288)

In this research site, a mixed poor area of Cairo, the 'flow of foreign commodities plays an increasing role in the satisfaction of the needs of even the poorest strata' (p.295). The adoption of consumer culture functions on three contradictory levels. First, the choice of cheap imported goods can be economically rational for poor consumers; second, consumerism 'is used by the people whom it subordinates as a veil to obscure the difficult material conditions in which they live' and it functions as a 'symbol of existence in contrast to the process of degradation which is also an outcome of the subordinating nature of consumerism' (p.299). Zayed's argument implies that once the culture-ideology of consumerism is adopted, poor people cannot cope economically, and a mode of resistance must develop. In the Muslim case this mostly manifests itself in religious extremism, whose target is as often Americanization as it is consumerism as such.

Zayed's research advances understanding of the culture-ideology of consumerism as a transnational practice one important step. It demonstrates that people are not 'cultural dopes' who mindlessly obey the instructions of an exploitative social order, even when these instructions are effective on a subliminal level. People, particularly poor people in the Third World, adopt the culture-ideology of consumerism for easily understandable reasons. In some circumstances, this is the only economically rational option open to them. It is often, perhaps always, a trap, but one that is entered not out of stupidity or even ignorance, but out of a lack of viable alternatives. It is a trap similar to the one that peasants enter when they feed seedcorn to their starving children. They have no alternative.

The culture-ideology of consumerism lacks this sort of drama and immediacy, of course. It is a process consisting of a series of practices that penetrate a society over a long period of time and in a variety of ways. While small minorities all over the world have criticized local versions of consumerism and the culture-ideology that promotes it, it is only very recently that it has been conceptualized as a global problem. This has tended not to happen as a direct critique of consumerism itself, but as a Third World protest at what was referred to above as cultural and media imperialism. One consequence has been the call for a new world information order.

A new world information order

Research on a new world information and communications order got under way in the 1970s, particularly through agencies such as UNESCO. This was conceptualized as a 'communications revolution' for the Third World, for example in an interesting collection of essays edited by Kumar in 1980, which dealt with global 'knowledge systems' and contained discussions on the ways in which TNC control over book publishing, news agencies, vocational training and education were having profound effects on Third World cultures (see also Nair, 1980). Interest in these questions intensified in the 1980s and the struggle for control of the electronic media is reflected in a growing volume of research on communications in the Third World (see Stover, 1984; Jefkins and Ugboajah, 1986; Meyer, 1988). Whereas political imperialism and economic neo-imperialism had focused attention on the economic and political consequences of First World hegemony over the Third World countries within their various spheres of influence, the 'communications revolution' of the 1980s has focused attention on the cultural-ideological sphere (see Becker *et al.*, 1986).

In the field of information technologies (IT), in particular, there has been both quantitative and qualitative advance. These technologies have created new services, new occupations and new cultural goods, such as cable television and video cassettes. In all these areas, the opportunities for hegemonic control are obvious and, indeed, have been enthusiastically seized by hegemon TNCs and transnational capitalist classes everywhere.

In his book, *Transnationals and the Third World: the Struggle for Culture* (1983), Mattelart identifies five theoretical stages through which the analysis of the 'Transnational apparatus of production of cultural commodities' has proceeded. He conceptualizes the present stage in terms of 'culture industries'. The contemporary culture industries, spanning everything from television through tourism to advertising, Mattelart argues, seek to transform the global audience into consumers of transnational commodities through the propagation of a set of self-serving notions of development, communication, organization, daily life and change. There are some who would regard Mattelart's views as one-sided and lacking in acknowledgement of the relative autonomy of Third World media of communication and the capacity of institutions and individuals in the developing countries to hold on to their own cultures and develop new forms for themselves. Nevertheless, as Bagdikian (1989) has documented, over the last few years and with the help of innovations in electronic technologies, the TNCs that largely control these technologies have created unprecedented opportunities to reconstruct global cultures to serve the interests of the global capitalist system. The extent to which the TNCs have actually seized these opportunities and the extent to which Third World elites and non-elites collude or resist the reconstruction of their cultures are still open questions. There has been a considerable amount of research on the issue.

One notable project was the 'World of the News' study, carried out by thirteen separate research teams and another team from the United States covering sixteen different media systems. In all, newspapers and broadcasting in twenty-nine countries were monitored for periods in 1979. Each news item was coded by location, source, position and nationality of actor, topic and theme. Politics dominated, as did regionalism, and there was not much cross-bloc coverage. A symposium in a major communications journal on the project usefully illustrates the different conclusions that can be drawn from such research. One participant concluded that the 'overall pattern of attention paid to certain kinds of events was remarkably similar' (Sreberny-Mohammadi, 1984, p.125); and another claimed that the 'pseudo debate' over media bias was exposed by the research. Lack of interest in what other people are doing rather than a lack of information is the issue, he asserts, and while coverage may be accurate though unbalanced: 'It is instructive to note how little of the news contained any themes' (Stevenson, 1984, p.234), proving, presumably, that the objective standards of professional journalism are universally maintained. Stevenson concludes that: 'Too much of the New World Information Order debate has focussed on assertions that were probably never true and are certainly no longer true. This study helps clear the air of the pseudo debate' (p.236).

Nordenstreng, who thought up the project in the first place, clearly disagrees. He complains that:

> The final project was dominated by 'vulgar' categories that capture *ad hoc* aspects of the media content, rather than a comprehensive image carried by the content . . . mainly determined by various pragmatic aspects – not least of which was the need to get a minimum common core of hard quantitative evidence across various national media systems. (1984, p.238)

Social scientists will recognize this as the typical positivist dilemma. Nordenstreng demonstrates the point well with his account of qualitative differences between reports in *The New York Times* and *Pravda* of the SALT II nuclear disarmament negotiations. On the 'vulgar' criteria used in the study, however, the reports were evaluated quite similarly.

In broadcasting, TNCs from the United States and Europe effectively control global flows, and barriers to entry remain formidable. A symposium on 'Africa in the Media' was told that the numbers of Western correspondents in the Third World and correspondents from the developing countries in the West were in decline. In the words of the commentator 'in a world of satellite technology, this seems absurd' (Palmer, 1987, p.247). The effects of this are to make it easier for the TNCs to 'dump' cheap news on the Third World, and restrict the flow of news from poor to rich countries.

There are, of course, alternative non-Western sources of news and information and, as critics of the media imperialism thesis always argue, no Third World country is forced to fill its media with material from any particular source. It is easy to forget that it may actually be more cost effective for a national television service or newspaper group from a poor country to buy in regional material, let alone overseas material from the well-developed Western sources, than to set up their own sources or rely on others as poorly endowed as themselves. Where alternative agencies have been created, there are often political forces ranged against them. For example, in a revealing history and analysis of the Inter Press Service, which was created to provide news for and about the Third World, Giffard (1984) documents how a disinformation campaign against it, originating from the United States, which was not supported by the facts about its coverage, almost destroyed the organization.[6]

In a sixty-nine country study of international television flows in the early 1980s, not much difference was noted from a similar study in 1973, though there were 'greater regional exchanges along with the continued dominance of a few exporting countries' (Varis, 1984, p.143). Among the more interesting, if hardly surprising, findings of this research are the extent of imported (mainly US) entertainment category programmes in most countries, especially in prime time when advertising revenue is at its highest, and that no socialist country Third World programmes were ever shown on prime time US television.

Control of global media markets

Important as the origin of media content is, it is not the whole story. In a study of television in Indonesia, where 25 per cent of programming is (mainly US) imports, Chu and Alfian (1980, p.56) found 'no case in any developing countries where television which has been introduced with Western aid has been able to operate completely free of Western influence'. What they are getting at is that even if there were no US or Western programmes on Indonesian television, the culture-ideology of consumerism would remain.

This is confirmed in a particularly striking fashion by Montoya Martin del Campo and Rebeil Corella (1986) in their paper on 'Commercial television as an educational and political institution'. This is a study of 480 students who watch the *Telesecundaria* programmes on Mexico's main commercial channel, *Televisa*. Commercial television 'has become in Mexico a vehicle for the transmission of North American culture, constantly eroding national identity and local cultures. Televisa classifies audiences as 'urban,' 'national middle class,' and 'Americanized middle class': peasants and Indians are nonexistent in this scheme' (1986, p.147). The selection of messages is not neutral, it rarely is, and ignorance is also an effect of television. The more commercial television the students watched the more they approved of, and accepted as natural and true, the American way of life, faithfully broadcast by *Televisa* (see also Sinclair, 1987, pp.169–81).

This research highlights some of the difficulties of the thesis I am arguing, but it highlights even more of the difficulties of the thesis of cultural and media imperialism. It would be possible to construct a project to measure the influence of 'the American way of life' in Mexican, or any other television, or media as a whole. It would be quite possible to do this on a series of variables of which consumerism would be one among many, and perhaps not the most important. But such research, based on a state-centred methodology, would miss how the global capitalist system works through the culture-ideology of consumerism, rather than through a glorification of the American way of life. There is a parallelism here with the opposition introduced above between the comprador class and the transnational capitalist class. In much the same way as political criticism of global capitalism can be deflected onto a more vulnerable and now dispensable comprador class, cultural-ideological criticism of consumerism, as the central value of the global capitalist system, can be deflected onto 'Americanization', also more vulnerable and now dispensable.

Thus, the central idea of the new world information order, that there is a global imbalance in communication, media capacity and influence, can be safely taken up by captains of industry in the First as well as by radical critics in the Third World. In Spring 1985, the prestigious US-based *Journal of Communication* ran a symposium on the US response to this imbalance, in the light of the decision of the US government to withdraw from what it considered to be an increasingly and unacceptably politicized UNESCO. The Independent Commission for World Wide Telecommunications Development, the Maitland Commission, a project to facilitate the progress of global communications in the less developed countries, played an important part in this.

Under the title of 'A U.S. effort to provide a global balance', William Ellinghaus (vice chairman of the New York Stock Exchange and ex-President of the US telecommunications conglomerate, AT&T) and Larry Forrester (Public Affairs Manager of AT&T International) observed that three-quarters of the world's 600 million telephones are in just nine countries. For more than 2 billion people, about half of the global population, there are less than 10 million telephones. What, they ask, can be done about this growing imbalance? (*Journal of Communication*, 1985, p.14). Maitland suggested a Center for Telecommunications Development and the AT&T men suggest that the US Foundation for World Communications Development, founded in 1984 to collect private sector funds for Maitland, could organize the private sector to this end. The public sector would then come in, and, implied but not actually stated, the American way of life could be transmitted, preferably on AT&T equipment, on a truly global scale.

This sentiment is also subtly conveyed in a letter from a US Department of State official to the Secretary General of the International Telecommunications Union on the subject of the Maitland Report. 'The needs and capacities of each developing country are unique, and for some it may be more beneficial to concentrate first on other telecommunications goals, such as perhaps high speed data access to international commodity markets' (Dougan, in *Journal of Communication*, 1985, p.21). Michael Gardner, chair of the US Telecommunications Training Institute, suggests that the reasons for the global inbalance are the expense of new communications technology, the low priority that most Third World governments accord to the sector and the rapidity of technical change. He argues that US action is needed on grounds of enlightened self-interest and estimates the global telecommunications market to be worth more than $410 billion. His Institute, set up in 1983 by the private sector and part-funded by the US government (over $100,000 from the US Information Agency), provides free hands-on training for students from the Third World inside US corporations. In its first two years it graduated 373 students from 71 Third World countries and is said to be doubling this output (*Journal of Communication*, 1985, p.38).

But how do First World TNCs actually control media markets in the Third World? A study of the practices of the Motion Picture Export Association of America, in India, provides one clue. It demonstrates how US TNCs operate a cartel to import and show US films, while Indian (and other Third World made films) are generally kept out of mass circulation in the United States. The same processes appear to be in operation for television and video distribution. The conclusion is that: 'the potential for profits [for the TNCs] and the current open-door policy of the Indian government are encouraging to further transnational involvement' (Pendakur, 1985, p.70).

The major mass media, radio, television, movies, records, audio and videotapes, books, magazines and newspapers, have all expanded in use in the Third World in the 1980s. They are not, however, entirely or even mostly under TNC control. Mass media control can be exercised directly through the production process and indirectly through marketing and distribution. The public media have held out the greatest promise for the developing countries in terms of their educational and instructional potential, and it is in this context that opinions are most sharply divided about the 'new communications technology', the role of the TNCs and the needs and wants of people.

As has already been suggested, however, research on the mass media in the Third World shows that it is the commercial rather than the educational purposes that are dominant. The record of the TNCs, independent Third World government efforts, or combinations of them, to put the 'new communications technology' to educational and humanitarian use has been spotty, to say the least. The promise of the 1970s that satellite television would revolutionize education, public health and nutrition, and eliminate illiteracy throughout the the urban and rural Third World, has been largely unrealized. It will not surprise the cynical to learn that INTELSAT, COMSAT and other glamorous projects, though they have an impressive spread of participants, have been utilized mainly for elite–elite communications (only those rich enough to use them speak to those who are rich enough to use them), the collection of military and commercially relevant information and for the global transmission of entertainment (Eapen, in Becker *et al.*, 1986;

McPhail, 1987). The alternative media that are somewhat less capital intensive, like desktop publishing, cable television and the constantly growing video industry, might in time challenge the hegemony of the TNCs in the mass media of the Third World as they may furnish more opportunities for independent production and distribution (see Hamelink, 1984).[7]

The enormous growth in the 1980s of the video-cassette industry in India and other Third World countries, has augmented the products of the Western TNCs with local material, and the two co-exist side by side in the marketplace (see Mowlana, 1985, pp.87ff.; Ganley and Ganley, 1987). Videotex, one-way or two-way data flows through television receivers, is another as yet unrealized potential for social progress in developing countries. Paradoxically, TNC generated information technology may increase the penetration of foreign 'messages' and at the same time increase the dissemination of indigenous cultures.[8]

In this vein, there are those who argue that informatics can make positive contributions to Third World development because of rather than in spite of the technological innovations of the TNCs. Stover, in his review of 'information technology in the Third World' (1984, pp.93–5), points out that in the 1980s four trends in IT give cause for optimism. Computers are becoming increasingly cost effective, for example a central memory of 1 million bytes now costs far less than 1 per cent of what it cost 20 years ago;[9] miniaturization has made computers more practical for small users; programming advances have increased the 'adaptation of software to user needs' and improved the chances that IT will address the developmental problems of Third World countries; and the integration of television, computers and telecommunications, telematics, permits global networking for the transmission of information and opens up new possibilities for resource and technology-scarce developing countries.

It is too soon to say whether Stover's optimism is justified, but the TNCs are already heavily involved in all these developments, and the potential benefits for the Third World appear to be very minimal compared with the profits to be made by the promotion of the culture-ideology of consumerism. It is through the device of advertising in the Third World that the culture-ideology of consumerism is expressed and the promise of the new world information order is exposed.

Advertising and the spread of consumerism

The transnational advertising agencies (TNAAs) are increasingly active in the Third World. They directly produce advertisements in Third World countries and indirectly tutor domestic agencies that will produce advertisements for TNC products and services through global marketing strategies. These take up more and more Third World radio, television and printed media space (Anderson, 1984; Sinclair, 1987). Studies of the TNAAs provide a good test for the view that we should be looking not at the increase or decrease of 'Americanization' in the Third World but at the inroads that the culture-ideology of consumerism is making in Third World societies.

According to Noreene Janus (1988), by 1980 the TNAAs derived more than half of their gross income from overseas, with the Latin American market expanding particularly fast.[10] Brazil, Mexico and Argentina are among the top twenty ad markets. Janus's approach is predicated on the claim that: 'lifestyles promoted in advertising include implicit and explicit agendas for social relations, political action and cultural change' (1986, p.128). She analyzes this in terms of the economic context, particularly through the promotion of nonessential products. In most countries advertising is concentrated on a relatively small group of consumer goods, soaps/detergents, tobacco, drugs, perfumes, deodorants, toothpaste, prepared foods, beer and soft drinks. Increases in the consumption of these, she argues, is less an indicator of *level* of development than *kind* of development. These tend to be high profit, high advertising to sales, high barriers to entry and high TNC penetration products.

This leads inexorably to the transnationalization of the local mass media. For example, in her own research, Janus finds that TNCs are responsible for most of the adverts on Mexican television and Latin American women's magazines, and for about one-third of non-government newspaper adverts in Mexico. The next stage in the process, the transnationalization of consumption habits, is not as unproblematic as is sometimes assumed. Janus argues for a 'perpetual confrontation between transnational expansion and local cultural expansion' (*ibid*, p.133) and cites as evidence the fact that TNCs such as Gerber (baby food) and Nestlé (instant coffee) have acknowledged that customer resistance is their main marketing problem in Latin America.

It is for this reason that the TNAAs are not simply trying to sell specific products in the Third World, but are engineering social, political and cultural change in order to ensure a level of consumption that is: 'the material basis for the promotion of a standardized global culture' (*ibid*, p.135). Those who find this difficult to accept might care to look at studies like that by Fejes (1980), documenting how the military regimes in Chile and Argentina used TNAAs to clean up their images. Similarly, Jefkins and Ugboajah (1986) in one of the few studies of the media in Africa, illustrate the point with reference to the media-induced following for Western culture heroes and products. And Mattelart shows how the mass media in Chile changed in the two years after the coup against the Allende government, when ad agency billings rose tenfold: 'There are no longer any political parties; there is no longer a congress; the mass media naturally become the superstructural party of the dictatorship' (Mattelart, 1978, p.33). The 'Pepsi Revolution' campaign in Brazil, for example, was deliberately designed as an alternative channel of youth protest in a repressive society.[11]

The way that the TNAAs achieve the desired societal changes is through projective advertising, the technique of producing new needs/wants as components of a new lifestyle, which is replacing suggestive advertising. The global advertising campaign, already used successfully by many TNCs, will be discussed in the section on 'the Cola wars' below. Janus tries to explain it in historical terms. While Gramsci argued in the 1930s that collective consciousness or common sense is unordered and inconsistent although directed by the dominant ideology, 'the dominant ideology of our times is consumerism and its particular strength may derive from the fact that it helps to order the unordered elements of the collective consciousness' (Janus, 1986, p.137). She cites Cathelat's idea that advertising is a 'supralanguage' where it is the products' associations rather than the products themselves that are crucial, prior to the use of language. Advertising is a vital link between material and social relations, transforming producers into consumers, by transforming captains of industry into 'captains of consciousness', as Ewen (1976) argues.

For most people in the First World and for small elites in the Second and Third Worlds, the contradictions of advertising and thus of the culture-ideology of consumerism, are blurred by the opportunities to consume at a high level on a more or less permanent basis. But what about those, most of the people in all but a few rich countries, who cannot afford to buy the products flaunted by the adverts? Can advertising and ultimately consumerism, be resisted? If they can be resisted, it will not be the transnational capitalist class, whether through its private entrepreneurial or its official bureaucratic or its comprador fractions, that will be organizing the resistance.

Global exposure

The global film, television and radio broadcasting industries, are increasingly organically linked and, are still dominated by the commercial interests of US transnationals. Although Hollywood actually produces only a tiny fraction of the worldwide total of films and television programmes, US control over marketing and distribution gives it an enormous input onto Third World screens. A report for UNESCO provides some data for the 1970s. In 1976, 36.5 per cent of Thai TV time was devoted to foreign, mostly US imports; and in 1973, almost 90 per cent of the films shown in Argentina were foreign made, 37 per cent from the United States (Guback and Varis, 1982, ch.4; but compare Mattelart *et al.*, 1984, part one). The research of Stover (1984) and McPhail (1987) on the ways in which the new information technology facilitates cultural dependency, and of Jefkins and Ugboajah (1986, pp.210ff.) on the 'Voice of America' fan clubs in Nigeria, illustrate how these trends intensified in the 1980s. The proposition that, in the words of the British media sociologist, Jeremy Tunstall, 'the media are American', has become a potent political slogan. A recent absurd example is the new Japanese 'fake festival of panty-givers'. Japanese confectioners take around 10 per cent of their annual sales on St Valentine's Day (whose name was unknown in Japan before the arrival of chocolate). Panty-giving Day 'is an attempt by the lingerie industry to join in the commercial exploitation of fake festivals'. The point is that the culture-ideology of consumerism produces the form, but the content is taken from the American film *Working Girl*, whose heroine is given underwear by her boyfriend. Mikiko Taga, the feminist author of a book on *sekihara* (sexual harassment) says: 'Japanese think this is an American custom and they imitate American actions' (see Sullivan, 1990).

There are those who would condemn all US culture products, as there are those who would as uncritically endorse them. This is not the point. The point is that Thailand, Argentina and Nigeria (and most other developing countries), as well as Japan and Western Europe, are exposed to media messages of US origin extolling the virtues of capitalist consumerism daily and at a high level of intensity. The balance between US/foreign and domestic origin mass media communication in key areas is skewed towards the former and Third World origin mass media messages practically never get exposure in the United States or other developed countries. Under the title 'What's hot on TV Worldwide?' *Advertising Age* (1 December 1986, p.60) produced a list of the top US and local shows on the television channels of nine Third World and eleven First World countries. Not one of the local shows had ever been networked in the United States. The most popular US shows for the Third World sample were *Knight Rider* (all the way from South Korea to Nicaragua), *The A-Team* and *Dynasty*. All of these programmes, and the many more broadcast in the Third World, present specific messages and convey specific myths about life in the United States, as indeed all popular television does in any country. The popularity of such programmes and the annual crop of multimillion dollar grossing movies that achieve global screening, also tell us something about the ways in which the media TNCs have successfully tapped into consumer preferences in the Third World. It must be remembered that these consumers are free to switch on or off, pay to see films or not. Intellectuals may bemoan the effects of US-influenced public mass media in developing countries, as they bemoan the onward march of the fast food and beverage industries due to the rise of global franchising, but it cannot be denied that these products of the TNCs are popular and widely sought after in developing countries. The inability or unwillingness of domestic producers, private or state, to compete effectively with the TNCs in these fields does not sufficiently explain the global success that the TNCs are currently enjoying.

An industry central to the culture-ideology of consumerism is processed fast foods. This has spread with remarkable speed in the First World, is accelerating in the Third World and is beginning to take off in the Second World. Of particular note is the TNC-controlled fast food franchising chain. Palmer (1985) argues that the international fast food sector has grown so quickly because it is seen as 'non-threatening' to the host countries. Fast food franchising outside the United States seems to benefit all the players, and its success is assured due to 'a growing preference for American fast food over local products' (Palmer, 1985, p.72). Catering to local tastes does not necessarily undermine the management philosophy of global standardization if the product itself has a strong enough image.[12]

The scale of global franchising in fast food and other industries is enormous. *Business America* (3 March 1986, pp.11–13) reported that about 500,000 outlets employing 6 million people were expected to sell over US $550 billion worth of goods in 1986. Franchising is highly concentrated, with about fifty companies accounting for half of total sales. In 1985, thirteen of these were in fast foods and nine in auto dealerships, but only 13 per cent of outlets were in the Third World. The prospects for growth there were considered to be very bright. Kaynak asserts, perhaps a little optimistically, that: 'Franchising is a potent source for socio-economic development of LDCs' (1988, p.50).

The peculiar significance of fast food franchising is its connection with the home and its effects on the reconceptualization of leisure time and family life. There is no better example of this than the McDonald's phenomenon. A United Nations Joint Unit has researched the fast food industry in the Philippines, Thailand and Malaysia. Findings from a study of the McDonald's chain in the Philippines highlights the impact of one very global TNC on a society with a long and contentious history of US intervention, some invited and some not.

The franchise system is the favoured method of operation of fast food TNCs. McDonald's opened its first outlet in Manila in 1981, followed rapidly by others. The positive effects on the economy of the Philippines have primarily been in employment (particularly of students), training of staff (McDonald's is renowned for its methods of instilling efficiency) and domestic linkages (the creation and/or encouragement of high standard local suppliers). The effect on the local Filipino chains was also very interesting. Originally, Filipino hamburger chains marketed their product on the basis of its 'Americanness'. However, when McDonald's entered the field and, as it were, monopolized the symbols of 'Americanness', the indigenous chains began to market their product on the basis of local taste. Filipino hamburgers are advertised in the context of Filipino life styles in contrast to the McDonald's appeal to the 'colonial mentality of the Filipino consumer' (ESCAP/ UNCTC, 1986, p.44).[13]

The entry of McDonald's into the Philippines brought competition to a local industry that was satisfying local demand. It is also responsible for an outflow of foreign exchange (repatriated profits) that the Philippines can ill afford. Nevertheless, it is possible that the Filipino hamburger is more efficiently and hygienically served (and perhaps made) than before.[14]

Delivering the goods

The question of how the culture-ideology of consumerism sets about delivering the products that it so assiduously promotes to Third World consumers, is rarely asked. Hill and Boya (1987) look at the ways in which consumer goods are promoted in developing countries, and provide some interesting information on a sample of sixty-one subsidiaries of nineteen food and drink, pharmaceutical, cosmetics and general goods TNCs. Many patterns of media use appear to be employed.

Another important issue is the diffusion of global retailing techniques to the Third World. Kaynak (1988, ch.1) lists recent changes in Third World urban retailing, such as the decline in the number and competitiveness of small grocery stores, the adoption of self service techniques, the expansion of large store operations, the differential growth rates of urban and metropolitan as against less-urbanized areas, wholesaler-initiated lobbying for a more independent grocery trade and more focus on operational efficiency. For example, shops are upgrading their perishables to compensate for the lower margins on groceries resulting from increased competition.

Kacker suggests some reasons for increased competition. Some TNCs have been involved in mass retailing in the Third World, for example Bata sells its own shoes, Singer sells its own sewing machines and Sears, Woolworths and Safeways between them sell almost everything. Transnational corporation presence, he argues, can be very beneficial, by transferring expertise and stimulating local suppliers. This often entails cutting out the middleman, as the experience of IBEC supermarkets in Latin America and Migros-

Turk in Turkey, showed, and competition between small domestic retailers can also result. Evidence suggests that most TNC retailers eventually rely mostly on domestic suppliers and that if they do raise prices, barriers to entry in the food sector are so low that those who do would instantly face fierce competition. Thus, by helping to transform retailing 'Sears, Roebuck is well-known all over the world for making a significant contribution in the creation of a middle class' (Kacker, 1988, p.40).

There is no substantial evidence that the revolution in Third World urban retailing has actually reduced or even stabilized the prices of food and other basic goods. Government policies on agricultural incentives, inflation and reliance on imports are all probably much more important determinants of prices than the retailing system. What the retailing system does do, however, is create the infrastructure for the culture-ideology of consumerism to flourish. Even if the poor urban or rural dwellers cannot afford to buy, they can still gaze in the windows of the boutiques and walk in the shopping malls that have sprung up in all but the very poorest Third World cities in recent decades.

One flaw in the argument of those who criticize the TNCs and the consumerism that they create, is the question of consumer sovereignty. As long as consumers in the Third, Second or First World have a choice, it may be argued, they are free to buy or not to buy what the TNCs are trying to sell. Advertising may be a hidden persuader, but no one is forced to obey. As long as what the TNCs are trying to sell is not directly life-threatening, surely TNCs are entitled to enter the marketplace.

It is important not to fall into the trap of moralizing. Most people in the Third World would be very happy to have the opportunity to share hegemon lifestyles, animated with the spirit of consumerism, the culture-ideology that encourages us to satisfy more than our biological needs.[15] All consumption due to *induced wants* has to be driven by external forces. In the final though neverending triumph of consumerism, wants becomes synonymous with needs. We may pause to distinguish the effects of consumerism in societies where affluence is the norm (though even here some people may be without the necessities of life) and societies where poverty is the norm (though some people may be very affluent). It is only in terms of these distinctions that the creation of new consumption needs by the TNCs in poor countries can be properly evaluated, but even with these distinctions it is difficult, if not impossible, to do more than identify what is happening. Seen in this light, consumerism creates cultural dependency. Elizabeth Cardova's definition is poignant, if controversial: 'Cultural dependency means people in our country have to brush their teeth three times a day, even if they don't have anything to eat' (cited in Stover, 1984, p.31). Most toothpaste and brushes are produced by TNCs.

Case studies in global consumerism

The baby bottle-feed case

The controversy surrounding the marketing of the Nestlé infant formula in the Third World is a *cause célèbre* in the history of both global consumerism and the consumer movement. The case is a classic in the stormy history of TNC–Third World relations, and the reimposition of the boycott on Nestlé products in 1988 points up its continuing significance.[16]

Nestlé, S.A., a Swiss-based transnational corporation, is the world leader in a variety of processed food and nutritional products.[17] The company has been producing and selling these products in the Third World for many years (see Nestlé, 1975). The public campaign against Nestlé began at a forum on nutrition sponsored by the UN in 1970, where a scientist claimed that the aggressive marketing of infant formula had caused a decline of breast-feeding in many Third World countries. A torrent of scientific and popular publications on the subject began to appear. Over the next few years the belief that infant formula was actually harmful to babies in the socio-cultural settings of the Third World snowballed and more and more individuals and groups (particularly Church groups) joined the campaign against the marketing of such products in general and the activities of Nestlé in the Third World in particular. Matters came to a head when a Swiss group accused Nestlé of 'killing babies'. The company sued for libel and in July 1977 an international boycott of all Nestlé products was announced.

The charges of the critics were quite straightforward. The infant formula producers were marketing their products in ways that discouraged breast-feeding, they were using salespeople dressed like nurses, they were ignoring the fact that many of their Third World customers did not have clean water or hygienic conditions in which to prepare the formula safely, they were not giving sufficient warnings against the dangers of overdilution, and they were pushing their products through Third World health professionals by methods ranging from persuasion to corruption (for one example in the Yemen, see Melrose, 1981). There is no doubt that some of the scientific issues became over-simplified in the course of the campaign (see Miller, 1983).

It was becoming increasingly clear that direct contacts between the boycott organizers and Nestlé were unlikely to be productive and both sides made attempts to bring in third parties. The boycott organizers, and Nestlé and other involved parties, put their cases to the World Health Organization. In 1981 the WHO promulgated a code for the marketing of breast-milk substitutes that adopted most of the recommendations of the boycotters. The vote was 118 to 1 (the United States), and represented a serious political defeat for Nestlé and the other infant formula companies. After many years of trying to play down the controversy, Nestlé began to realize that it needed a more systematic strategy if it was ever to have the boycott lifted. In 1981 it created the Nestlé Coordination Center for Nutrition, Inc. (NCCN), a group of public relations experts with a generous budget to hire anyone needed to resolve the problem. NCCN, and in the following year the Nestlé Infant Formula Audit Commission (NIFAC), went on the offensive.

By accommodating critics' complaints, dividing the opposition and shrewd targeting of winnable objectives, these organizations won reputations for independence and objectivity and the boycott coalition began to crumble. In 1984, the boycott was called off. This prompted a social marketing and communications expert to comment:

> The lesson to be learned here is that the absence of sophisticated regulatory mechanisms in the Third World should not be misconstrued as an open invitation to free-wheeling marketing behaviour. One suggested rule-of-thumb for international markets: If you can't get away with it at home, it's better not to try it elsewhere. (Manoff, 1984, pp.16, 20)

However, the case was not closed. The anti-Nestlé campaigners continued to monitor the situation carefully and throughout the 1980s Nestlé and other TNCs were charged with continued violations of the WHO code of practice. Nestlé hotly disputed these accusations and argued that the campaigners were misinterpreting the WHO code. In 1988 the boycott was reinstated.[18]

What are the lessons of the Nestlé case? Although there is now recognition on the company side that there are questions of morality and social responsibility involved, neither Nestlé nor the infant formula industry has ever seriously acknowledged anything more than 'free-wheeling marketing behaviour' (in Manoff's ambiguous phrase). Nestlé and other companies have never conceded that they owe reparations of any sort to the bereaved parents and stunted children in countries where their (allegedly now-discontinued) malpractices actually did lead to death and ill-health. Nevertheless, governments and health workers in beleaguered Third World countries appear still to want infant formula, and most seem satisfied that the WHO code sufficiently protects mothers and babies.[19]

The lesson for the TNCs is that there are now groups of activists operating transnationally to monitor the activities of the TNCs on a permanent basis, particularly where there are health implications for people in the Third World. When the *Wall Street Journal* (25 April 1989, B6) revealed that Nestlé's public relations advisors, the major transnational advertising agency Ogilvy and Mather, had proposed a 'Proactive Neutralization' campaign to infiltrate the company's opponents and discredit them, this caused a storm and boosted the renewed boycott.[20]

Drugs, health and profits

The pharmaceutical-medical drugs industry, for obvious reasons, has also attracted a great deal of attention from those for whom global consumerism is problematic (Gereffi, 1983). Medical drug sales in both developing and advanced industrial societies are often highly controversial. The pharmaceutical industry claims that its research and development and testing costs put it in a special category compared with most other industries, but critics have drawn attention to the fact that the industry's extremely high ratio of advertising expenditure to sales revenue is what makes it unusual. What is undeniable, however, is that many TNCs in the pharmaceutical industry have over the years adopted systems of differential pricing in different markets, and that consumers in many developing countries have been paying far more for their internationally branded medicines than consumers in some First World countries. It has also been established that labelling practices vary quite dramatically between markets in rich and poor countries, leading to widespread charges of unethical behaviour against the companies.

It is important to acknowledge that the pharmaceutical industry is a special industry (along with other medical and hospital products industries some of which are integrated with it) in terms of its direct and intimate connection with human life and well-being, but like most other industries it only survives as long as it makes profits. The main contradiction between the activities of the drug TNCs and the needs of the Third World is that the bulk of TNC research and promotional effort is directed towards the relatively expensive drugs designed to combat the perceived health problems of the rich countries, while the poor countries of the world require, for the most part, relatively simple and cheap preparations to cope with the illnesses of the mass of their populations (see Medawar, 1984).

A clear illustration of this is the treatment of diarrhoea, a major killer in most Third World countries, and especially dangerous to infants. Pharmacies in some parts of the Third World will routinely recommend expensive antibiotics and anti-diarrhoeal drugs. These are in most cases (though, of course, not in all cases) quite unnecessary and can even be dangerous. One notorious example is the hydroxyquinolines, some of which were withdrawn in the United States in the mid-1970s but continue to be available over the counter in many Third World countries. The best treatment for diarrhoea, universally recognized by health professionals, is a simple rehydration solution (boiled water, sugar and salt) which most people could prepare for themselves at low cost, even in conditions of substantial deprivation. It is clearly not in the short-term financial interests of the local firms, the TNCs producing the superfluous drugs or the pharmacies selling them to have these facts widely known. One of the most discussed cases of unethical marketing of such drugs by a TNC in the Third World is that of

Searle's *Lomotil,* exhaustively documented by Medawar and Freese (1982).

As in the marketing of infant formula, there is also a voluntary International Code of Pharmaceutical Marketing Practices, adopted by the International Federation of Pharmaceutical Manufacturers Associations (IFPMA) in 1981. While consumer groups in many countries have been watching the transnational activities of IFPMA members for decades, two issues have come to the fore in recent years, namely the export of drugs and chemicals banned in their countries of origin (Norris, 1982); and the larger question of 'inappropriate' drugs for the Third World (Silverman *et al.,* 1982).

The debate over export to the Third World of products banned in the First World highlights many of the problems surrounding any attempt to evaluate the culture-ideology of consumerism in the Third World. From the point of view of the TNC, if a sovereign state in the Third World allows a product to enter then the attitude of the United States, or any other country, should be irrelevant. There is even some research suggesting that in the area of environmental pollution the TNCs actually have a relatively good record in the Third World, despite the tragedy of Bhopal (Leonard, 1986; but compare Ives, 1985). More specifically, there are arguments that cannot simply be ignored that the benefits of, for example, malaria control in a Third World country resulting from the use of a pesticide banned elsewhere, may be sufficient to offset the risks to health involved, and may justify the marketing of a range of 'hazardous' pesticides. Third World governments and planners often accept this privately.[21] From the point of view of First World governments, seriously worried by the loss of markets for manufactured goods to foreign competition, anything that makes it more difficult for their manufacturers to export is rarely welcomed. Nevertheless, there is clear evidence that Third World consumers are not being properly advised by drug TNCs.

In the case of the United States, the Food and Drug Administration sets what are probably the most exacting safety standards in the world, and so it could well be argued that the balances of benefits and costs in poor countries, which have quite different priorities, are not the same as in rich countries. It is often noted that few, if any, Third World countries can reasonably be expected to have the capacity to monitor imported drugs and chemicals for themselves and, therefore, the best system of testing is to encourage the TNCs to regulate their own activities and so hold themselves responsible for any avoidable mishaps (compare Norris, 1982 and Peretz, 1984). The TNCs argue that they cannot be held responsible for incorrect or inappropriate use of their products and that as long as they are not breaking any rules in the countries in which they are selling, the rules of their home countries cannot fairly be applied to inhibit their business. This continues to be a contentious issue.

This is the reasoning behind the several voluntary codes of conduct that attempt to control the uses of drugs and chemicals. In the case of direct danger to life the issue is straightforward, if often technically very complicated. In the case of 'appropriateness', it is rarely straightforward. In 1977, the WHO developed a list of between two and three hundred 'essential' drugs to help Third World medical personnel choose from the tens of thousands available on the market. It is a little baffling to learn (from Medawar, 1984, p.34) that in Norway in the early 1980s there were about 1,000 branded drugs available for prescribing, while in India there were about 15,000. And India is by no means unique in the Third World in this respect.

Several Third World countries at one time or another have restricted imports of drugs not on the WHO list (for example, Bangladesh, Zimbabwe, Mozambique) and others (for example, Mexico, Nicaragua, Costa Rica and Kenya) have developed 'essential drugs projects' through which a small number of the most useful medicines are made available very cheaply through government dispensaries in the countryside. These initiatives are not necessarily antagonistic to the interests of the TNCs, as most of the drugs are still imported or, where produced locally, are often manufactured by the local subsidiaries of the TNCs. However, they do fundamentally question the way that the pharmaceutical TNCs do business in the Third World, and there is little evidence to suggest that the corporations are prepared to abandon the questionable business practices that have brought lucrative rewards over the years. It is also the case that in many countries of the Third World cheap generic drugs do not displace the more expensive branded drugs.

The advertising of drugs and health-related products obviously plays a part in this. One study sponsored by the International

Advertising Association reviewed the control of pharmaceutical advertisements in 54 countries and found that there was very little serious monitoring of the claims of drug advertisements. Most TNC advertising was devoted to the over-promotion of general health products (like laxatives, vitamins and diet supplements) of doubtful medical value.[22] The bewildering variety of 'tonics' on sale in most Third World countries is testimony to the power of the TNCs (and local companies) to sell promises in liquid, tablet and lozenge form. The struggle for global regulation of the marketing and sale of drugs and health-related products rests on an uneasy compromise between the TNCs and organizations such as the WHO, with little sign of progress to the point where the real medical needs of the mass of Third World peoples will be adequately met (see Melrose, 1982).

The solution to this serious problem appears not to be the replacement of the TNCs by indigenously-owned drug companies. One study of the Turkish pharmaceutical industry in which large Turkish-owned and TNC companies share the market, demonstrates than in most important respects large drug companies, whether foreign or domestic, act in a similar manner. It concludes: 'Both the TNCs and the large comparable local drug firms similarly rely more heavily on the production of those drugs which do not provide cures for the major causes of mortality in the country' (Kirim, 1986, p.521).

What, then, is the solution? Claudio Schuftan (1983) suggests that the only solution is to sever the links between the TNC dominated 'Western' health-care model and the Third World. He argues that in general TNCs and the type of organized medical systems they work through cannot meet the needs of the poor and the sick masses in the Third World and the treatments that they offer tend to do as much harm as good.[23] Schuftan's approach mirrors the experience of the 'barefoot doctors' in China in the 1960s and 1970s. The fact that the Chinese authorities saw fit to downgrade this experiment should not lead one to suppose that it was a failure or that something better was put in its place.

Once again, dilemmas abound. The TNCs that sell drugs in the Third World have undoubtedly saved countless lives, even if their practices have also caused unnecessary suffering and fatalities. The culture-ideology of consumerism in the Third World holds out a vision of health and bodily well-being, for consumerism would lose much of its positive meaning without this. The drug companies have always been very active in promoting these absolutely commendable values even if the products through which the values are promoted have been found to be wanting in many cases. Medawar (1979) illustrates this in his case studies of how health and nutrition themes pervade processed food advertising, particularly in the Third World. Foods and drinks lacking in nutrition or providing nutrition in an inappropriate and deceptively expensive fashion are, indeed, a highly profitable component of TNC-induced consumerism. The case of 'the other baby killer' (sweetened condensed milk) as researched in Malaysia (see Consumers Association of Penang, 1981) is a tragic example of this. The case of the cola beverages is another good, if less deadly, example of the clash between consumerism and inappropriate consumption in the Third World.

Cola wars

The so-called *cola wars* provide a telling example of how the TNCs have gone about the creation of a culture-ideology of consumerism in the Third World. Coke (Coca-Cola), the market leader, has been active outside the United States since the beginning of the century. In an article to celebrate the hundredth anniversary of the product and what it stands for, *Beverage World* (May 1986, pp.48–51) under the revealing title, 'Ambassador to the world', provides an insight into how the industry sees the product. In it we learn that by 1900 Coke was already international and by 1929 it was operating 64 bottling plants in 28 different countries. Recalling its diplomatic skills and its very special role as a symbol of the American way of life, the article describes how Coke survived the India–Pakistan War by turning its plants into blood donor stations, how it survived the Arab anti-Zionist boycott, and how it has recovered after its major diplomatic setback, losing the USSR market to Pepsi. Coke is found in 155 countries, over 60 per cent of its sales are outside the United States, and more than 300 million Cokes are drunk every day (1986 data). It is truly global!

Only in the last 20 years or so has the pressure of competition, particularly from its great rival PepsiCo, led Coke and its competitors to a more public global strategy, and a specific targetting of

Third World markets (see Clairmonte and Cavanagh, 1988, ch.7 and 8). In the early 1980s it was reported that the annual consumption of Coke overseas was 49 6.5 oz. units per person, compared with 272 units in the United States. The potential for growth is thus in other First and selected Third World areas, rather than in any major expansion of domestic consumption (see *Advertising Age*, 29 October 1983, pp.2, 86).What have been labelled the *cola wars* illustrate one phase in the continuing TNC campaign to structure new consumption needs, or more accurately *induced wants*, particularly in the Third World.

This is true not only for Coca-Cola. Well over half of total world soft drink consumption takes place in the United States. Since the mid-1960s, US per capita consumption of soft drinks has more than doubled while that of water appears to have halved. Soft-drink consumption now exceeds water, coffee, beer and milk (see *Beverage World*, February 1989, p.45). While, no doubt, North Americans can always be persuaded to have another one, the greatest challenge for the TNCs is to persuade consumers elsewhere to develop the same habit. As one industry analyst has proclaimed:

> because the international soft drink market is yet in its infancy, the successes of both Coke and Pepsi will serve to grow the entire world market. Their success, in part, hinges on their ability to change the way consumers in foreign markets regard soft drinks . . . . So as a strategy, Coke will target an increasingly younger consumer in an attempt to shape his [*sic*] drinking habits to consume more soft drinks instead of alternative beverages. (Hemphill, 1986)

One indication that the beverage industry, organized from the United States, was gearing itself for an onslaught on the drinking habits of the global consumer came in 1984 when InterBev'84 was staged with 15,000 delegates from nearly 30 countries. Two years later, under the slogan 'Selling the World', InterBev'86 brought together 25,000 people from 80 countries to ponder the thought expressed by a prominent industry representative: 'You have billions of people around the world that have yet to be exposed to soft drinks'. Even Coca-Cola, the market leader, had half its sales in only five countries (*Beverage Industry*, September 1986, pp.1ff.). The cola wars were well and truly underway!

Announcing that 'Cola wars move to foreign shores', *Advertising Age* (26 August 1985, p.6) described how Pepsi and Coke were locked in global combat in Europe and Asia; in 'Latin soft drink wars' (11 November 1985), how Pepsi's 7UP and Coke's Sprite were engaged in a lemon-lime battle for the allegiance of potential South American consumers; and how Schweppes was challenging in Australia (18 December 1989). 'Pepsi in China' (*Beverage Industry*, April 1986, pp.15, 20) recounts how PepsiCo will invest $100m over 10 years to develop the Chinese soft drinks industry, and secure the company's place as the prime purveyor of non-alcoholic beverages in the Communist world. PepsiCo has operated a bottling plant in Canton since the early 1980s, and along with its joint venture Happiness Soft Drinks Corporation in the Shenzhen Special Economic Zone, serves the Chinese and South East Asian markets. Coke, however, is fighting back, and the Chinese authorities have had a certain degree of success in playing the two corporate giants off against each other.

India, too, has had its own cola war. The Coca-Cola presence in India dates from 1950 and, in alliance with a local bottling company aligned with the politically dominant Gandhi family, it prospered until 1977 when it was forced to withdraw rather than give up its total control (as IBM had also done when threatened with indigenization). A local soft drink, 77 Cola, flopped because of marketing and flavour problems, but a rival Coke clone, Campa-Cola, was more successful (*Advertising Age*, 28 January 1985, p.63). The cola wars in India were sustained by the bold actions of an Indian entrepreneur, who tried to keep Pepsi out of the country, while sneaking his own brand of fruit juice into the United States (*Forbes*, 22 September 1986, p.207; updated in Chakravarty, 1989). The wars rumble on, in India and all over the rest of the Third World, where TNC advertising budgets are sometimes not far short of state expenditures on education.

There are very few parts of the world in which the effects of the cola wars have not been felt. In even the most remote places Coke and Pepsi and their ubiquitous marketing slogans and logos symbolize the American way of life and the prospect that anyone, however poor, who can afford a bottle or a can, can join in the great project of global consumerism, if only for a few moments. The transnational practices of the global capitalist system fade into the background as the joyous promises of 'Coca Cola is It' or membership of the 'Pepsi Generation' flood the foreground.

Now this may be very welcome news for those who oppose the consumption of alcohol by the young, and it may also be good news for those involved in bottling plants and distribution networks in the Third World. It is hardly up to the outside observer to decide whether one or other of the colas is 'appropriate' for Third World consumption. Nevertheless, it is legitimate to draw attention to the massive marketing budgets and the battery of promotional skills put to work by TNCs like Coca-Cola and PepsiCo in poor countries, and to acknowledge that they really can create new consumption needs for nutritionally worthless products, and dictate the means to satisfy them largely on their own terms.

It is not irrelevant that most of the players in this game are from the United States and that what is being marketed is not simply a soft drink but a style of life, specifically a (North) American style of life. An executive of a small Cola company puts the point plainly when he says:

> our emphasis in Third World countries is to reinforce to the consumer that we are an American soft drink and we do have the quality the consumer has been looking for and not always finding . . . there is a tremendous potential for expanding per capita consumption . . . through impacting lifestyles in the same manner that we have here in the U.S. (in Jabbonsky, 1986, p.188).

This statement expresses well the complex relationship between 'Americanization' and the culture-ideology of consumerism in the capitalist global system.

Conclusion

These brief studies of global consumerism set out to document the spread of the culture-ideology of consumerism in the Third World.[24] The choice of high prestige, relatively costly non-essentials is deliberate, because it is precisely the contradiction inherent in these 'mass-luxury' products of foreign origin that symbolizes the problem that the global capitalist system faces in extending itself over the whole world. The questions remain: can capitalism ever achieve its global goal of transforming all the people into genuine consumers? Can it even meet the basic biological needs of the world's people? Despite the ingenuity of the TNCs, the efforts of the transnational capitalist class, and the hegemony of the culture-ideology of consumerism, the answers are by no means clear.

This sentiment encapsulates what many Third World thinkers fear most about the impact of the TNCs on their countries in the future. The spread of the new international division of labour (NIDL), in its widest sense, has indeed brought many jobs and a good deal of prosperity to the transnational capitalist class and other groups in the Third World. Nevertheless, many in the Third World believe that, despite the apparent successes of the culture-ideology of consumerism, the material benefits, such as they are, will never percolate through to the masses.

These views range from the cautious to the catastrophic. James and Stewart (1981, p.106), on the basis of a study of eight products, find: 'tentatively, that products developed in advanced countries are likely to have inegalitarian effects when introduced to poor countries and may, under certain conditions, cause losses among some or all consumers'. More dramatically, Jayaweera (1986) says: 'capitalism will also have left behind in the Third World, as its most enduring contribution to Third World development, an almost unfettered and wild consumerism, undergirded by the new electronic entertainment technologies'. He concludes on the grim note that 'when production pulls back to the metropolitan centers, and the offshore enclaves are dismantled, those tastes and aspirations will remain, along with the TV and video networks that nourished them' (Jayaweera, 1986, pp.42–3). Not many people share the view that capitalism in the Third World will end in this way, but most would agree that the TNCs have played a crucial role in raising consumerist expectations that cannot be satisfied within the forseeable future for the mass of the population in the Third World.

Notes

1.   This is exactly the rationale under which it was introduced to China in the 1980s, (see Chapter 6).

2. Relevant here is the 'cultural discount' thesis of Hoskins and Mirus, who argue convincingly that 'US dominance follows naturally from the characteristics of television programming, its production and trade' (1988, p.500). See also Meyer (1988) on media dependency; and Gould and Lyew-Ayee (1985) on television in Jamaica.

3. These headings derive from Lee Chin-Chuan's discussion of media imperialism (1980), but my interpretations are radically opposed to his. The differences between cultural and media imperialism are irrelevent in this context.

4. See Schlesinger (1987) on the contested concept of 'national identity' which is crucial to this issue; and the wide-ranging discussion in Mattelart *et al.* (1984).

5. A statement from an East African newspaper editor articulates well the way in which Americanization becomes detached from the system of global capitalism: 'My fight for intellectual freedom is more important to me than the fight against Americanization' (cited in Smith, 1980, p.40). For many insights into the complexities of First World-Third World cultures, see Worsley (1984).

6. For a critical review of the problems of Third World entry into news markets see Samarajiwa (1984). Merrill (1983) is full of useful information.

7. Relevant here is the work of IPAL (an Argentinian-Peruvian research centre) on Information Technology, see Atwood & McAnany (1986); also the special issues of *Latin American Perspectives* on 'Culture in the Age of Mass Media' (Winter 1978) and 'Cultural Production and the Struggle for Hegemony' (Spring 1989).

8. An extraordinary example of this was the 'pornographic' videotape allegedly smuggled into the Philippines which was actually a cover for a Japanese documentary on the assassination of Benigno Aquino (cited in Mowlana, 1985, p.88). Ganley and Ganley (1987) suggest that there was no shortage of media reports of the killing in the Philippines and so the pornographic videotape story may be apocryphal.

9. Salinas Bascur (1985) argues, however, that this has led to wasteful and expensive overpurchase (and consequent under-utilization) of computer facilities in Latin America. For an extension of the argument to the First World, see Caulkin (1989).

10. Nicholson (1988) reports that while only the United States spent more than 2 per cent of its GNP on advertising in 1986, fourteen other countries spent more than 1 per cent including Argentina, Bolivia, Costa Rica, Dominican Republic, Israel, Panama and Venezuela. Asian advertising is also booming, according to this source. A table in *Advertising Age* (24 July 1989) shows that at least seven of the top eleven ad agencies in Latin America are foreign-based. See also Sinclair (1987).

11. See Fejes (1980). In this connection, a research project on the 'global teenager' (Baker and Rappaport, 1989), though methodologically

problematic, is of interest. I am grateful to John Ryle for this reference.

12. The rapid spread of McDonald's hamburgers in East Europe confirms this. For their ecstatic reception in Moscow see *US Today* (1 February 1990) and *The Guardian* (29 January and 1 February 1990). See also the special issue of *Journal of American Culture* (Summer 1978) on McDonald's.

13. Other food TNCs have been quick to capitalize on this. The chief of the Heinz Corporation (which markets in 200 countries) is quoted to the effect: 'In the Far East, Western habits are really catching on – O'Reilly intends to profit from the "McDonaldisation of Asia" ' (in Gabb, 1989, p.69).

14. In an interesting analysis of the case of breakfast cereals in Kenya, Kaplinsky (1979, p.90) argues: 'a move from traditional, appropriate products to new, less appropriate ones significantly increases the nutrient cost to consumers and, moreover, results in the introduction of inappropriate production techniques'.

15. As Garnsey and Paukert (1987, pp.69–70) argue, some consumer goods have undoubtedly made life easier for women.

16. Unless otherwise stated, this account is based on Pagan (1986); Muskie and Greenwald (1986); and Sethi *et al.* (1986); Nestlé (1985); Chetley (1986); and Salmon (1990).

17. See Clairmonte and Cavanagh (1983, pp.109–18). In addition to its most famous product, Nescafé instant coffee, Nestlé also currently owns Carnation, Chambourcy, Crosse and Blackwell, Findus, Libby, Buitoni, Rowntree and many other brands (see *Ethical Consumer* [Manchester], July-August 1989, p.17).

18. Code violation is a controversial question and rests, to some extent, on company claims that they have little control over what actually happens with their products in the Third World. The interested reader could compare the Nestlé press release of February 1989 and *IBFAN Africa News*, December 1988.

19. In an interesting paper, Howard and Mayo (1988) illustrate concretely how the corporations could build in safeguards to prevent misuse of their products. But this would raise costs.

20. Though Nestlé rejected the proposal it retained the advisors! See *Multinational Monitor* (May 1989, pp.21–3); the sensationally titled, but very informative 'Forget the dead babies. Nestlé's PR firm spins feel-good line,' *Voice* (2 May 1989, pp.14, 18); and the *Action for Corporate Accountability* press release, 'Infant health activists angered by Nestlé's "PR only" response' (26 April 1989).

21. See 'Too much fuss about pesticides?' in *Consumer Reports* (October 1989, pp.655–6) illustrating that this dilemma is one that consumer movements in the First World also face.

22. The research (reported in *Advertising Age*, 22 April 1985, p.55) was carried out by Jean Boddewyn, whose recent book on self-regulation in the advertising industry (1988) is a good guide to the subject.

23. This argument has parallels with Illich's thesis of 'clinical

iatrogenesis' and related theories of 'commerciogenic illness'. All are based on the idea that it is profit-inspired medical intervention that makes people ill.

24. Space precludes the inclusion of more cases. Suitable candidates for this type of study would include the tobacco industry (see Nath, 1986; Taylor, 1984); the private car (*New Internationalist*, May 1989, and references therein); mass tourism in the Third World (Hong, 1985; McKee, 1988); and children's comics and cartoons (Dorfman, 1983; Dorfman and Mattelart, 1975).

6

Socialist societies in the global system (1)

Proletariat of all countries – Sorry! (slogan on an independent march in Moscow, Revolution Day, 7 November 1989)

Up to 1990 between twenty and thirty countries considered themselves communist or socialist. They can be split up in several ways. Economically, they fall into two groups, those that belong to the Council for Mutual Economic Assistance (Comecon) and those that do not. The Comecon group comprises most of the East European countries where communism followed the Soviet victory in Europe in 1945, plus Cuba and Vietnam. The other group includes Third World countries that opted for some variant of socialism when they were granted independence by the colonial power, like Tanzania, or after revolutionary wars, like China and the African states of Angola, Mozambique and Zimbabwe.

We can also divide them up into Second World, the East European states and Third World, the remainder. Scholars working principally on socialist states in Africa have suggested another classification, namely populist socialist and scientific socialist states (see Keller and Rothchild, 1987). However we divide them up, we would be well advised to try to define what is meant by communism and socialism.

Communism and socialism defined

There are different ways of defining socialist and communist societies. The terms are sometimes used interchangeably, but usually *socialism* is seen as a stage on the road to *communism*, a sort of transitional society. Both these usages can be defended, but the second is more useful. *Socialism* is defined as the social system based on the principle 'to each according to work, from each according to ability', while *communism* is defined by 'to each according to need, from each according to ability[1]'. As will be immediately obvious, while this definition does distinguish socialism from communism, and tells us that no society in the world has achieved communism, it does not really distinguish either from many other social systems. There are, however, several structural features of socialism that do distinguish it. These would certainly include the attempt to break the power of private capital over the economy and to establish mechanisms of democratic planning for the eventual transition to communism (see White *et al.*, 1983, p.1). In addition to these common structural features, there are also many sources of heterogeneity between societies that have embarked on the road to socialism. Among the most important are the widely varying initial conditions of their birth, the brand of socialism adopted, and the point in the socialist development reached at the time of the analysis (Forbes and Thrift, 1987, Introduction).[2]

The analysis of Rothchild and Foley (1987, pp.282–4), though intended for the study of Afro-Marxist regimes, has a much wider application. They suggest seven criteria of socialism, as follows:

1. Commitment to a specifically African (or presumably any other regional) scientific socialism but still true to orthodox Marxist-Leninism. (The reference here is to Gromyko's distinction between revolutionary but petit-bourgeois ideology as in Tanzania and Algeria; and a wider range of revolutionary transformations as in Angola, Mozambique and Ethiopia.)
2. Focus on class analysis rather than a populist analysis based on the 'people as a whole'.
3. The leading role of the vanguard party representing, but not necessarily led by, the working class.
4. Commitment to strengthening the state.
5. Open acceptance of revolutionary transformation to bring about a new social order, using coercion if necessary and including the reduction of the penetration of foreign-based capitalism.

6. Commitment to the creation of social and economic conditions for the redistribution of wealth and the triumph of socialism.
7. Finding natural allies in the socialist bloc.

This can be criticized on various grounds, for example that Marxism is actually anti-state, and that there are problems involved in the relationship between coercion and democracy. But Rothchild and Foley are inclined to argue that these regimes are trying to achieve socialism under very difficult conditions, and that this will inevitably lead to 'reluctant pragmatism'.

An important determinant of reluctant pragmatism is that the socialist societies of the 1980s could no longer operate as if they could insulate themselves from the global capitalist system, which is what they had previously been trying to do to a greater or lesser extent. While not everyone agrees that the socialist countries now actually operate within the orbit of global capitalism, few will now wish to deny that economic, political and cultural-ideological practices from the First World are penetrating socialist societies in ways that would have been considered unthinkable 20 years ago.[3]

Many remarkable developments occurred in the communist world in the 1980s, notably the opening-up of the People's Republic of China (PRC) and other socialist Third World and East European countries to capitalist transnational practices, particularly in the economic sphere. Political and cultural-ideological changes have also been spectacular, but more unpredictable. This chapter will deal first with the question of the options open to socialist societies presented by their increasing exposure to capitalism. The effects of economic, political and cultural-ideological transnational practices in China are then discussed. The next chapter briefly reviews what is happening in the rest of the socialist Second and Third World.

However they classify themselves or we wish to classify them, in the late twentieth century these countries face a struggle over the choice between three different systems based on three different world views. These are the continuing drive towards the utopian Marxist vision of the classless communist society, the restoration of capitalism and an, as yet not very well articulated, 'Third Way'.

Choices for socialist societies

In many socialist countries the 1990s have brought important economic reforms. These are invariably in the direction of a freer market, reducing central state controls on the economy and permitting individuals more autonomy in their economic activities. In some countries, like China, Poland and Hungary, these processes have gone some way along the road of 'market socialism' (or partial restorations of capitalism), in others, like Albania and North Korea, the changes have been less spectacular. Nevertheless, all socialist governments do appear to be trying to find ways to satisfy the visibly growing economic aspirations of their peoples.

In the political sphere, the record is less uniform. While the economic changes in Poland, Hungary and China have many similarities, the contrasts in the political sphere at the beginning of the 1990s could not be wider. Although these differences are mostly explicable in terms of their widely varying domestic circumstances, the recent emergence of embryonic *transnational capitalist classes* in the socialist world play a key role in these developments. The forces behind re-unification of East and West Germany and the developments in Hungary, are vivid illustrations of this.

The cultural-ideological sphere follows the economic more than the political, in the sense that under the influence of the global capitalist system, even in socialist societies, economic and cultural-ideological changes appear to reinforce one another in ways that political changes do not. As will be clear from the drift of the argument in the previous chapters, the connections between the market-oriented economic changes and the promotion of a culture-ideology of consumerism in socialist societies is of the first importance.

Of the three choices facing the socialist world, the utopian communist dream of a classless society is a truly transnationalist humanitarian vision that would obviate the necessity for war, hunger and deprivation of all sorts. It would also remove the social conditions that aggravate the human predispositions to anger, hate, envy, depression, boredom and violence, and secure the social conditions that promote the equally human predispositions to tolerance, altruism, love and enthusiasm. This vision has almost disappeared throughout the world, largely because the state forms that Stalinist communism encouraged have led neither to increased human freedoms for their populations nor to general increases in prosperity sufficient to compensate the masses for the deprivations they suffered in the revolutionary process. This is, in some cases, a very harsh judgement even if it is true. For example, the people of Nicaragua did not seek the US economic blockade and the CIA-funded Contra terrorism that stifled their revolution (see Walker, 1987), nor did the Mozambicans choose to become embroiled in a war against South African financed MNR terrorists that is destroying the material conditions for the construction of socialism in their country.[4] But that is what is happening. The communist parties and governments of East Europe have had no such excuses for decades, and many of their peoples appear to have rejected the communist vision too, though it is less clear that capitalism is what they want.

Many Marxists see the main cause of discontent in the socialist world in the absurdity of the idea of 'socialism in one country' created by the Stalinists to sustain the national integrity of the Soviet Union. Communism is an international theory and practice or it is nothing and the prospects for isolated socialist states, breakaway socialism as it is sometimes labelled, in a global capitalist system must always be bleak. As one writer puts it: 'the continued strength of world capitalism, especially as it operates in the interstate system, have pushed these [socialist] states in the direction of reintegration as functional parts that reproduce the logic of the capitalist world-economy' (Chase-Dunn, 1982, p.9).

It may be intellectually sounder to argue that actually existing communist states have no genuine connection with the communist ideal. This is my own view, but it is hopeless to try to argue the case with the victims, for they have suffered too much to be willing, far less enthusiastic, to give the communists another chance. This is the message of some of the recent extraordinary elections in East Europe. But these changes appear to be restricted to East Europe, for the time being. As the repression in China of June 1989 suggests, Third World socialist regimes are not ready to tread the same path. What are the choices open to them, now that the communist ideal has been rejected?

The restoration of capitalism is the first option that springs to mind. It involves a complex set of ideas, particularly in societies that have never really experienced capitalism. In a very real sense, the tremendous changes that are taking place in most communist societies are the results of attempts to come to terms with the economic, political and cultural-ideological practices of contemporary capitalism. The global capitalist system, mainly but not exclusively through the culture-ideology of consumerism, has very successfully projected its vision of the 'good life' (as opposed to socialism's vision of the 'good society'). The culture-ideology of consumerist capitalism appeals to individualism, private enterprise and the idea of choice. Most socialist societies, despite some very impressive rates of economic growth in the past, appeared in the 1980s to be in economic crisis. This is true, but only in terms of the criteria of the global capitalist system, namely their inability to satisfy ever-growing demands for consumer goods (see Birman, 1989), than in terms of their own goals, namely the provision of a basic minimum standard of living for everyone. As we have already seen in Chapter 5, while some demands for consumer goods may be genuine, others may be artificial. It is always very difficult to decide in a particular society where the dividing line is and, indeed, the dividing line is not fixed over time.

The economic 'reforms' in East Europe and the socialist Third World are regularly labelled moves towards the restoration of capitalism, approvingly by capitalists eager to cash in, and disapprovingly by theoretical communists defending the purity of their beliefs. These judgements of right and left are predicated on conceptions of capitalism that monopolize individual enterprise and entrepreneurship. This has the unfortunate effect of making it virtually impossible to criticize inefficiencies in socialist economic and social planning without appearing to advocate the restoration of capitalism, at one extreme, or sounding hopelessly naive on the question of human motivation, at the other. The simplistic belief that 'privatization' will solve all ills is as false in the Second World as it is in the other two (as Cook and Fitzpatrick, 1988 demonstrate). This goes to the very heart of the dilemma faced by all the socialist societies that embarked on processes of reform in the 1980s. We could ask why it is that more than 70 years after the Russian revolution and more than 40 years after the Chinese revolution, few appear to believe that 'communism' works. If the leaders no longer appear to believe, then it is not surprising if no one else does.

The Chinese authorities, for example, have been accused of the restoration of capitalism, at least since 1978. The argument hinges on the extent to which socialist development depends on the promotion of transnational practices that are *capitalist* in origin. The contradiction here is apparent, not real. *Capitalist* practices have a different significance in socialist as opposed to capitalist societies, though they may not, it is true, have very different immediate consequences for the individual worker or citizen involved. Just as *socialist* practices, like socialized health services and public housing, have a different significance in capitalist and socialist societies, *capitalist* practices, like the freedom of employers to fire workers and to declare an enterprise bankrupt have, as we shall see below, a different significance in socialist as opposed to capitalist societies.

The perceived need to introduce *capitalist* practices into socialist societies is due to the political primacy of economic growth, particularly state-sponsored export-oriented industrialization, in current development strategies.[5] This has repercussions for class structure in socialist societies, in terms of the tendencies to favour the urban proletariat over the peasantry, despite communist-populist rhetoric, and the growth of an urban-based (and biased) bureaucracy. Though Marxists argue that under communism the state will wither away, it is precisely in communist societies that state control has grown to enormous proportions. The characterization of communist societies as state capitalist began with the labelling of the Soviet Union and, since Milovan Djilas wrote *The New Class* (Djilas, 1957), the idea of a state bureaucratic ruling class in communist society has been widely discussed inside and outside Marxist circles. What the reforms in China in the 1980s (and elsewhere) have introduced is the idea that an actual *capitalist bourgeoisie*, as opposed to the *party or state bourgeoisie*, is emerging in these societies.

A comprehensive analysis of embourgeoisement in a socialist society is Ivan Szelenyi's study of socialist entrepreneurs in rural Hungary. Hungary appears to be the only case of the re-emergence of family entrepreneurship in East Europe, and Szelenyi develops a complex theory to explain how four class processes of proletarianization, the formation of a new working class, embourgeoisement and cadrefication, have simultaneously taken place. An elaborate methodology predicts, through life histories and the inheritance of 'cultural capital', how the new entrepreneurs emerge.

> The kind of embourgeoisement we are describing here – at least until
> now – has not led to 'capitalism'. Rather, a new, state socialist type of
> mixed economy is emerging, with a uniquely new dual system of social
> stratification. It is as different from laissez-faire or welfare state
> capitalism as it is from the Soviet style of monolithic, redistributive,
> state socialism. (Szelenyi, 1988, p.13)

I shall pursue the *socialist entrepreneur* idea with reference to the
class structure in China.

Szelenyi draws two main theoretical conclusions. The transition
from self-employed petit bourgeois to capitalist entrepreneur or
pure proleratian may not be as simple as Marx imagined; and
concepts like market and entrepreneur need to be 'converted' before they can be used for non-capitalist societies, like that of a state
socialist mixed economy.

In late 1987 the Chinese Communist Party adopted the theory of
the 'Initial Stage of Socialism', undoubtedly a form of state socialist
mixed economy. Cynics, inside and outside China, interpreted this
as an ideological rationale for the whole reform package started in
1978. Nevertheless, the rejection of practices simply because they
occur in capitalist societies is dogmatic and contrary to the spirit of
scientific reasoning. *Capitalist* practices, as noted, do not necessarily
have the same significance in capitalist as in socialist societies.

If the introduction or restoration of capitalist practices into
socialist societies does not necessarily mean the restoration of capitalism itself, what does it mean? The answer to this question is one
version of the Third Way. The many possible Third Ways are the
societies that emerge from attempts to combine elements of capitalism and communism. Interpretations of the Third Way range
from one party parliamentary 'democracies' whose economies are
largely centrally controlled, to totalitarian states that do not inter-
fere at all in the economy at the grass roots. Some of the countries
of the Third World already claim to have found a Third Way, but
as a societal form it is still very embryonic. As I shall argue in the
discussion of China and in my concluding chapter, the choice may
not be between socialism and capitalism. The choice may be between a bureaucratic state socialism or state capitalism and some
third way which combines practices that are proven to be economically efficient without being socially inefficient (some of which are
characteristic of rich capitalist societies) with practices that are
politically more democratic without at the same time unduly en-

couraging the exploitation of powerless large minorities by privileged small minorities (a combination that few societies of any type have managed to achieve to any great extent).

New China[6]

The Chinese economic reforms of the late 1970s, the 'post-Mao' economic policies, clearly represented a real shift in strategy for the Chinese government, but whether they represented a real shift in goals is less easy to determine. Chinese policy, even during its most isolationist periods, was aimed at harnessing the best of foreign technology and methods. Reluctance to become dependent on foreign capital and technology to the same extent as other Third World countries, at least up to the 1980s, was a result of the bitter experience of the Sino-Soviet split in the late 1950s, and a keen eye for the worst consequences of neo-colonialism elsewhere. The policy of self-reliance did not mean 'rely on ourselves for everything' but 'do not rely on foreigners for anything we can do for ourselves'. Even during the Cultural Revolution, turnkey projects for large chemical fertilizer factories were concluded with foreign companies.

Mao's economic policy was thoroughly tempered by strategic military thinking. Throughout the 1950s and the 1960s China felt threatened by actual wars conducted by the United States and its allies on its borders with the declared aim of defeating communism, and by potential war from a hostile Soviet Union. Regional self-sufficiency in the 1960s was reduced to village level with the exhortation that everyone should 'store grain, and prepare for the eventuality of war'. The military rationale of these decentralizing processes declined in the 1970s as China's entry into the United Nations in 1971 and the Nixon visit to Beijing in 1972 reduced China's isolation. However, exposure of the economic inefficiencies of the policies had to wait until the death of Mao in 1976 and the defeat of the 'Gang of Four' and their followers shortly after.

The opening door

The economic reforms of the late 1970s inaugurated a process of selective decentralization. By the early 1980s a form of regional decentralization was being encouraged that presaged a radically new theory of development for China, and one that owed little to Mao Zedong. It is in this context that the general opening up of the Chinese economy to foreign influence and the creation of the Special Economic Zones (SEZ) must be placed.

China is the most populous nation on earth, with a population of over 1 billion people, most of whom are young. One of the most visible effects of the economic reforms of 1979 and since, has been the transformation from a low income, low inflation and low consumption economy to one in which there are substantially increased incomes for numerous groups, significant inflation and a veritable consumer boom in the cities and some parts of the countryside. A sign of the times was the announcement in 1984 that peasants were to be subject to personal income tax, where previously a fixed percentage of production had been levied as a tax on the collective. The fact that even a small proportion of Chinese workers and peasants now have money to spend after they have bought the necessities of life, means that there are many millions of extra potential consumers in the global marketplace.

The south of the country has always provided the bulk of Chinese emigration, principally to South East Asia but also much farther afield. Apart from Hong Kong, about half of whose people were actually born in the PRC, there are important Chinese communities in Malaysia, Singapore, Thailand and Indonesia. In all of these countries the Chinese are over-represented in business, and they have always been wooed by the authorities in the PRC who have consistently seen these 'overseas Chinese' as economically and politically worthwhile allies. Services and facilities for them now constitute a growth industry throughout China. The official interest parallels and is thoroughly nurtured by strong clan, village and kin links. Overseas Chinese consider investment in China as both a patriotic duty and a convenient way to help their relatives.

From the early 1980s there was a general liberalization of the economy accompanied by changes in political and cultural-ideological practices, some quite incredible from the perspective of previous decades. For example, the lifting of restrictions on various forms of private enterprises led to an embryonic 'stock market'. One manifestation of this was in the attempts by some entrepreneurs to sell shares in public as well as private enterprises.

The difference between buying shares in private companies, which no one in China had experienced since the 1940s, and deposits in bank or cooperative savings accounts, which have been widespread and secure throughout the whole period of communist rule, was not at all clear to the uninitiated. As a result, many people lost money, some no doubt cheated by unscrupulous speculators. The official visit of John J. Phelan (then chairman of the New York Stock Exchange) to China in 1987 served to give Chinese stock dealings a measure of legitimacy but this has not been matched by adequate regulatory law.

In the cities, the economic reforms have resulted in tremendous growth in small businesses, particularly personal services. For example, beauty parlours have mushroomed, encouraging an expanding clientele to seek social and psychological fulfilment through cosmetic surgery for the creation of Western facial features. By 1988, it was reported that 20 per cent of all China's doctors and nurses were in private practice, many of them specializing in such fields (Schell, 1988).

The growth of the tourist industry in China has also been extraordinary, but only in contrast to the situation up to the late 1970s, rather than in comparison with what is common in the rest of the Third World. Now, at sites throughout China, tourists are accosted by multitudes of peddlars selling local curios and other objects of uncertain origin, often undercutting the prices of the official state shops. At the most popular attractions, like the Ming Tombs outside Beijing, and the Terracotta soldiers outside Xian, large peasant markets catering to the tourist trade have implanted themselves. Whereas visitors in the 1960s and 1970s had complained that the reticence of the salespersons made it difficult to buy anything, now the complaint is that hawkers will not leave tourists alone.

These may be seen as interesting if rather peripheral examples of what has been happening in China since 1978. More central to the future of the society and more salient for the analysis of the impact of transnational practices on it, is the open-door policy. In 1988, the east coast 'open belt', China's *gold coast*, covered a total area of 320,000 km^2 with a population of 160 million, about 15 per cent of the national total. The open region is made up of three parts, namely the four Special Economic Zones (SEZs), the coastal open cities, and the larger coastal open economic areas (Zheng Yiyong, 1988).

The SEZs were established in southeast China in 1979–80. The largest and most important is at Shenzhen, directly across the border from Hong Kong's New Territories. In order to facilitate the utilization of foreign investment in 1983 the Chinese authorities announced the establishment of eight zones for priority investment. These were large areas, like Beijing–Tianjin–Bohai Bay, the nine municipalities and 57 counties of the Shanghai Zone, the Wuhan Zone and the Pearl River Delta Zone. They already contained about 90 per cent of China's foreign investment. The plan was, and largely still is, to concentrate most of the future FDI in these areas where, it is argued, it can be put to the most effective use most quickly. Two hundred and twenty-two key cities (later increased to 287) were designated to transmit development to the backward areas that surround them.

In 1984 fourteen coastal cities were opened up to relatively unrestrained foreign investment. The rationale for this policy was the 'trickle down effect', now somewhat discredited in the eyes of most planners. While it would be rash to prejudge the issue, several decades of development planning experience would suggest that this strategy has little to commend it. It is only fair to add, however, that there is no single development strategy with very much to commend it on the available evidence. The choice of investment priority areas and 'open ports' seems to be a predictable first step in any process of industrialization.

In 1985, in yet another open-door initiative, Coastal Open Economic Areas were established in 52 Pearl River delta cities and Yangtze River delta cities and counties and in Fujian. These were already relatively prosperous areas, but links with the outside world through foreign investment and foreign trade have made them even richer.

Similar policies are now pursued all over China, and, in the words of an open-door policymaker, the 'long time isolation from the world economy, a product of many historical factors, has become a matter of the past' (Zhang Ge, 1988, p.70). However, the more prosperous areas must pay a certain price for their new economic opportunities. In return for greater autonomy the open door region is expected to do the following:

1. Increase its output of technology intensive products as well as

its export of labour in order to earn the foreign currency that China needs to import equipment and materials.

2. Encourage the growth of international as well as domestic cycles of production through the use of both domestic and imported inputs for exports.

3. Increase all forms of foreign investment.

4. Import more foreign technology and use it for both import substitution products and R&D.

5. Selectively learn from foreign managerial expertise.

6. Train various kinds of personnel (*ibid*).

The Chinese government has invested heavily in infrastructure to improve the foreign investment climate, particularly in Shenzhen, and this has provoked a good deal of criticism. One indication of the resentment felt at the over-generous treatment Shenzhen has received from the centre can be gauged from the vote at the National People's Congress (China's 'Parliament') in 1989, on special rights for Shenzhen. These were opposed by 274 out of 2,688 deputies, with 805 abstentions, 'the largest opposition debate and votes in the history of the congress' (*Beijing Review*, 17–23 April 1989, p.5). It would be incorrect to see this as a vote against the open door as such. Nevertheless, there has been some criticism of the emphasis on exports, partly because Chinese goods are not very competitive internationally, but to a greater extent because the level of unsatisfied domestic demand is very high. However, China, in common with many other Third World countries locked into export-oriented development strategies, considers it necessary to export in order to earn the hard currency to import.

Of particular significance for Shenzhen, and indeed the growth of the whole Pearl River delta, is the relationship with Hong Kong. There has been a substantial trading link between Hong Kong and the rest of China for decades (see Youngson, 1983). Indeed, Hong Kong could hardly have prospered in the way that it has since the 1950s without supplies of relatively cheap food, raw materials, labour and latterly oil from the PRC. The trade, however, is decidedly two-way. While the value of Chinese exports to Hong Kong increased almost twentyfold between 1960 and 1980, Hong Kong exports to China increased over fifty times in the same period, most of the increase being in the 1970s. PRC exports to Hong Kong are commonly trans-shipped to third countries, indicating both the shortcomings of the Chinese transportation network, and the residual resistance that some countries still have to doing business with China directly. The volume of trade and trade-related contacts between the south of China and Hong Kong increased enormously in the 1980s. Most of these contacts take place in Canton and in the Shenzhen Zone.

While Chinese society has rarely been as thoroughly egalitarian as some of its more enthusiastic erstwhile supporters have imagined, in general communist party policies have managed to keep intra-regional inequalities in check more successfully than inter-regional differences. The economic changes since the late 1970s, and particularly the exhortations to the workers and the peasants to enrich themselves as fast as possible, within the somewhat elastic bounds of socialist legality, may well have increased local inequalities. But, as tends to be the case in communist societies, this depends on the characteristics of the family (age and labour status) and not directly on the ownership of land or property. The benefits of economic growth in the coastal regions as a result of foreign investment in particular, and transnational economic practices in general, therefore, are liable to be spread relatively evenly across the mass of the population of these areas, and other regions may well share some of these benefits. The question that is increasingly posed is whether the overall benefits of the economic reforms are sufficient to compensate for the income and other differentials they will clearly produce, and for the corruption and nepotism that are widely reported, even in the official media.

The TNCs have played an important if muted role in all of this (see Teng Weizao and Wang, 1988, Part III). Most of the foreign investment that flowed into China in the 1980s came from small to medium-sized companies, usually based in Hong Kong and overwhelmingly run by ethnic Chinese. However, a small number of very large TNCs, for example, PepsiCo from the United States, Sanyo from Japan and British Petroleum, have invested in Shenzhen SEZ and the adjoining Shekou Industrial Zone (Wong and Chu, 1985; Sklair forthcoming). Outside the SEZs, many large TNCs have been operating since the 1970s. A spate of regulations to encourage foreign investment continually reinforced the impression that, irrespective of what was going on in the sphere of domestic politics, the TNCs continued to be very welcome in China.[7]

As always, it is difficult to distinguish the specific impact of the TNCs from the more general 'modernization' effects that arise from any type of contact with the First World. Nevertheless direct links between transnational practices and changes in China's economic, political and cultural-ideological structures can be found in a number of areas and can be illustrated through analyses of the labour market (economic TNPs), changes in 'class' structure (political TNPs); and the creation of new consumption needs (cultural-ideological TNPs).

The labour market

Up to the beginning of the 1980s the basis of Chinese Communist employment policy was the 'iron rice bowl'. This meant that most enterprises in China were obliged to employ many more people than they really needed, and to maintain employment irrespective of conditions of operation, both in the urban and the rural economies. Therefore, although many Chinese enterprises achieved high levels of production, very few achieved high levels of productivity per worker. When the foreign investors began to do business in China, there were many disputes between them and the Labour Services Bureaux (the state organizations that provided workers to the firms) over employment levels and labour discipline. Both sides faced serious problems. The TNCs, most of whom were quite small, had come to China precisely to taken advantage of lower wages (as well as more and cheaper land for industrial expansion). Though wages in less industrially advanced areas in China, principally those distant from the coastal regions, are very low, those in the major cities and in Guangdong province, adjoining Hong Kong, where most foreign investment has been concentrated, tend to be relatively high.

Full wage costs to foreign employers in Shenzhen SEZ, for example, have been about half of those in Hong Kong for some time, and so there were not the huge labour cost savings that are to be found in some other Third World locations. This meant that the TNCs were less willing to tolerate either excess labour or unsatisfactory workers than they might otherwise have been. Under this pressure a definite crack appeared in the 'iron rice bowl' but, despite efforts to make it more substantial, it remains limited because the Labour Bureaux are still responsible for finding alternative jobs for those allocated to but not employed by the enterprises in the SEZs.

From the point of view of workers surplus to requirements and/ or those who fail to match up to the demands of TNC labour discipline, this is the thin edge of the wedge. However, it can be argued that it was precisely to learn from foreign capitalists about how to run modern factories efficiently that the economic reforms were introduced and the TNCs were allowed in, in the first place. It was with this problem in mind that a retired West German engineer was appointed general manager of the Wuhan Diesel Engine factory, the first foreigner to run a state factory. There are other similar stories of how seriously the Chinese authorities are taking the task of modernizing Chinese industry.[8] The rationalization of labour figures prominently in most Chinese analyses of economic reform, and there is no doubt that practices introduced by TNCs are beginning to have an impact on employer–employee relations in China.

It is not only at the worker end of the labour force that the impact of the TNCs is being felt. Since the early 1980s a revolution has been going on in the practice of enterprise management, and many academic management theorists and working management consultants (sometimes the same people) have been invited to China to instruct Chinese managers and administrators in the art and science of management. A highly visible symbol of these activities has been the establishment of several US and EC-sponsored MBA programmes through the Chinese university system and other management training schemes (see Warner, 1987). There is a link between this development and debates that have raged throughout the PRC since its birth over the questions of 'red versus expert', political versus technical expertise.

This takes us to the core of the fundamental dilemma that a communist society like China faces in its struggle to modernize and in its relations with the TNCs, the bearers (and often the owners) of the technology and techniques that are widely believed to be necessary for modernization. The history of enterprise management in the PRC has seen violent swings from 'reds' (those with the correct political attitudes) in control, to 'experts' (those with technical expertise irrespective of political attitudes) in control. These two states were summed up by the reported assertions by followers of the 'Gang of Four' on the one hand, 'better socialist weeds than capitalist rice', and, on the other, Deng Xiaoping's famous saying, 'it doesn't matter whether the cats are black or white, as long as they catch mice'! It would be naive to assume that all enterprise managers in China are now 'experts', and that the 'reds' have been entirely eliminated (or, for that matter, that these two categories exhaust all the possibilities). Transnational corporation operations in other Third World countries have often been seen to depend as much on finding people who 'know their way around the corridors of power' (or, at least, the foreign investment bureaucracy), as on finding indigenous managers who are technically competent. From the point of view of the TNC trying to gain a foothold in China, perhaps the local 'expert' is less vital than the 'red' who can work the political system. From the point of view of those who bear the responsibility of enterprise management in the new conditions of profit and loss accounting, the problem is increasingly: where is the economic liberalization policy leading? (See, for example, Sullivan, 1988; and Sklair, in Warner, 1987.)

The other side of the foreign investment coin is, of course, the jobs that are lost in other places when a factory relocates, a central economic transnational practice of the global capitalist system. During the 1980s, hundreds of thousands of jobs were shifted from Hong Kong to Shenzhen and the Pearl River delta, particularly in the garment, electronics and toy industries. According to one trade union source: 'workers in Hong Kong helplessly watch their employers move the production lines across the border and gradually their wages eroded since they are paid on piece-rate basis' (Lee Cheuk-yan, 1987). The Hong Kong Clothing Union mounted a job saving campaign in the 1980s which, among other things, highlighted the shady practice of keeping plants 'open' for minimal production in Hong Kong to secure false certificates of origin, thus making it possible to sidestep First World quotas and continue exporting. The result is underemployment of the workforce rather than mass redundancies. Surveys showed that many employers were routinely deceiving Hong Kong customs. Under these circumstances, it is difficult to see how international socialist solidarity can be built between Hong Kong and Chinese workers.[9] This raises the issue of the 'class' nature of the open-door policy in China.

'Classes' in the New China

There are those who see the attempted reform of the labour market as a clear indication of the capitalist nature of the PRC. Charles Bettelheim, the French economist and historian of the Soviet economy, has characterized both the Soviet and the Chinese systems as state or party capitalist. Bettelheim (1988) argues that despite quite respectable growth of industry between the 1950s and the 1970s, the Maoist strategy is condemned because of poor progress in agriculture, a reduction in the share of services in the national economy, growth in urban unemployment and a gradual reduction in the marginal efficiency of investment. 'Communist' China, according to Bettelheim, has always been a society ruled by a party bourgeoisie, and since 1978 has embarked on a 'new road' which could lead either to a *mixed* or a *predominantly private* capitalist system.

The theme of capitalist restoration (or re-creation) is becoming very familiar in the analyses of all socialist societies.[10] However, not everyone agrees that a capitalist restoration is taking place in China. Solinger (1989), in a closely argued paper based on first-hand research, labels the situation at the end of the 1980s, 'Capitalist measures with Chinese characteristics'. She demonstrates that the reforms are state-centred, not centred on private enterprise. Their rationale is that they are intended to recoup state losses incurred over the years as a result of subsidizing inefficient enterprises, and to turn bureaucrats into better managers. Enterprise bankruptcy regulations, takeovers of loss-making by profit-making companies, the spread of shareholding and embryonic stock markets, are all responses to the dire lack of state funds. 'There is no privatization of any significance going on' (Solinger, 1989, p.22).

She shows, for example, how *shareholding* and *bankruptcy* differ in communist China and the capitalist system. The Chinese system of shareholding is based on shares that are really state and enterprise bonds, holding no risks, rather than capitalist-type speculative shares. State enterprises are prohibited from issuing more than 30 per cent of their capital in shares, and these shares are often used as extra welfare payments and bonuses for the workers.[11] The system of official warnings for near-bankrupt state enterprises often leads to firms being turned round rather than going to the wall.

The question is often asked: why do party bureaucrats in China and other communist countries appear to tolerate such apparently capitalistic practices? The simple answer may be that Chinese (and East European) bureaucrats generally support these changes because they provide many commercial opportunities for them. For example, Solinger argues that state organizations like material supply bureaux, industrial companies set up by local authorities, trade associations, investment companies and economic and technical cooperation committees, all stand to benefit from the reforms. She concludes, not unreasonably in my view, that capitalistic measures are forced to adapt to Chinese communism rather than vice versa!

Is a new class emerging in China? My own research has focused on the Shenzhen SEZ, just across the border from Hong Kong. While the assertion that there is a new 'class' emerging in Shenzhen (let alone in the rest of China) as a consequence of the open-door policy is highly controversial, the assertion that there are new 'strata' (groups that have qualitatively new positions and interests) can hardly be denied. Generalizing from Shenzhen and other areas that are clearly within the orbit of the global capitalist system, we can identify at least three new strata from which a transnational capitalist class could theoretically emerge: the *officials* who deal with foreign capitalists as representatives of state or parastatal agencies; *private entrepreneurs*, many of whom do business with foreigners; and the large group of PRC Chinese, *expatriate red capitalists*, who live and work in Hong Kong and abroad.

Officials

One distinctive feature of Chinese (and Soviet-style) political economy is that officials have enormous power in the economic and commercial spheres. Everyone knows that the economic reforms have created opportunities for corruption that the government has signally failed to control. The special relationships between officials and entrepreneurs (foreign and Chinese) are plain for all to see and there is incontrovertible evidence that these relationships are increasingly corrupt. This is openly discussed in the Chinese media and Shenzhen is often singled out for criticism in this regard. In 1988 Li Hao, Mayor and Party Secretary of Shenzhen, admitted that corruption had seriously discredited the SEZ with the public.

In Shekou, the industrial zone west of Shenzhen, the seriousness of the situation was illustrated in early 1989 by the promulgation of four new regulations concerning the widespead phenomenon of public officials involved in private enterprise. The Shekou authorities offered the following conditions: holders of concurrent public and private posts must declare their interests, hand over excess income and receive half back. Corrupt earnings and brokerage income, if declared and returned, would be excused (*Shekou News*, 6 February 1989).

Although many appear to blame the SEZ for the rapid increase of corrupt cadre practices, it is clear that such practices have been widespread throughout the country for some time. The PRC magazine *China Market* (November 1988, p.15) reported that many of China's 390,000 companies were 'briefcase' (or paper) companies. One such company in Zhejiang Province, for example, made over a million yuan in its one and only transaction, namely buying 3,000 tonnes of urea from the state and selling it at 70 per cent above the official price! Chinese critics argue that such practices are undermining the market for many goods, and though the authorities know about them, they are not cracking down hard enough. These criticisms have been given theoretical form by Hua Sheng and his colleagues at CASS (Chinese Academy of Social Sciences), who argue that the failure to separate economic from political power is destroying the reforms because the bureaucrats who monopolize the supply of raw materials are corrupt and this makes a rational pricing and allocation policy impossible to put into practice.

Private entrepreneurs

In 1988 it was reported that there were over 13 million private businesses in China. But only 115,000 of these employed 8 or more people. According to Zhang Houyi and Qin Shaoxiang of CASS, a new social stratum of owners of private enterprises is emerging and they are becoming politically organized. One survey even suggests that 15 per cent are members of the Communist Party.[12] All over the country entrepreneurs' clubs and magazines are springing up and many sources express the opinion that a new 'entrepreneurial culture' is becoming established in China. 'Getting rich quick' and 'putting money above everything', while not entirely unchallenged, are sentiments officially legitimized by the view that the pursuit of individual wealth is a necessary precondition of national prosperity in contemporary China. Under such conditions, it is hardly surprising that an entrepreneurial stratum is rapidly growing. Often the entrepreneurs and the officials are the same people. But do they constitute a class, and are they allied with others sharing the same (protocapitalist) interests?

For those who suspect this to be the case, the influence of Chinese expatriate capitalists is crucial. Chossudovsky (1986, pp.140–4) argues that what he labels the Chinese 'expatriate bourgeoisie' plays a key role in the process of class formation in the post-Mao period. Overseas Chinese often have close kin connections with the national patriotic bourgeoisie, and since 1978, they have been involved in foreign trade and investment policy making (for example, in the SEZs).[13] Entrepreneurs from Taiwan have also begun to invest in southeast China in growing numbers. *Business Week* (19 September 1988, pp.18–21) has raised the prospect of a 'Greater China' combining China's labour, Taiwan's skills and Hong Kong's financial might.

Since the mid-1980s there has been an unprecedented level of contact between foreign entrepreneurs and PRC Chinese, both in China and in Hong Kong, but nowhere more so than through Shenzhen. Two hundred thousand mainlanders visited Hong Kong between 1983 and 1988, including many young people keen to see capitalism at first hand. In the other direction, the number of ferry passengers between Hong Kong and China rose from 300,000 in 1979 to 2.8 million in 1987. Many of these passengers are foreigners who work in Shenzhen, some on a very long-term basis.[14] As travelling between Hong Kong and Shenzhen becomes easier and border facilities become more streamlined (it is about 40 minutes by train from Kowloon to Shenzhen and about 1 hour by ferry from Hong Kong to Shekou), more and more Hong Kong residents commute to the SEZ. This increases the opportunities for interactions and business. The Shenzhen and Hong Kong media often carry stories of business visitors to and from the SEZ,[15] and there is now more or less a free flow of persons and ideas from Hong Kong, long (though not entirely accurately) regarded as the epitome of free enterprise capitalism, to Shenzhen. The entrepreneurs of the New China, it may be said, have some of the most ruthless, if not the best, teachers in the world. Their instruction also takes place in Hong Kong itself, and this leads us to the third new stratum.

Expatriate 'red capitalists'

In preparation for 1997, when Hong Kong is reincorporated into China, there is a rapidly increasing body of mainland Chinese living and working in Hong Kong (see Shih, in Kaynak and Lee, 1989). There are said to be around four thousand PRC-funded offices, some very small and some very big. The China Resources Corporation, resplendent in its new office block on the Hong Kong waterfront (representing the Foreign Trade department of the State Council in Beijing) is the largest of the Chinese Holding Companies. It handles imports and exports between China and the rest of the world and it has a multitude of subsidiaries. Other well-known names in Hong Kong, like Everbright Holdings, the Bank of China and China International Trust and Investment Corporation (CITIC), have in the 1980s carved out a substantial chunk of Hong Kong for China. The China Merchants Company has represented Chinese shipping in Hong Kong for more than 100 years, and now has many diverse interests there. It has a direct link with Shenzhen SEZ through its management of the Shekou zone.

Resentment built up against PRC cadres working in Hong Kong throughout the 1980s, on matters concerning both their business practices and their personal life styles. This came to a head in late 1988 when several scandals rocked the 'PRC in Hong Kong' business community and led the Chinese authorities to demand that all these enterprises be re-registered and thoroughly examined. This was carried out at a high level as it was a very sensitive matter, for example the military were said to be using these firms for speculative purposes. Chinese working abroad may bring back 'eight big things' (consumer durables) duty free, but the question was: on such low salaries, where do they find the money (around HK$25,000) to buy them? There is also a lucrative parallel goods market of products smuggled out of China and sold cheaply in Hong Kong, undercutting Chinese exports.

Many administrative departments in Hong Kong also run businesses. For example, Xinhua (the official Chinese News Agency), the highest level representative office in Hong Kong, has dozens of enterprises in Hong Kong and Macao. Ex-Xinhua cadres have retired to Hong Kong and Macao and run trading companies there, strictly against PRC rules. Such 'red capitalists' are charged with having extravagent life styles not only outside the country but when they return to spend time in China. The problem for China has been how to stop the rot in Hong Kong without destroying the confidence of the foreign investors. A complicating factor is that 'foreign' partners in many joint ventures are really Hong Kong affiliates of Chinese state and provincial bodies, acting as brokers rather than genuine traders, whose main function is often to solve foreign currency problems.

The influence of Hong Kong in Shenzhen is undeniable. The Chinese currency (RMB) is not welcome in the Zone. Many foreign banks have branches there for corporate and personal accounts and it is estimated that about 50 per cent of the money circulating in Shenzhen is Hong Kong dollars (and foreign exchange certificates equivalent to HK$). It is no wonder that Hong Kong dollars are popular because the official exchange rate in 1989, about two HK$ to one RMB, vastly overvalued the Chinese currency. Foreign currency is almost indispensable for economic success in Shenzhen and, although it is becoming easier to acquire, access to Hong Kong and its unrestricted foreign exchange market is certainly a commercial advantage that many 'red capitalists' use to the full.

It is as well to be clear that the title 'red capitalist' is not always necessarily one of disapproval. To put no finer point on it, these people were sent to Hong Kong and abroad to make money, connections and trade for China (as indeed are those who work in foreign-related business within China). The problems arise, naturally, when they begin to make money, connections and trade for themselves. The question of *class* arises when they begin to make alliances with others whom they perceive to have common interests in the pursuit of private profit through the accumulation of capital.[16]

All of these three strata do have common interests and have begun to forge some systematic linkages. One highly significant linkage, common throughout China, is that the officials, private entrepreneurs and expatriate 'red capitalists' are often members of the same family. Cadres and their children frequently engage in private business and combine their state and private connections very profitably. The government publicly acknowledges this but it is not yet clear whether it has the political will or the bureaucratic muscle to eradicate the corrupt practices that result from the combination of economic and political power.[17] While in the short term the party and the government may prevent any or all of these strata from becoming a class for itself, as history teaches, new classes can crystallize independent of official approval.

So, is there a new 'class' emerging in China? And if there is, is it in any sense a *transnational capitalist class*?

If a new 'class' is emerging out of these strata it is most likely to be based on an alliance between private capitalists and entrepreneurs who have a connection with the state and/or party apparatus and, in places like Shenzhen, Chinese who are part of the foreign economic relations network. Though the foreign direct investment at work in China is still quite limited, and most of the TNCs active in the country are actually small overseas Chinese operations, there is no doubt that the centres of economic power of the global capitalist system have considerable interest in China, both as a source of cheap labour and as a potential market. This is clearly expressed in a UN 'China Round Table on Foreign Direct Investment' held in Beijing in 1987. 'Once having abandoned the ideological hang-ups against accepting the role of foreign direct investment that have inhibited so many developing countries, China is likely to want to continue to take advantage of it' (Richardson, 1987, p.25). The haste with which the TNCs flocked and were welcomed back to China after June 1989 suggests that the sentiment is mutual.[18]

The reality of corruption is presently highlighting the potential effects of such a new 'class'. The next stage in Chinese development could bring the clash of the quasi-capitalist entrepreneur and a new 'socialist entrepreneur' dedicated to the creation of wealth for all the people without individual exploitation and excessive differentiation between the richer and the poorer groups. It would be unduly cynical to define the quest for efficiency among the Chinese managers and technicians in foreign-invested enterprises in a way that contradicts the, as yet only vaguely formulated, notion of *socialist entrepreneur*.[19]

The future of the urban working class is just as difficult to predict. We can only speculate that some might resist the private entrepreneurs as their working conditions worsen, while others might take advantage of the new opportunities that economic and social changes bring. White (1988) makes the plausible suggestion that the labour reforms may well produce a more militant unionism and a more organized managerial representation. If this happens, and there are small signs that it may already be beginning to happen in Shenzhen and in the rest of China, then the open-door policy will have had the totally unintended consequence of sharpening a class struggle that the Chinese authorities had hoped to bury in the 1980s.

The sexual division of labour in the workplace and the status of women in the domestic economy have both been affected where they have come into close contact with the open-door policy and the TNCs. In Shenzhen, unlike most other zones, the numbers of female and male workers are roughly equal and this reflects Chinese employment practices in general, the mediating effects of the labour supply authorities and the mix of industries. It is also worth noting that the Chinese household, while not by any means free from patriarchal domination, might be somewhat more sexually democratic than households in other Third World countries. However, as both domestic and foreign-invested enterprises become more profit conscious, the relatively generous maternity and other benefits that they enjoy are beginning to work against Chinese women.[20]

These issues have been highlighted by Chinese media reports of a village where 95 per cent of the employed women were said to have returned to the home. Most rural women over 40 are reported to have given up their paid jobs, and even for young women, doing housework has a new meaning, namely 'doing special labor as the masters of society and the household rather than slaves'. Is going to the city to be a housekeeper an advance over staying at home and being a housemaker? For one uneducated woman:

> it was a great pleasure for her to see that her husband eats and
> dresses well, to raise her child and to keep her home in good order.
> Can we say she is ideologically backward or that she has backtracked
> to the status of household slave? I am afraid we cannot say so'.

The (male) commentator concludes that if women have the choice and they choose to stay in the home, this can be a socially useful occupation.[21] The forces promoting and the forces inhibiting the industrial employment and general emancipation of women in China are finely balanced as the country seeks its own *Third Way*.

New consumption needs

While China is still a very poor country, with large pockets of absolute deprivation in its vast hinterland, there is no doubt that in the 1980s a huge urban and rural-suburban consumer demand was created as a result of government policies. Since 1978, the responsibility systems in the factories and in the countryside, under which people and enterprises paid the costs and reaped the rewards of their own economic actions, and official encouragement for individual enrichment, have started to transform the whole country. Millions of small family businesses have been permitted to flourish, serving needs that had either been suppressed or neglected in the previous period. Western styles of clothing, personal goods and a wide variety of consumer durables can be seen on the streets and in homes in all the main cities, and increasingly in the countryside too.

Prior to 1978 there were relatively few retail outlets in China. Of those shops that did survive the destruction wreaked by the Japanese and the civil war, most were closed down in favour of the new state-run marketing and supply cooperatives. It is estimated that between 1957 and 1978 the number of retail outlets in China fell from 2.8 to 1.3 million; outlets per 1,000 persons in urban areas fell from 10 to 1.5; and employment in distribution fell from 1.4 to 1 per cent of the total workforce (Mun, 1988).

Due to the policy of transforming what had been consumer cities into socialist producer cities, and also to some extent to the traditional Chinese downgrading of traders and merchants, there was little notion of consumer sovereignty in China. Since the late 1970s, the most important changes in the distribution of goods and services have been the re-emergence of the rural markets, particularly in the suburbs of cities, the rocketing numbers of individuals and families that have become traders, the growing demand for better quality products (not unconnected with the one-child family policy) and the growth of multiple sources of goods, both for stores and their customers. For example, the much visited Nan Fang Department Store in Canton is said to have increased the numbers of its suppliers from 20 to 1,000, and the products it sells from 19,000 to 27,000 in the 1980s.

China has some supermarkets, usually single units rather than chain stores, relatively small compared with the gigantic structures found elsewhere, and with a very limited range of customer services. They also tend to be more expensive than small stores, as they are targetted at better off and better educated people, who are prepared to pay higher prices. The goods they sell are not necessarily imports, but they are often in foreign styles. These stores are sometimes restricted to customers who have Foreign Exchange Certificates or hard currency, like the so-called Friendship Stores specifically designed for foreign tourists and expatriate Chinese.

Chinese (and most other communist country) retailing differs from retailing in other parts of the world on several counts. First, there is controlled market entry, which makes it difficult, if not impossible, for private individuals to open shops. China relaxed controls considerably in this respect in the 1980s, but the enormous increase in retailing outlets has come from market stalls and itinerant traders rather than from shops as such, though the state and the municipalities have opened more shops than in previous decades. Second, China has an inadequate supply of consumer goods, especially high quality goods. This is a result of the overemphasis on heavy industry as against light industry, and the rigid state control of foreign trade, particularly the import of consumer goods. Both these policies have been changing since 1978. During the 1980s the government committed itself to increasing supplies of the big consumer durables (washing machines, refrigerators, television sets), and by partially decentralizing foreign trade it opened the door to local imports of consumer goods, particularly from Japan and other countries whose products were transshipped through Hong Kong. Finally, until recently, TNCs had no consumer goods manufacturing facilities in China to serve the Chinese market.

The TNCs have clearly been observing these developments with great interest. Both Coca-Cola and PepsiCo have bottling plants in the PRC. Foreign soft drinks are still too expensive for all but the most prosperous Chinese, but a cheaper local soft drink Xingfu Cola ('Lucky' Cola), a fairly blatant copy is, as it were, softening up the market.

The fast food industry is also growing rapidly in China, as US chains such as Kentucky Fried Chicken, Pizza Hut and McDonald's negotiate with the Chinese authorities for franchise agreements. The Chinese welcome companies such as these into the country for the advanced food processing technology that they bring, and they are being used to upgrade the local food and drink industries (see Elliot, 1984). The Chinese authorities obviously feel that the risks involved in exposing the population directly to products that are global symbols of advanced capitalism's favoured lifestyles, are more than offset by the potential industrial benefits. The 'cola wars' (discussed in Chapter 5) are being fought in China as well as elsewhere in the Third World.[22]

There are now many global consumer products available in China: the beverages and fast foods of the franchisers, the soaps, toothpastes and cosmetics of the leading TNC manufacturers, the consumer electronics from which no part of the world is entirely immune and, increasingly, European and American fashion garments. This flood of 'Western goods' (a convenient if inaccurate label because so many of them come from Japan and other Asian sources, including China itself) is most noticeable in the big cities, but it is evident to a greater or lesser extent all over the country. With it has come a perceptible change in the appearance and values of the Chinese people, particularly the young (see Bai, in Reynolds, 1987). How much this is due to the impact of the TNCs and how much to the general exposure to Western (and Eastern) capitalist influences is very difficult to say, though we can assert that the most important bearers of these influences as they affect China are the foreign investors and traders, a mixture of many very small companies (mainly from Hong Kong) and a few very large TNCs (mainly from the United States, Japan and Europe).

Some of the largest TNCs active in China are the transnational banks. Although several of them have had representative offices in the major Chinese cities for some time, the lucrative credit card business was closed to them until 1986, when the Mastercard and Visa networks, followed rapidly by American Express, were granted access. In 1988 China had fewer than 3,000 credit card outlets and very few state enterprises were willing to accept them. Total credit card turnover in China was worth only about 10 per cent of Hong Kong's, with a population two hundred times greater (Lim, 1988). The recent introduction of MasterCard's Great Wall card and the others that followed will undoubtedly increase their use in China and play a part in the formation of China's transnational capitalist class.

The culture-ideology of consumerism places all poor countries in a terrible dilemma, and China is no exception. The official policy of concentration on heavy industry and producer goods that drove the economy and politics during the Maoist era, meant that China, once it started to change its economic priorities, was under the most intense pressure to supply its people with consumer goods. The government has, since the 1978 reforms, proclaimed a policy of rising standards of living for the masses. In order to carry out the policy in the cities, local authorities and state enterprises awarded pay rises on declining revenues. This led to great increases in personal consumption in many places, a phenomenon encapsulated in the slogan: 'Celebrating the Spring Festival at the expense of the state' (meaning that food was sold at prices subsidized by the work unit at holiday times).

The three most prized consumer items of the 1960s and 1970s, watches, sewing machines and bikes, were replaced in the 1980s by refrigerators, washing machines, televisions and radio-recorders (and in the 1990s probably by colour televisions, videos, fridge-freezers, washer-driers, stereos and electronic cameras). In urban areas production more or less doubled in the 1980s, money income more than doubled, and purchasing power rose about three times. This was achieved by printing money and by foreign loans, and inflation naturally followed, a situation not improved by chronic waste of resources. As one source puts it, the Japanese mentality of 'living in a poor nation' seems to have vanished in China![23]

Throughout the 1980s the Chinese government was ever announcing its intention to control more strictly the import of consumer goods like wines, cigarettes, canned drinks, cars and household electrical appliances and the demand for them grows all the time. In the words of a high-level Chinese research team: 'In recent years, a consumer psychology has been created by the premature consumption, and a high-level consumption drive has been touched off by the "demonstration effect" of opening to the outside world' (Xia and Li, 1987, p.105). This raises an issue that has been seized upon by the critics of the culture-ideology of consumerism in communist China, namely the polluting influence of Western capitalist values.

In 1983–4 the Chinese government unleashed a campaign against 'spiritual pollution' in an attempt to foster its alternative 'socialist spiritual civilization'. The targets of the campaign were, confusingly, the remnants of the 'Gang of Four' *and* those who were accused of spreading corrupting capitalist practices through foreign investment and superfluous foreign trade. The campaign trod a very narrow path. While the authorities did not want to scare off foreign investors they did want to send signals to them and their Chinese associates that the 'open door' did impose some restrictions, though these were not always very clearly specified. The campaign against 'spiritual pollution' did not last very long but others like it have reappeared in various guises. In particular, attempts to apply the brakes on internal reforms that were evident in 1986–7, and since June 1989, and the ongoing campaigns, sometimes explicit and sometimes implicit, against 'bourgeois liberalization', keep up the pressure to ensure that the open door does not let everything in.

One example from Shenzhen will illustrate the complex issues involved. An article in *China Youth News* in 1988 reported that ten Shenzhen massage parlours had advertized in Changsha (a city in central China) for masseuses, and this had outraged the local people. On investigation, the parlours turned out to be perfectly respectable. However, conditions in many TNC assembly plants in Shenzhen were described as 'unbelievably bad' and child labour and excessive compulsory overtime were found. The local cadres were accused of 'doing anything for money' (Becker, 1988). It is as if direct attacks on capitalist economic practices themselves are prohibited by the open-door policy, but the culture-ideology of capitalism can be attacked, and through it, capitalist economic practices can be challenged.

The connections between this and the democracy movement, its suppression in June 1989 and subsequent events are highly convoluted, but it is surely of great significance that the first public statement of Deng Xiaoping after the Beijing massacre was to reassure foreign investors that the open-door policy was unchanged and would continue.

As I argued in Chapter 3, the interests of the TNCs are best served by a stable business climate that gives opportunities for individual and corporate wealth creation, and that the TNCs are indifferent to democracy. The Chinese authorities realize this. There is no evidence to suggest that the TNCs play any part at all at present in Chinese political life, though there is certainly a rapidly growing stratum of Chinese whose interests, both private and public, are identified with the success of the 'open-door policy' and by implication with the advance of TNC activity in China.

Whether this stratum will develop into a 'transnational capitalist class' is a question that still waits for an answer. If such a class ever becomes established in China it will be within the state apparatus as much as outside it. In this case its political influence, and the political influence of the TNCs in China, will be powerful.

One of the most visible changes in the China of the 1980s and 1990s, directly connected with the impact of the TNCs and the creation of new consumption needs, is in the extent, forms and contents of advertising. From the mid-1960s until the late 1970s, there was practically no product advertising in China. In his book on advertising in Asia, Anderson (1984, ch.9) presents a rare glimpse into the rebirth of the advertising industry in the People's Republic of China. Radio commercials first appeared in January 1979, and in March 1979 a television commercial (for 'Lucky' Cola) was broadcast. The first commercials for foreign products were shown in April on Canton television (for US cigarettes and Japanese watches) and many more followed. In 1982, CBS made a deal with the Chinese authorities by which the Chinese gave 320 minutes of airtime for commercials on Chinese television in exchange for 60 hours of US television programmes. This opened the floodgates for the rapid expansion of the Chinese advertising industry, which rocketed from 10 (state run) agencies in 1980 to 7,000 (mostly not state run) in 1988 (Schell, 1988).

Large advertising billboards are now a common sight in Chinese cities, and the once-austere *Beijing Review* (the main print vehicle through which the Chinese government communicates to the world) has been carrying vivid advertisements for some time. By the mid-1980s, several of the world's largest advertising agencies had a presence in China. The Japanese agency Dentsu, one of the biggest, has been in association with the Shanghai Advertising Corporation since 1979; the New York giant Young and Rubicam has been training Chinese advertising staff in New York since 1980; McCann-Erickson, also of New York, handled the Coca-Cola account in China and the China National Airline account abroad; Ogilvy and Mather handled the first Chinese advertising campaign (for Chinese herbs and drinks) in the United States; and so on (Anderson, 1984, ch.9). Thousands of selected foreigners received a 'confidential' letter in 1987 from Zhao Ziyang, then Premier of China, inviting attendance at the 1987 Beijing International Advertising and Marketing Congress.

The Chinese here, as in other areas, are careful to point out the difference between socialist and capitalist practice. Whereas under capitalism, it is argued, advertising is mainly devoted to ensuring that a product or service fights off its competitors, under socialism advertising is more of an educational and informational medium. There are contradictions in this view for all parties.[24]

The central contradiction revolves around the very valid point that although a consumer revolution has occurred in China, so far it has reached a relatively small proportion of the population (probably fewer than 25 per cent, mostly concentrated in and near the coastal region). China does not seriously regulate the personal imports that individuals carry on entry to the country. Hundreds of thousands of Overseas Chinese (largely, but by no means exclusively, from Hong Kong) have brought huge quantities of consumer goods for their relatives and friends in China. Many TNCs have found it worthwhile to advertise to create product differentiation for the PRC citizens likely to want such products. Now Chinese television not only advertises TNC products but also Chinese products, despite the widely recognized chronic shortage of consumer goods in the shops.

Transnational corporation advertisements for global brands bring in foreign currency to China, and they also nurture more 'modern' styles of mass media which create a more consumer-oriented public. The Chinese are as aware as anyone else of the merits (some might argue the necessity) of communication skills, for internal social control and external public relations. The advertising TNCs are widely seen as the vehicles through which these skills are generated and perfected. In the short term, therefore, in the early-learning stage, the socialist purpose of advertising is lost in the rush to master techniques. It is worth remembering, too, that most advertising executives, when in philosophical mood, will claim that their practice is educational and instructional, though not necessarily directed towards socialist goals.

The long-term contradiction likely to be created by the impact of these TNCs in China is a consequence of the fact that, for the foreseeable future, there will be little mass consumer market for non-essentials, though a market for what are defined, at least for contemporary urbanites, as essentials is certainly growing all the time.[25] The policy to encourage some people to get rich quick has not yet come to terms with the fact that, increasingly in China, a small but rapidly expanding stratum is already in the market for luxury goods while most of the population is barely in the market for essentials. How the domestic and the transnational advertising industries are permitted to handle such a situation remains to be seen. The problem tends to resolve itself in capitalist or non-communist Third World societies, as the TNCs orient themselves to the better-off strata. As Zimmerman (1986) shows, in his study of the marketing strategies of 31 US TNCs active in China, where the potential domestic market of a Third World country, even a communist one, is very large, the corporations can afford to be patient.

Notes

1. For an interesting discussion of the principle of 'distribution according to work' (DATW) see *Social Sciences in China* (1989). Sociologists might like to compare DATW with the functionalist theory of stratification and consider the point that it is the criteria on which different jobs are evaluated that distinguishes capitalism from socialism.

2. Post and Wright (1989), which came to hand after this chapter had been written, seems to me the best available discussion of Third World socialism. See, for example, the discussion of seventeen conditions of socialism, derived from Marxist and post-Marxist experience (pp.11–17).

3. See Girvan's 1975 essay (reprinted in Sklar, 1980); Frank's rousing article (1977); and more generally, Chase-Dunn (1982). For the interesting case of rock music in East Europe see Ryback (1989).

4. In the words of a Christian Aid report:

   > The objective of the MNR is to make life unbearable for the farmer and the peasant by making it impossible for them to grow their crops and by making them homeless. ... Their paymasters want to point to the chaos in Mozambique ... where else the bottom line of this war except the survival of white minority rule in South Africa? (Knight, 1988, p.14).

This is the same so-called 'low intensity' strategy in operation in Angola and Nicaragua. The recent electoral defeat of the Sandinistas in Nicaragua was widely seen as a statement about the war rather than domestic policies.

5. Which explains, for example, the introduction of Western-style business school courses into China (see Warner, 1987).

6. All unattributed Chinese language sources were translated by Huang Ping, research student in the Sociology Department, London School

of Economics. I have also used translations from the US-based *Foreign Broadcast Information Service* (*FBIS*) and the BBC's *Summary of World Broadcasts* (*SWB*) series.

7. This is confirmed by the increasing attention given to foreign trade and TNC-related matters in Chinese economic publications, for example, in *China Market* (published in Hong Kong) and *China Economic News* (published in Beijing).

8. See 'Riding China's capitalist road', *The New York Times* (10 May 1987, p.4F), Zamet and Bovarnick (1986) and, for a post-June 1989 discussion of a Matsushita JV, Han Guojian (1990).

9. This problem exists in many parts of the world. For example, the Mexican *maquilas* (in-bond plants) are accused of causing massive job losses in US manufacturing industry (see Chapter 3); and in Germany the TNCs are similarly accused (Gensior and Scholer, in Elson and Pearson, 1989). I have no doubt that many jobs will migrate from West to East Europe in the 1990s.

10. In this context, see Chossudovsky (1986, ch.7–9) on China's limited capacity to resist the overtures of the TNCs.

11. This was the case in the Beijing Minibus Company, whose leading management group I interviewed in April 1989.

12. In 'Features, practice of private economy viewed', *FBIS*-235 (7 December 1988, pp.32–6). See also Rosen (1987/1988). For a revealing account of one entrepreneur with transnational connections, see 'Going it alone', *Beijing Review* (27 February–5 March 1989, pp.19–22).

13. Though Chossudovsky gives no source for this assertion, I can confirm it from my own interviews with Hong Kong entrepreneurs active in the Shenzhen SEZ. See, more generally, Han Guojian (1990).

14. In 1986 there were 2,300 non-PRC specialists working in the SEZ, most from Hong Kong. See 'Outside experts aid Shenzhen', *China Daily* (17 February 1986). For the travel data, see *FBIS*-192 (4 October 1988, pp.73, 74).

15. One among many examples is the visit of the International Public Relations Association to mark the establishment of a SSEZ branch (*Shenzhen Daily*, 17 September 1988).

16. For a discusssion on the attitudes of enterprise cadres by the Chinese Economic System Reform Research Institute, see Yang *et al.* (Reynolds, 1987, ch.5)

17. In August 1989, relatives of the top Chinese leaders were said to have given up their private business interests. Whether they have all actually done so is another question.

18. See 'Turmoil won't close open door', *Beijing Review* (26 June–2 July 1989). Indications after June 1989 that the open-door policy might be seriously curtailed appear to be dissolving.

19. I have in mind those Chinese managers I interviewed in 1983–4 and again in 1988–9 in Shenzhen and Shekou who saw no contradiction between an efficient enterprise and the goals of socialism.

20. See 'Paper urges solving women employment problems', translated in *FBIS*-165 (25 August 1988, pp.42–3); and 'Women struggle for equality', *SCMP* (9 January 1989).

21. Quotes from ' "New Thinking" on women's liberation', *FBIS*-189 (29 September 1988, pp.51–3). See also, on more general issues of gender in China, Croll (1984).

22. See 'Coke and Pepsi vie in Chinese, Asian markets', *Journal of Commerce* (24 January 1986, p.5A).

23. See 'Article says consumption "running wild",' *FBIS*-172 (6 September 1988, p.37–8).

24. As Hansen says in his early and still useful study of advertising and socialism: 'It is not so obvious how advertising fits into an economy of the Soviet type' (1974, p.6).

25. The distinction between essentials and non-essentials is not as clearcut in practice as it might seem in theory. For an interesting case of long term planning of one US food industry TNC that is sensitive to this issue, see 'Sara Lee cooks up new China recipe', *Advertising Age* (23 June 1986).

7

Socialist societies in the global system (2)

Transnational practices and East Europe

Few people, even ten years ago, would have predicted that the two Russian words most broadcast in the world's mass media at the beginning of the last decade of the twentieth century would be *perestroika* (restructuring) and *glasnost* (openness). While the first refers to efforts to make the domestic economy and system of administration more efficient, the second has come to imply a receptivity to progressive ideas and influences from inside and outside the Soviet Union. Both *glasnost* and *perestroika* appear to be sweeping the whole of East Europe in the direction of global capitalism, or at least towards an opening to the practices of the global capitalist system. Birman's recent analysis (1989) of the dramatic gaps between personal consumption in the United States and the Soviet Union (and, by implication, the rest of East Europe) makes it less difficult to understand the force of the pent-up consumer demand that is propelling these changes so rapidly.[1]

Although these movements appear highly dramatic, unforeseen, even cataclysmic, the historical record shows that as long ago as 1957, Poland attempted to embark on a process of economic reform and was rapidly followed by most of the other members of Comecon (see Korbonski, 1989). These attempts were not successful, nor were they carried out very systematically. The point, however, is that the classic communist strategies, far from overtaking the prosperity of the capitalist centre, were unlikely even to provide for the necessities of their own citizens. East Europe did not suddenly wake up in the mid-1980s to find that it was falling behind global capitalism. It has been conscious of this fact at least since the 1960s.

In the 1950s Comecon rejected the global capitalist project, in particular the culture-ideology of consumerism, and therefore could choose to ignore it. By the 1980s the politics and culture-ideology of 'modernization' in the industrial societies of East Europe combined with the power of capitalism to communicate on a global scale, had changed the situation irredeemably. The political leadership in East Europe could no longer pretend that the West was failing to feed, clothe and house its people. The aspirations of the masses in the socialist countries began to find a voice in more responsive leaders, principally Gorbachev, and these leaders were forced by the perceived necessity for change and their own need for political survival, to adopt the culture-ideology of consumerism and to emulate the project of global capitalism. As a headline in *Advertising Age* so unsubtly puts it: 'Eastern Europe beckons!' (20 November 1989).[2]

Though the political changes have been sudden, the underlying economic changes have been more gradual. The countries of East Europe have been actively engaged in the global system for at least 20 years (Frank, 1977). Since the 1970s Bulgaria, Czechoslovakia, East Germany, Hungary, Poland, Romania and the Soviet Union have had transnational corporations operating in most countries of the world (see McMillan, 1987). Indeed, until very recently, the Comecon countries were far more active in the rest of the world than capitalist TNCs were in them.

Comecon direct investments (CDIs) tend to be equity investments in locally incorporated joint stock companies. Though banks and insurance companies establish branches directly, subsidiaries are more common in most other sectors. McMillan suggests that this is seen as the best way to avoid the hostility of the host country, but subsidiaries themselves often establish branches. The equity split is very variable, but the Comecon partner usually takes the majority share (for example, in retailing, technical services, banking and transport). Local personnel are frequently used.

By 1983, there were CDIs in 23 First and 75 Third World countries. Comecon TNCs in the Third World are concentrated in a small number of countries. Nigeria, Morocco, India, Singapore, Lebanon, Iran, Mexico and Peru account for about half. Activity in the First World is mainly in support of exports, while Comecon TNCs in the Third World are mainly involved in resource exploitation. The typical Comecon TNC tends to be small, between 10 and 50 employees (none were found to have more than 500). Like capitalist TNCs in the Third World, they relied largely on the local market for investment funds (McMillan, 1987).

In the mid-1980s there were at least 600 'red TNCs', worth at least 1 billion dollars. About one-third were active in the Third World. However, this represents only about one-tenth of 1 per cent of global foreign investment. The pattern of Soviet-style foreign trade organizations predominates, though manufacturing ventures appear to be on the increase. One survey showed that 377 of 403 Comecon TNCs in the First World in 1986 were in the service and construction industries. The spread in Third World countries was rather more even.[3]

There is abundant evidence to suggest that the growth of the 'red TNCs' was a consequence of the even more substantial growth of Comecon trade with the Third World since the 1960s. Nayyar (1977, ch.1) reports that between 1960 and 1970 the share of the Third World in Comecon exports rose from 8 per cent to 15 per cent and its share of Comecon imports rose from 9 per cent to 11 per cent. Asia took 40 per cent of this trade, while Africa and Latin America took 30 per cent each. However, as with the 'red TNCs' a limited number of countries were involved. Only fourteen countries accounted for 70 per cent of the total, with India and Egypt by far the most important trading partners. These two countries received about 30 per cent of socialist bloc aid in this period, which was also very concentrated.

Comecon–Third World trade tends to operate within bilateral agreements for the exchange of commodities, cash transactions being in local rather than hard currencies. This is obviously very useful for most Third World countries, which tend to be short of hard currency. Soviet credits have been important for development projects and have contributed to import flexibility for many poor countries.

Trade does not necessarily benefit all parties equally, and there have been cases of Comecon countries dumping Third World goods that they have received in barter deals on to the world market. Theoretically, a Third World producer could find its exports undercut by goods that have already been exported to a Comecon country. This works both ways. Comecon countries accept goods that they do not want in order to supply a Third World partner with goods that it cannot afford to pay for. However, to the extent that Comecon mainly exports machinery and transport equipment and other manufactured goods, and imports mainly textiles and raw materials from the Third World, long-term agreements between the parties do tend to lead to more price stability for Third World commodities than they enjoy in the world market.[4]

TNCs in East Europe

By the 1980s the countries of East Europe began to respond to the global consensus on the beneficial effects of foreign investment. The Soviet Union made a serious attempt to attract FDI through joint venture regulations established in January 1987. These had an immediate effect and by March 1987 there were more than 100 applications, about 20 under negotiation, and 3 already in the stage of filing for endorsement (Ivanov, 1987). However, most of the 40 or so agreements operational up to mid-1989 were reported to be losing money.

One exception was Applied Engineered Systems (AES), a joint venture between a Soviet state firm and Combustion Engineering, a US firm that had been doing business in the Soviet Union for some years. Combustion Engineering had something that Soviet policy makers considered essential for their industrial modernization plans, namely process-controlled equipment. The Soviet personnel in AES began by assembling kits of components supplied from the United States, under the management of Combustion Engineering technical staff. They then graduated to assembling whole units by themselves and to manufacturing some of the parts in the Soviet factory. The aim of the company is eventually to manufacture the whole product in the USSR from domestically-produced components for the domestic market, and also to export (Copetas, 1989).

The first genuine capitalist foreign direct investment in the Soviet Union was announced on 28 November 1989, when Fiat signed a deal worth over a billion dollars for a factory near Moscow to manufacture, market and export Fiat-badged cars. This is a qualitative step beyond the production under licence through which Fiat already turns out local-badged cars in Russia, Poland and Yugoslavia. One Fiat executive 'believes Eastern Europe will become the new Korea of the motor industry, except this time cheap production will be available on our doorstep' (quoted in *The Guardian*, 2 February 1989, p.4). Volkswagen are also considering East Germany for the same purpose.

Soviet planners are well aware of the economic potential of manufacturing for export. They are also, no doubt, aware of the costs. In 1988 a decree established the Soviet Far East as a special region of 'joint entrepreneurship' and Odessa, Estonia and Sochi, among other places, were said to be keen to follow suit. Advocates of this opening-up policy speak of Nakhodka, a port east of Vladivostok, as 'a new Singapore' (Hansen, 1989). In September 1989, at an international meeting in Moscow sponsored by the UNCTC, the creation of three free zones (Nakhodka, Vyborg and Novgorod) was announced.

Parallel initiatives are also to be found in other communist states in East Europe. Nawrocki (1987) describes the history of recent foreign direct investment (FDI) legislation in Poland. In 1976, a regulation permitted FDI in small businesses, but this was re-stricted to those of Polish descent. In 1982, shortly after the brutal (but, of course, temporary) suppression of the Solidarity move-ment, the Law on FDI in Small Industry allowed foreigners or TNCs to set up wholly owned subsidiaries and offered various tax and currency incentives. A Chamber of Industry and Commerce (InterPolcom) set up in 1977, facilitates FDI. The policy has had a certain degree of success. From 3 foreign enterprises in 1977, the total grew to almost 700 in 1986, but total FDI was valued at only $100 million. These enterprises employed about 60,000 workers (less than 1 per cent of the total workforce), and over half of these worked in firms with less than fifty workers. They are mainly in textiles and garments, chemicals, wood and engineering, oriented to the domestic rather than export market. New laws were passed in 1986 to encourage foreign investment in larger enterprises and in the service sectors, and there is some prospect that the efforts of Western countries to help the Solidarity government of 1989 will encourage more FDI.[5]

Martonyi (1987) discusses similar moves in Hungary. The legal framework for joint ventures in Hungary dates from the early 1970s, when it was restricted to R&D, commerce and services. In 1977 it was widened to include manufacturing industry. Foreign interest, however, was slight, only growing from 8 JVs worth about $10 million in 1980, to 66 worth $80 million in 1986. Normally in Hungary the foreign partner is only permitted a minority of the equity, but there are exceptions, mainly for exporting and high technology ventures and in banking and tourism. Since 1982, joint ventures have been allowed in special zones offering a certain degree of legal extraterritoriality. But the price of isolation in these offshore joint ventures appears greater than the costs of operating under full domestic regulations.

Measures to promote FDI have improved since 1986. For example, there is said to be less bureaucracy, better tax benefits, and more legal (especially international) protection for foreign investors. In the words of a responsible official, 'the policy of promoting joint ventures in Hungary forms an integral part of an economic policy whose main objectives are the further progress of economic reform and a fuller integration of the national economy in the world economy' (Martonyi, 1987, p.53).

The process of 'Westernization' (for want of a better term) and the spead of the transnational practices of the capitalist global system, has gone further in Hungary than anywhere else in East Europe. Since the first wave of decentralization in 1968, and particularly since the 1980s, new forms of individual and partnership enterprises have flourished in many areas of the economy. A vivid example is the new economic zone (housing an extremely busy branch of Marks and Spencer) that has been established in Sopron, on Hungary's border with Austria. Only hard (Western) currency is accepted. A visit to the zone has led one commentator to suggest that 'unbridled consumerism is what perestroika is really all about'.[6]

Even in Romania, before the Ceauşescu regime was overthrown, the heavy hand of the state was not total, particularly in the retail and professional sectors, where something like a free market existed. In his study of the SKALA Cooperative department store chain in Bucharest, Naor (in Kaynak, 1988) shows how entrepreneurial forces worked in the retail sector, for example in the development of franchising.

Problems of reform

As I have already noted, the most thorough analysis to date of a potential Third way is to be found in the work of Szelenyi and his colleagues on Hungary. Hungary is the only clear case in East Europe of the re-emergence of family entrepreneurship, but with the appropriate economic conditions and political encouragement, it could spread (as it appears to be doing in China). Szelenyi compares three theories about private farmers in socialist society. The first, the proletarianization thesis, holds that they are a necessary but a temporary phenomenon while rural collectivization is being completed. The fact that, in Hungary at least, in the 1980s the family farm was producing and selling more than ever before and that agricultural collectivization did not seem to be displacing it, makes this theory implausible. The second theory argues that a new form of peasant-worker will emerge, making the best of both agriculture and industry. To some extent this is already happening, but it seems not to be a very dominant tendency. The third theory, the one that Szelenyi prefers (indeed, more or less creates), is labelled 'interrupted embourgeoisement' (Szelenyi, 1988, ch.3 and *passim*). To put it briefly, this theory argues that the advent of the communist party to power in Hungary interrupted processes of rural embourgeoisement, and in so doing, changed its nature, thus producing socialist entrepreneurs.

These three processes, proletarianization, the formation of a new peasant-worker class and rural embourgeoisement (plus the creation of a cadre stratum), take place simultaneously, leading to different 'destinations' of different social types. Most Hungarian family farmers, Szelenyi argues, believe that they would go under in a market system, and so, quite rationally, they prefer to operate in the 'market' sector of the state socialist system. There is some evidence that this sentiment is not restricted to Hungarian farmers, or even Hungarian workers in state enterprises, as the discussion of the iron rice bowl in China illustrates. The welfare implications for those whom the new 'social market' of reformed communism leaves behind will be a central issue for the 1990s (see Kagarlitsky, 1989), as it has been in the United Kingdom and the United States under the 'free market' of the 1980s.

There are indications that this is already creating problems in the Soviet Union. Walker (1989) reports on the daily Aeroflot–Pan

Am flight 30 from New York to Moscow, known as 'the flying vacuum cleaner' because of the volume of consumer goods that homecoming Russians bring with them. This has led to rapid increases in burglary and the private security industry in the Soviet Union. The rouble is losing value against the dollars necessary to buy the much sought after imported consumer goods; extremist nationalist groups, embittered by the 'get rich quick' mentality that perestroika has encouraged, use the weapon of anti-semitism; more and more credit-card-only outlets point up the increasing gap between rich and poor; and intellectuals talk openly of the possibility of social chaos (see Bonnell, 1989). Ironically, in the short run at least, *perestroika* and *glasnost* may have made the Soviet Union less like the First World it was intended to emulate than like the Third World.[7]

The socialist Third World

As already noted, the socialist bloc of East Europe, led by the Soviet Union, established its own alternative to the global capitalist system, Comecon. Though only two Third World countries (Cuba and Vietnam) have joined,[8] Comecon has economic relations with most of the countries of the Third World, through its import and export trade and the activities of its transnational corporations, discussed above.

In some countries at some periods, for example in Egypt under Nasser, Ethiopia, Ba'athist Iraq and Syria, Cuba from the 1960s and North Vietnam, Soviet influence has been much stronger than Western influence.[9] The most thoroughly researched case of the transnational relations between the Soviet Union and a Third World country is probably Cuba. The issue is usefully posed in terms of the argument that Cuba simply exchanged US imperialist exploitation and dependency for Soviet imperialist exploitation and dependency.

Cuba

When Cuba freed itself from the Batista dictatorship in 1959 it was not at all certain that Fidel Castro and his supporters would automatically ally with the socialist camp. A combination of US and Cuban provocation, however, led gradually to this outcome. Cuba is typical of many Third World countries in that its economy is highly dependent on one product, in Cuba's case, sugar. Before 1959 the United States guaranteed a market for Cuban sugar, after 1959 it was the Soviet Union that bought most of it. This brutal economic fact makes plausible the conclusion that Cuba exchanged one master for another. This is a very complex question, involving economic, political and cultural-ideological judgements.

We can make no progress until we disaggregate the composite term *dependency*. Packenham (1986, p.66) usefully does this. Comparing Cuban dependence before and after 1959, he concludes:

monoculture of national production	no change
overall trade dependency	no change
monoculture of exports	no change
trade partner concentration (USA/Comecon)	no change
trade partner concentrations (USA/USSR)	less dependent
capital dependency	no change
debt dependency	more dependent
energy dependency	more dependent
technological dependency	no change.

There is little disagreement about the details of Cuba's relationships with the Soviet Union, though the interpretations of these details can vary widely. For example, in another analysis of Cuban dependency, LeoGrande shows that for sixteen out of twenty-eight indicators Cuban dependency seems to have declined, while Mesa-Lago points out that ten of these sixteen indicators involve trade dependency.[10] The nub of the differences is the view, plausible to some and ridiculous to others, that dependency on the Soviet Union is non-exploitative and more benevolent than dependency on the United States. Fidel Castro himself and many Latin American anti-imperialist writers have argued that the influence of the Soviet Union is benign. Whether this is true or not, the fact remains that Russia could cut off most of Cuba's oil, and a substantial part of its imports of food, raw materials and capital goods, as well as most of its weapons. The export market for at least half of Cuba's sugar is also vulnerable. However, and this is a central part of the argument, this only proves that the Soviet Union can exercise policy leverage on Cuba, not that it exploits Cuba economically. Indeed, the evidence, complicated as it is, suggests that over the years Cuba may well have earned more from its sugar deals with the Soviet Union than it would have earned on the world market.

There are other considerations, too. Cuba joined Comecon in 1972, and since then it has closely followed Soviet planning and organizational methods. The thesis that Cuban society has been 'Sovietized' in a variety of ways cannot seriously be denied. Changes in Cuba's domestic social structures, its political and cultural life and foreign policy, all testify to increasing Soviet and decreasing Western influence since the 1960s.

It is, however, difficult to deny that Cuba is still a part of the global capitalist system. The 'Sovietization of Cuba' thesis may be true, but in common with most other socialist Third World countries, Cuba's links with the capitalist world economy have grown substantially in the 1980s, and the fact that Cuba is now open to selected foreign investment suggests that the trend is set to continue. One could replace 'Cuba' with the name of many other countries and still agree with the judgement that 'Cuba can restrict and regulate, but not eliminate, relations with Western bloc countries. It is socialist in name, ideology and intent, but it must come to terms with capitalist forces in its international relations' (Eckstein, 1980, p.270). The Soviet Union's diminishing ability (and, one may surmise, will) to sustain its Third World client states economically, creates the opportunities for global capitalism to do the job in its own way.

Nicaragua

Only two socialist Third World countries, Cuba and Nicaragua, have so far joined Comecon. The rest have had to work out their transnational relationships with the Soviet Union and the rest of the world on other terms. For many, the best option appeared to be membership of the Non-aligned Movement (NAM). Nicaragua, a neighbour of Cuba, likewise the sometime victim of US military aggression, was led by the Sandinistas in the struggle to build socialism (see Rosset and Vandermeer, 1986), until their electoral defeat in 1990. Nicaragua used its membership of NAM to mediate its relationships with both great powers.

By 1979, when the Sandinistas defeated the Somoza dictatorship in Nicaragua, NAM had almost one hundred members, including many in Latin America. The sixth NAM summit meeting in Havana in 1979 provided the ideal base for Nicaragua to seek and express support for all those involved in revolutionary struggles. The siting of a NAM extraordinary meeting in Managua in 1983 was one indication of the success of its policy, eloquently summarized as 'the unity of the weak' by Daniel Ortega, when he first addressed the UN as leader of his country. Membership of NAM (rather than Comecon) afforded Nicaragua a more independent and flexible foreign policy than was possible for Cuba, and this has led to a higher level of international support for Nicaragua in the NAM and elsewhere, for example the UN. It has even been suggested that this diplomatic and solidaristic activity has helped restrain the United States from actually invading Nicaragua, though not from funding the Contra terrorists (Vanden and Queiser Morales, 1985).

Despite its genuine progress in the fields of education, health, land reform and the environment (Rosset and Vandermeer, 1986, pp.398–432), the key problem for Nicaragua (and for all other socialist countries), is the viability of socialism within a capitalist global system. The rapid encroachment of the TNCs, the emergence of transnational capitalist classes and the onward march of the culture-ideology of consumerism, has become an everyday reality for the socialist Third World.

African socialism

Although the intensity of capitalist transnational practices in these countries increased dramatically in the 1980s, the seeds of the process can be quite clearly seen in the 1950s and 1960s when the proclamations of 'African socialism' rang through that continent. The inability of the African socialist countries either to break from global capitalism or to make domestic political progress in the last two or three decades leads inexorably to the conclusion that they have never really stopped being capitalist or capitalist dominated societies. It is useful to distinguish between those states that achieved their independence through a process of negotiation with the colonial power in the 1960s (Tanzania is the classic example), and those who liberated themselves through revolutionary struggle in the following decades (for example, Zimbabwe and the ex-colonies of Portugal). These cases are often referred to as first wave, socialist-humanist and second wave, Marxist-Leninist regimes, a more useful guide to original ideology than present practices.

As Keller and Rothchild point out in their introduction to *Afro-Marxist Regimes* (1987), in both francophone (Algeria, Mali, Guinea) and anglophone (Ghana, Tanzania) Africa, populist socialist ideas were common in the struggle against colonialism. These were often non-Marxist, and sometimes, as in Kenya, not even anti-capitalist. Lack of effective administrative control (the so-called 'soft state') made it difficult to put socialist ideas into practice. As populist socialism declined, scientific socialism bloomed. In 1969, Ngouabi proclaimed the People's Republic of the Congo, the first Afro-Marxist regime to reject populist socialism, and many others (like Somalia, Madagaskar, Benin, Mozambique, Angola and Ethiopia) followed. It was not until the military interventions of the Cubans in Angola in 1975 and of the Soviets in Ethiopia in 1977, that the West began to pay serious attention to communism in Africa.

It is difficult to see how, under the conditions of the capitalist global system, 'African socialism' could be much more than a form of state capitalism where bureaucracies try to run the economy with very limited resources. It is even doubtful that the level of autonomy they have permits them to *run* the system in any very meaningful sense. As Keller argues: 'In every case, these regimes are heavily dependent on foreign capital, mostly provided by bilateral and multilateral aid agencies' (1987, p.16). The key point is: in whose interests do the bureaucrats run the economy and society? From the point of view of the workers and the peasants, state capitalism is similar in at least some of its essentials to private capitalism. The direct producers in the factories and the fields may still have to struggle against their bosses. Though they are employees of the state, these bosses may identify more with bosses elsewhere than with the masses in their own country. There are undoubtedly many state and party bureaucrats in the socialist Third World who do take the socialist project seriously (see Fitzgerald and Wuyts, 1988; Forbes and Thrift, 1987; White *et al.*, 1983). Nevertheless, one is left with a distinct impression that, leaving aside the corrosive effects of corruption and nepotism, these 'socialist entrepreneurs' are outnumbered by entrepreneurs and bureaucrats of a more orthodox kind. These are the most important elements in the emergence of transnational capitalist classes in the socialist Third World.

Each region has its own structures, institutions and personnel to promote the global capitalist project. In sub-Saharan Africa, the Republic of South Africa is the core of this system and fulfils a strategic global function for capitalism in the whole continent. The transnational corporations have for decades used South Africa as their base from which to extract minerals, food and industrial crops from the region, and from which to sell their goods (see Hauck *et al.*, 1983).[11] It is sobering to reflect that even the most militant socialist opponents of *apartheid* in Southern Africa, Mozambique, Angola and Zimbabwe, have been unable to cut themselves free from dependence on the global capitalist system as it operates through the South African economy and society.[12]

Tanzania

The twin necessities of socialism, to create a political base and to seize the commanding heights of the economy from both domestic and transnational capital, have not happened to any great extent anywhere yet in Africa. Tanzania exemplifies some of the main problems. The parastatal enterprises, publically owned but effectively run on private enterprise lines, are controlled by foreign managers and local bureaucrats whose commitment to the goals of socialism have constantly been questioned at home and abroad. Nationalization in Tanzania was carried out with 'full and fair' compensation, which left the new companies on a feeble economic footing. The belief in 'neutrality of management' and the recipes of foreign consultants (like McKinsey) left little space for socialism. Capital–labour relations have likewise been subordinated to management needs (Loxley and Saul, 1975).

Where the TNCs initiate their own enterprises, they tend to be capital intensive projects established to maximize profits rather than labour intensive projects that serve Tanzania's needs. The Mwanza textile mill, for example, built by French investors, cost three times as much as the Chinese-built Friendship textile mill, and produced the same value of goods with one-third of the work-force. Increasingly, under the influence of foreign experts, the World Bank and other purveyors of the capitalist global project, relations between capital and labour in Tanzania are subordinated to the requirements of the external capitalist environment. Writing of 'the silent class struggle' Shivji (1976) calls the new ruling class the 'bureaucratic bourgeoisie'.

The key to Tanzanian socialism lies in the struggle between two strategies. The *ujamaa* (familyhood) tradition based on an African past, much of which was destroyed during the colonial period with the intrusion of capitalist agriculture, was encapsulated in the call for land to be returned to the communal cultivators. The other strategy, promoted in the First Five Year Plan (commended by a World Bank mission in 1961 who had blamed stagnation on con-servative peasants and poor extension services), directed resources to progressive farmers and the resettling of people on more fertile lands.

The Arusha Declaration of 1967 was a turning point. The First Five Year Plan had not worked, it simply reinforced the tendencies to classic export promoting dual economies. In Arusha, President Nyerere identified capitalism as the main obstacle to Tanzania's development, and began a process of nationalization of foreign interests, particularly the banks. The new policy, with the slogan of 'mass participation and equality in distribution', broadcast throughout Africa a vision of development based on self reliance and peasant agriculture, but also industrialization (see Mittelman, 1981).

The Guidelines of 1971, partly in response to the threat posed by Idi Amin's Uganda, went even further. Expensive private houses were expropriated, causing the departure of one-fifth of the Asian population and a massive brain drain. All official salaries were reduced. But in 1977, 10 years after Arusha, the government was forced to admit that Tanzania was neither socialist nor self reliant, though it claimed to have halted nascent capitalism.

The *ujamaa* experiment, begun in the mid-1960s, was based on the communal ownership of land. Most small farmers were unwill-ing to organize in collectives and by 1970 a campaign of 'persua-sion' more or less signalled that the voluntary phase of *ujamaa* had ended. As long as the government had something to deliver to the villagers, they would cooperate, but there were never enough resources and outright compulsion was introduced after a severe drought in 1973. While villagization did bring welfare and social services to the countryside, it failed the production test decisively. It is, therefore, not surprising that Tanzania has slowly abandoned its socialist policies, thrown its lot in with the World Bank and embarked on state expenditure cuts, privatization and a greater reliance on the market.

Between 1967 and 1977, foreign borrowing rose from a quarter of development expenditure to more than half. By the 1980s, the World Bank was more or less dictating the country's export and import trade through a system of tied aid. Financial support for village projects now comes through World Bank loans and the *ujamaa* programme has become something of a showcase for foreign investment! The decision of the major international financiers to support *ujamaa* villages, once the symbol of creeping African socialism, might be seen as part of a strategy to keep Tanzania stable and to inhibit the production of manufactured goods that might cut out First World (and even Second World) imports. Meanwhile, as in most of the Third World, the foreign debt grows.

An important aspect of this process is what Bryceson (1981) terms the 'proletarianization' of women in Tanzania. Most Third World policymakers believe that removing people from their means of subsistence and forcing them to become wage labourers will encourage the transition to industrialization. A rather precise sexual division of labour had been imposed on peasant women by the colonial authorities in the 1930s, and Tanzanian women saw proletarianization as a means of escape from male domination.

Since the 1940s women have been migrating to the towns, to join their men or to seek work, or both. Women are part of the small industrial labour force, but tend to be replaced by men when factories are automated (for example, in matchmaking and coffee-curing). Bryceson notes that the Maternity Leave Act of 1975 resulted in some employers refusing to hire women (as in China recently). There are large numbers of unmarried women with children who rely on their own labour power and, to that extent, have escaped from the sexual subordination of peasant women. But many of those who cannot find jobs are forced into prostitution by the 'freedom' of the market. This is a pattern that is by no means unique to Tanzania, or the socialist Third World for that matter (see Brydon and Chant, 1989).

Mozambique

An instructive comparison can be drawn between Tanzania, the leading first wave African socialist state and Mozambique, often identified as a hard-line second wave Marxist-Leninist state. Their paths to independence could hardly have been more different. For Tanzania, independence was 'granted' by a British government, anxious to rid itself of colonial responsibilities while maintaining the economic stake of its TNCs, while for Mozambique the revolutionary movement, Frelimo, had a long and bloody struggle for freedom from a ruthless, but eventually exhausted Portugal.[13]

By the time Frelimo came to power in 1975, the Portuguese farmers who had dominated the economy had largely sabotaged agriculture when they abandoned the country. Food supplies for the cities were the top priority of Frelimo and to achieve this a policy of state farms and agricultural cooperatives, reliant on imported tractors and chemicals, was embarked upon. Mozambique proceeded rapidly to implement socialist policies. The banks were nationalized in 1978 with compensation, and although the government sought to take over the commanding heights of the economy, private property was sustained in housing and land. Private medicine, law and education persisted, as did private business. 'Dynamizing groups' of Frelimo cadres worked at the grass roots, in the countryside and in the towns, where a serious commitment to industrialization was made.

The exodus of the Portuguese did not, of course, entirely end the influence of Portugal. Policy decisions to support the modern sector, and encourage what Raikes (1984) terms an 'essentially Portuguese urban diet' are explicable only in terms of a curious but by no means unusual mixture of communist ideology and the legacy of colonialism on its erstwhile victims. It is not only in Mozambique, or even in Africa, that the peasant sector has been starved of resources due to an oversimplified conception of agricultural modernization based on foreign rather than local standards of living. The government took the pattern of consumption under colonialism for granted, and tried to maintain European standards, though attempting to establish them as the norm rather than the privilege of the elite. This meant that it was forced to support cash crops rather than food crops to pay for imports, and to favour relatively expensive rather than basic foods. The inevitable consequence was that the family commercial sector was left to stagnate and resource-wasting state farms took most of the available investment. As a result, the peasants trade on the black market and the state agencies are chronically unable to deliver food and other commodities to the masses.

The government actually signalled the end of the free welfare state and 'the persistent spirit of getting things for nothing' (to quote the Finance Minister, Baltazar) in 1984. A free market in a variety of goods and services was announced then, and private foreign investment was heralded as 'the main engine of change'. The official news agency admitted that it would not be easy to defend socialism because capitalists 'leave behind them a petty bourgeoisie and government absolutely corrupted by the crumbs from the neocolonial banquet'. Despite this, the new course was seen as the only prospect for development.[14]

The salience of the official analysis is entirely borne out by the establishment of three agricultural plantations by the British TNC Lonrho, representing an investment of $40 million. In at least one of these, the Nhamatanda estate, which grows cotton and food crops in a joint venture with the Mozambique government, the classical conditions of enclave development are reproduced. The estate has its own import and export facilities, and the workers are paid in tokens which can be exchanged for goods in the company store. Poor socialist (and capitalist) African countries are forced into such alliances.[15]

By the mid-1980s, the cumulative effects of the terrorist war waged by the South African-funded Renamo dissidents, poor policy decisions, drought and the consequent destruction of the rural and urban economies, resulted in a World Bank/IMF sponsored Economic Rehabilitation Programme (PRE) being forced on the government of Mozambique (Torp, 1989, ch.3). Between 1981 and 1986 production fell by 30 per cent and per capita consumption by 45 per cent. Contradictions abound. By the late 1980s the minimum wage was less than the cost of the average food basket, let alone other necessities of life, though the urban middle class (including a number of wayward party cadres) was growing and there were goods in the shops for those with money to buy. The new policy looks to market forces, but the basic weaknesses of economy, low productivity and imports for consumption financed through foreign aid, persist.

The PRE was a typical World Bank restructuring exercise, with devaluation, cuts in state spending, reduction in price subsidies and investment increased at the expense of consumption. As Torp (1989, p.53) puts it: 'The programme aims to transfer resources and initiatives from the public sector, to the private sector, including the peasant family sector and to encourage exports'. A massive injection of external resources, spare parts for industry and consumer goods to stimulate peasant production have resulted in some growth. But the urban poor are going hungry, school rolls are falling, health facilities are closing, and the prospects for socialism in Mozambique are dimming. All the evidence suggests that the World Bank makes the policy, while Frelimo explains it to the masses. The demand for higher levels of production is gradually being replaced by the demand for pre-independence structures, mostly initiatives in the private sector. This should not prove too difficult a task to accomplish, as most agree that the basics of the colonial capitalist economic system are still in place.[16]

The re-introduction of capitalist and colonial practices under pressure from the global system does not affect men and women in exactly the same ways. While Mozambican resistance in the war against Renamo terrorism undermined the patriarchal authority of the home, the persistence of female subservience to men contrasts with a new female sexual self-confidence. The Frelimo socialist project for reconstruction promised to make space for the feminist project of gender equality, as appeared to have been implied by the revolutionary method of *self-empowerment*, but this did not happen (Urdang, 1989). As has been argued in an informative study of the Mozambique Women's Organization (OMM): 'the political programme of modernization and the exclusion of gender struggle often amounts to a tacit support for male power, whether intended or not' (Arnfred, 1988, p.12).

Is there anything left of the socialist project in Africa? Rothchild and Foley, in their analysis of ideology and policy in Afro-Marxist regimes, argue that the experiments of Mozambique and Angola with nonsocialist economic practices, like private trading, peasant production and relations with TNCs, represents 'a shift of emphasis intended to strengthen the country to deal with a hostile environment, not a substantial retreat from basic Marxist-Leninist principles' (1987, p.311). Mozambique's 'liberal investment code' guarantees repatriation of profits and compensation against nationalization; and in addition to the plantations revived by Lonrho, General Motors are contracted to transport coal around the country.

In Angola, although the regime remains committed to Marxist-Leninist ideology:

> it has excellent business relations with a wide array of prominent multinational firms. Angola's state oil corporation, Sonangol, in partnership with Chevron, Texaco, Elf Aquitaine, Conoco, and others, is actively exploring the country's rich offshore deposits, and prominent Western banks such as Chase Manhattan play an important role in financing the country's development'. (Rothchild and Foley, 1987, p.312)

If Keller and Rothchild are correct for socialist Mozambique and Angola, even allowing for the ravages of the South African-promoted wars of destruction, then prospects for both the TNCs and socialism in Africa are perhaps not quite so bleak as might be imagined. But, it must be said, most scholars today would regard the prospects for the TNCs and the prospects for socialism to be mutually exclusive.

Conclusion

The socialist Second World, and to a much lesser extent, the socialist Third World, have in the past enjoyed a certain measure of autonomy from the global capitalist system. Comecon for some time served to insulate the countries of East Europe from having to compete on the world stage with global capitalism. The available evidence suggests that the countries of the socialist Third World, like those of the capitalist Third World, never really managed to free themselves entirely from global capitalism, and perhaps some of their leaders never intended this in any case. The Soviet Union did achieve a high level of transnational independence but as the communist project began to collapse, it has become increasingly attracted to aspects of the global capitalist project, particularly the culture-ideology of consumerism. This is now more or less true for all the countries of East Europe.

Recent evidence suggests that the feeling is entirely mutual. Representatives of the transnational capitalist class from all over the First World have been flooding into East Europe making deals, setting up joint ventures, opening consultancies and generally teaching erstwhile communists how to operate within the global capitalist system. Illustrations of this are legion: from the 'blue pimpernels' of Prague (see Gott, 1990) to the 1990 Leipzig Trade fair where 'The East is open for business' (Farr, 1990); from the Soros Foundation's International Management Centre, the first to be opened in the communist world (*The Economist*, 15 July 1989, p.50) to the transformation of a US government official in Budapest to the manager of the private Central European Development Corporation (*Newsweek*, 5 February 1990, p.45). Neither the TNCs nor the politicians nor the ideologues of 'free enterprise' are in any doubt that capitalism has triumphed over Stalinist communism because it has delivered the goods. It satisfies the demands of the consumers. Or that is what it looks like from the East.

In order to implement the culture-ideology of consumerism, socialism, just like capitalism, needs transnational corporations to produce the goods for domestic consumption and export, and transnational capitalist classes to organize the system politically. These are emerging, embryonically, in the socialist Third World, notably in China and in Central Europe. I have argued that all these developments do not necessarily point to the restoration of capitalism, indeed I find this to be an unlikely scenario, even in the face of apparently contradictory evidence such as the 1990 election results from East Europe and Nicaragua. In my concluding chapter I shall outline what I consider to be the more likely outcomes of the present transnational collision between socialism and the capitalist global system.

Notes

1. That this is not exactly what the original intention of the policy was, is clear from Gorbachev (1988). See also the critique by Petro (1989) of pro-*perestroika* Soviet scholars.
2. See also *Advertising Age* (19 February 1990) for more on the East Europe market. Rosati and Mizsei (1989) discuss the pressures on East Europe to adopt what I have been calling export-oriented industrialization and the capitalist global project.

3. See 'Socialist countries' enterprises abroad: new trends', *The CTC Reporter* [UN], 24 (Autumn 1987, pp.17–22). China has been particularly active in this field in recent years.

4. Nayyar (1977) contains informative essays on trade relations between Comecon and Tanzania, Egypt, Ghana and Nigeria, India and Pakistan, as well as the impact of Soviet oil, and China's aid and trade with the Third World. See also Skak (in Caporaso, 1987) on East/South (NICs) economic relations.

5. As King (1986) shows, the Polish government began to market imported global products aggressively as early as 1985. This paper provides solid evidence for the culture-ideology of consumerism in Poland.

6. Ian Traynor in *The Guardian* (London), 11 May 1989. For a similar situation in Zahony, on the Hungarian–Russian border, see *The Economist* (22 July 1989, p.44).

7. Kis (1989), in a thought-provoking essay on reforms in Hungary, suggests that this is what appears to be happening there.

8. Mozambique was denied full membership because the Soviet Union would not commit itself economically as it had done in Cuba and Vietnam (Jinadu, in Keller and Rothchild, 1987, pp.239–53).

9. See Laiodi (1988) for an unusually interesting collection of essays on how the Soviet Union is *perceived* in Black Africa, Iraq and Syria, Turkey, the ASEAN Countries, Vietnam, India and Latin America. This makes a welcome change from the innumerable works that discuss how the Soviet Union *treats* such countries.

10. For references to these works and further discussion on the issues, see Packenham (1986). Useful collections on 'Cubanology' from opposing perspectives are Roca (1988) and Zimbalist (1988), which provide information on all the issues discussed below.

11. This helps to explain the struggle over the sanctions weapon against *apartheid*. For a thought-provoking examination of the question of transnationals in Southern Africa see Seidman *et al.* (1986), which is useful both for South African-based TNC activity and the efforts of socialist countries in the region to resist and create their own structures.

12. Mezger (1978) clearly illuminates the roots of this dependency for the mining industry in the region.

13. See Mittelman (1981) and Moore-Lappe and Beccar-Varela (1980), for (rather different) systematic comparisons between the two countries. Both works provide useful background for understanding the developments of the 1980s.

14. Quoted in 'Revolutionary Mozambique puts its money on capitalism', *The Guardian* (9 May 1984, p.10). This is by no means a unique case. As Steinberg (1982, p.119) commented on Burma: 'Ironically, the attainment of Burma's socialist goals is increasingly dependent on foreign capitalist economies'.

15. As Dowden (1987) concludes: 'profitable enterprises are being handed over to foreign companies such as Lonrho. There is no popu-

lar capitalism in the privatisation of Africa. Increased production benefits only foreign companies or individuals who do not reinvest their profits locally'.

16. The same case can be made for many other Third World socialist countries. Stoneman (1978) makes it for the transition from Rhodesia to Zimbabwe; and Khaing (1986, p.41) says of Burma: 'Any time that the inner councils of the state decide to return to capitalism, the people will be ready with the skills they have kept alive, and the wits they have made even sharper in the pursuit of profit under socialism'.

8
Conclusion

Although the presence of a group of transnational corporations may seem relatively innocuous when compared with the total industrial and commercial life of a whole country, one or a few of these TNCs may have gross assets that are larger than the GNP of that country. While a few government officials, local business people and the foreign business community may seem not very important compared with the domestic political rulers, the transnational capitalist class may entirely dominate certain sectors of a country (for example, manufactured exports or finance). And while the global media images may seem harmless enough, the culture-ideology of consumerism advances daily.

All these forces may have profound consequences for the distribution of economic, political and cultural-ideological power, particularly in Third World countries in which the TNCs are involved. There is a profound paradox in the way in which these issues are conceptualized which exactly parallels the ideological chasm that divides those who largely support the TNCs and those unswervingly opposed to them. As I have documented in previous chapters, under the influence of dependency theory a great weight of research has accumulated to document the harmful effects of TNC involvement in the Third World, countered by an equally great weight of research documenting both the benefits that TNCs bring to the Third World and the hazards that they face in doing business there. As this involvement has grown and the complexity of TNC–Third World transnational relationships has come to be increasingly realized, new positions have emerged that focus on the possibility of reversing dependency and improving the bargaining strategies of those in the Third World. Governments and social strata that abandon outright hostility or subservience to the TNCs take serious risks in putting over such policies to their internal and external constituencies, some of whom may be violently opposed to 'Western imperialism' or 'the communist threat'.

There was a notable change in the 1980s compared with the 1960s and 1970s, when most Third World countries appeared, to a greater or lesser extent, hostile to TNCs. With the spectacular reversal of Chinese policy at the end of the 1970s, the symbolic floodgates were thrown open. Today, practically all Third World and most Second World countries in a position to absorb foreign direct investment are producing incentive packages to lure the TNCs into opening up factories, relaxing restrictions to attract foreign capital and, perhaps a little more cautiously, welcoming the transnational culture-ideology industries. As a result, a changing set of conditions has emerged for the embryonic transnational capitalist classes. While there are still groups in the Third and the Second Worlds (though a decreasing number) who continue to accuse those who collaborate with foreign capitalists of betraying national interests, most are eager to enlist the support of TNCs for national development.

In the context of increasing impoverishment and a gradual deterioration of public services in many Third World countries (see Cook and Fitzpatrick, 1988, *passim*) it is not difficult to believe that those directly and indirectly connected with the TNCs are indeed better-off than those entirely untouched by the TNCs, even though the effects (for example, for those in rural areas impacted by global agribusiness) may be mixed blessings. If this is the case, then Third World industry and trade, and the bureaucracies responsible for facilitating them, as well as labour movements dependent on TNC employment, and those in the informal sectors also dependent on the presence of foreign investors, may well be recruited to the support of the TNCs in the Third World. The transnational capitalist classes see their best interests and the best interests of their countries served by more foreign investment, not less. Under these circumstances, TNCs need feel no necessity for hostile intervention in host-country economies, politics or culture-ideology. The tide, of course, could change again.

TNCs and development

Much writing on development gives the impression that Third World governments and institutions stand idly by while the bearers of transnational practices wreak havoc on their societies. Nothing could be further from the truth. Most Third World governments and a multitude of local and transnational organizations wage ceaseless campaigns to highlight abuses. Nevertheless, it is necessary to acknowledge that at the present historical juncture the whole of the Third and most of the Second World is in something of a double bind with respect to the economic, political and cultural-ideological transnational practices of the global capitalist system. No one (apart from capitalism's most uncritical proponents) denies that there are negative effects of these practices, but the balance of opinion (apart from dogmatic anti-imperialists) has clearly swung behind those for whom the positive benefits are overwhelming.

Much effort has gone into the question of how to enhance the positive and minimize the negative effects of, for example, foreign direct investment in developing countries. The 1980s saw continual attempts by transnational and quasi-governmental organizations to legislate on the relations between TNCs and the developing countries in which they are to be found. While more or less all countries have made it easier for TNCs to enter, they have been pressing for more stringent rules to govern the conduct of TNCs. There is no necessary contradiction here, in fact it makes good sense to try to control the operations of an institution that you wish to encourage.

Though there is no logical contradiction, there might be a sociological one, to the extent that the larger the presence of the TNCs in a country, the more likely it is that they will make the transition from quantitative to qualitative domination in the industries in which they are active. These tend to include the industries at the leading edge of technology and those that provide valuable manufactured exports for developing countries. Where these conditions apply, the balance of power between the TNCs and Third World countries will tend to favour the TNCs, particularly when conflicts arise. However, the changing nature of the global and national systems makes it less likely that conflicts will arise in many developing countries because of the conjuncture of export led industrialization strategies and the levels of support (grudging or enthusiastic) of Third World elites and other social strata for TNCs.

Thus, for those who wish to 'modernize', there is an element of self-fulfilling prophecy about the economic, political and cultural-ideological success of the TNCs and, by implication, the global capitalist project, in the Third World. As long as the TNCs maintain their dominant position in the transnational marketing and communications industries, hostile or alternative forces to the TNC world view can rarely achieve a national, let alone a global, audience. The TNCs monopolize the symbols of 'modernity' for themselves and for their supporters. 'Modernity' becomes what global capitalism has to offer.

The somewhat one-dimensional view of the Third World presented by the TNCs can, of course, lead to extreme myopia on the part of the First World, as in the case of Iran in the period leading to the overthrow of the Shah (see Bassiry and Dekmejian, 1985), but in general the myopia does not lead to such serious consequences. This is testimony to the winning combination of successful marketing of the Western (specifically US consumerist) way of life, the actual benefits that the TNCs have brought to developing countries, and how these benefits have been highlighted and the costs increasingly pushed into the shadows.

The economic, political and cultural-ideological impact of the TNCs in the Third World can only be measured over time and social space. There can be no doubt that for most people in the Third World the major short-term benefit that the TNCs bring is jobs. In addition, TNCs bring foreign currency, and even though little is retained, without it social and political stability would be even more fragile than it already is. In the longer term, however, it is unlikely that many people outside their immediate ambit see the TNCs as the key to mature development. The unresolved question remains whether their presence actually improves developmental prospects over the long term. This opens up the issue of social space.

The TNCs have been instrumental in creating quite new social strata in the Third World, some frankly subservient and parasitical in the old sense of 'comprador', but others more creative and even patriotic in a rather new sense. These are the transnational capitalist classes. Such groups now wield economic and political power in an unprecedented manner in the Third World. The struggle for cultural-ideological power, to capture the symbols of national identity and progress and to identify them with what global capitalism has to offer and can deliver, is on the agenda all over the world.

The great issue is whether there are any viable alternatives to the TNCs and their local affiliates in the economic sphere, to transnational capitalist classes in the political sphere and to the culture-ideology of consumerism in the sphere of values. As Chapters 6 and 7 documented, the communist ideal has faded dramatically in the last decade. Is there another way, a Third Path? The age of *perestroika* and *glasnost* has stimulated many attempts to bring capitalism and socialism into some transcendental harmony (see, for example, Halal, 1989). However, such attempts retain coherence only through the device of ignoring the conflicts of interests that persist nationally and transnationally between labour and capital, even after centuries of stunning capitalist material progress. I am fully aware that most of the conflicts in today's world appear to be based on race, religion and nationalism, rather than class. It would take quite another book to argue the view that these are secondary rather than primary causes. Nevertheless, it is true to say that there is no adequate theory of how class relates to race, religion and nationalism in the economic, political and cultural-ideological spheres, nationally or transnationally.

My own version of the Third Way assumes that conflicts of race, religion and nationalism, real as they are, actually stand for something else even where they obviously take on lives of their own. What they stand for is the fear of the opposing groups that their conditions of existence are at risk. These are material conditions, but they reverberate in the economic, political and cultural-ideological spheres. It appears to be the case that only capitalism can develop the productive forces to a level that would begin to offer material security to enough of the global population to make the difference. However, it does this under constant conditions of class and other types of struggle, sometimes violent, but mostly peaceful, if robust. This is the opening that social democracy, as practiced by Social Democratic and Labour parties have exploited. Because I cannot accept the optimistic hope that capitalism can become much more humane globally than it already is, or that communism can become more productive in any society; in my view the next step in this historic quest for human progress has to be in the transformation of social democracy into democratic socialism.

Democratic feminist socialism: a Third Way?

In the first chapter I suggested that there is an alternative, democratic feminist socialism, but that as a global project it has hardly begun to make an impact in either material, political or ideological terms, in comparison with the bounding successes of the global capitalist project. Indeed, the whole book has been organized around the premise that, despite serious challenges and widespread cynicism, no other secular world view has come anywhere near the ideological force or the practical achievements of the global capitalist system.

Democracy

All three terms of this alternative are highly controversial and hotly contested under capitalism. Democracy, of which capitalism claims a monopoly, has at least two senses, namely *parliamentary democracy* (the capitalist sense) and *participatory democracy* (the socialist sense). The differences between these two types of democratic practices are profound. Parliamentary democracy is based on a system of professional political parties whose activists organize candidates to compete for the votes of the electorate at (generally) fixed intervals. Once the election has decided a winner, or a coalition of losers, the electorate is expected to withdraw from active politics and let their representatives get on with the job, until the next election. While extra-parliamentary activity is usually legal, it is rarely encouraged and only when it becomes violent is it given much attention in the mass media. Democracy here means the freedom of the individual to choose who is to govern and, under certain circumstances, to become a candidate for election.

Participatory democracy is based on the concept that people do not cease to be politically active or aware between elections. On the contrary, people as individuals and as members of interest groups, through those they delegate to act for them, are entitled to have an ongoing voice in what is done in their names. Thus, while participatory democracy has need of parliaments (or similar bodies), it is people rather than parliaments that are supreme. Therefore, sub-parliamentary elected bodies are necessary to act as channels of communication (in both directions) and decision-making between the people and their government. Characteristics of this type of democracy are frequent reporting back of delegates, representations of popular opinion to policy makers, open government and referenda on important questions.

This is, of course, a very cumbersome system and its critics argue that under such constraints nothing will ever be accomplished. As it has never been tried on a large scale, it is not possible to know with any degree of certainty whether this system would actually be any more efficient than the gargantuan bureaucracies that govern most contemporary states. A somewhat less efficient system might be a bearable price to pay for an increase in the volume of democratic practices. This, surely, is an open question, and one that parliamentary systems are often forced to grapple with. In any case, this is the sort of democracy I mean, and perhaps what some in East Europe mean, when they call for a new type of democracy. Only under such a system can ethnic and national-cultural conflicts be dealt with fairly.

Feminism

The feminist project is just as problematic. For a variety of reasons, which competing theories have tried to explain biologically, historically, sociologically and psychologically, there are no societies in which women have achieved equality of opportunity with men in the economic, political and cultural-ideological spheres. This structured social inequality is often labelled *patriarchy*. Individual women, of course, have succeeded in their chosen fields, but in general all over the world women earn less than men for comparable work, have fewer positions of political power and are less influential in culture and ideology (Iglitzin and Ross, 1976) . Although capitalism clearly did not create patriarchy, capitalism appears both to reinforce and channel it for women of all classes, albeit in different ways.

Many progressive writers simply incorporate 'the liberation of women' into the democratic and/or socialist project, arguing that patriarchal democracy (or patriarchal socialism) is no democracy (or socialism) at all. The histories of women's movements, nationally and internationally (see Jayawardena, 1986), suggest that this is not good enough. I have already commented critically on the widespread assumption that 'modernization' and the penetration of the capitalist global system would inevitably bring equality of opportunity for women. Evidence from the First World and the richer parts of the Third World shows that this is not the case.

There have been many attempts to theorize this problem, for different countries and for different institutional settings. Judith Van Allen (1976), for example, attacks the 'myth' of the positive Western influence on the emancipation of African women. The assumption that Western women's roles are *ipso facto* 'modern' has served to make African women more dependent on male-dominated society. She argues that: 'This pattern of dependence may not be "functional" for the development of female autonomy; it is for the economic system' (1976, p.30). The traditional bisexual spheres of male and female authority that characterized so much of pre-colonial Africa have been eroded by 'modernization'. She makes the important point that colonialism did have some positive consequences for women, particularly women traders, and helped protect them from male violence, but that the net effect of 'modernization' has been to increase female dependence on men, particularly in the economic sphere. Barbara Callaway (1976) documents a similar process at work for Akan-Ashanti women in Ghana, even during the supposedly quasi-socialist Nkrumah period.

Marxists, under the influence of the Engels' thesis (that exploitation by sex is a consequence of the more general division of labour, particularly under capitalism, and will disappear when capitalism is transcended) would obviously not be surprised by the inability of capitalism to eradicate the exploitation of women. But has socialism liberated women, as Engels predicted? Though the evidence from East Europe, China, Cuba, etc. suggests that women may well have improved their positions compared with the old societies, by no stretch of the imagination does it permit us to draw the conclusion that socialism has *liberated* women. Indeed, the consensus of opinion is that where women are drawn into the labour force, as they are massively in socialist societies, they end up with a double burden of waged work and domestic labour. Despite some national variations, this is the case for Russia (see

Holland, 1985), China (Croll, 1984), Cuba (Murray, 1979) and Mozambique (Urdang, 1989).

This raises the question of what would constitute progress for Second and Third World women. While the conventional view is still that 'modernization' and 'Westernization' will eventually improve their lot, there are other views gaining ground as more feminist scholars become interested in the study of development. Several of the writers in Monique Gadant's collection on *Women of the Mediterranean* (Gadant, 1986), for example, argue that Third World women want change, but not necessarily to become like women of the First World.

This is an issue whose class dimension is in constant tension with its gender dimension. Much research suggests that there are groups of women in many (most? all?) poorer societies who aspire to emulate First World women. Riddell (1976) describes the female political elite in Mexico, characterized by a European–North American style, making no pretence of its admiration of the US way of life; and Van Allen (1976) provides a good sketch of how upper-class women in West Africa set about 'acquiring wifely skills of Western "ladies"' (pp.43–4). Zamiti-Horchani (1986) on Tunisia and Morokvasic (1986) on Yugoslavia demonstrate the complex age, class and gender dimensions at work in the creation of positive and negative images of 'the modern woman'.

Capitalism gives a definite, though sociologically ambivalent, place to most women, men and ethnic minorities, in terms of their class positions. It may well be the case that the extremely low level of support that feminist socialism has won from working-class women (let alone men) is due to their perception that they might have more to lose than to gain from it. This is why the participatory democracy of socialism is so important, but only if the feminist socialist project ensures women equal opportunity with men to participate in it. This will necessitate a fundamental restructuring of the sexual division of labour in general as well as the sexual division of domestic labour.

Socialism

The socialist part of the project is the most difficult to specify with any degree of plausibility, particularly with the so-called socialist world in such turmoil. The socialism that seems most likely to emerge out of the global capitalist system is not going to come about as a result of a revolutionary seizure of state power (this method has failed miserably wherever it has been tried), but as a result of a successful period of social democracy in which the hegemony of global capitalism is increasingly and effectively challenged by a combination of domestic and transnational democratic innovations. Although there can be no specific formula for the transition from social democracy to democratic socialism appropriate for all countries, some general principles might be suggested.

Experiments in 'workers' democracy' and cooperatives, for example, are already well established all over the world, particularly in East Europe, as Jones (1989) illustrates. As long as these do not become tyrannies of producers, they point towards some democratic alternatives.

The role of the consumer is generally neglected in socialist thought, though a new school calling itself 'rational choice Marxism' might open up some possibilities in this direction. Marx's call to destroy the dehumanizing division of labour that turns people against one another, finds echoes in the call to destroy the division between producers, marketers and consumers. The origin of the antagonism between producers, marketers and consumers, as I tried to show in my analysis of the culture-ideology of consumerism, is that the motive for production under capitalism is not to satisfy human needs but to accumulate capital, while the motive to consume beyond our basic needs is often (not always) to satisfy induced wants. This ends up by embroiling us in a trap of unsatisfiable false needs. This is not a healthy situation for individuals or for societies, but the global capitalist system depends upon it for its survival.

As long as the mass media are directly, or indirectly through commercial leverage, under the control of the transnational capitalist classes, it is difficult to see how the socialist project can get a fair and balanced hearing in the newspapers and on television and radio. Nevertheless, and not for the first time, global capitalism is caught in a contradiction of its own making, namely its commitment to freedom of choice. This ensures that alternative points of view do get heard and seen, even if not on prime time or on the front pages. In some countries, the new communications technologies could be creatively transformed into vehicles of democratic decision making.

What is more difficult to imagine is the idea of socialist transnational practices. This raises the question of whether or not the transnational corporation is inherently a capitalist phenomenon. As I have argued in previous chapters, much of transnational trade, commerce and production is highly exploitative, particularly where First World TNCs are dealing with Third World producers. It is not clear how genuinely socialist transnational practices could prevail with the current system of nation-states. Theoretically, transnational socialism would make the nastier side of nationalist ideologies unnecessary but, practically, the way to achieve this is far from clear at this point in time.

Democratic feminist socialism is one alternative. It is an organic project and no one part can be detached from the whole. But it exists only in the thoughts of those who think it and, perhaps, in isolated places for more or less isolated groups of people. At present, it appears to pose no serious threat to global capitalism. However, the global capitalist system, though dominant, is not entirely coterminous with the world as it is today. Those outside the system, though not untouched by it (in the socialist and non-capitalist Second and Third Worlds and some groups in the First World), are obviously attracted by its ability to deliver the goods and what the culture-ideology of consumerism promises.

Nevertheless, even if it was once believed, few now imagine that the streets of New York or West Berlin (or anywhere else) are paved with gold. The evidence of private affluence and public squalor, and the Third World in the First World (pockets of poverty and dreadful deprivation jostling for survival in the richest areas of the richest countries) are visible daily on the same screens and pages that advertise the consumer goods that the poor are crying out for. Perhaps not as visibly as the symbols of consumerism, nor as ubiquitous, but the same 'freedom of choice' that propagates the culture-ideology of consumerism also propagates its negations: homelessness, unemployment, child abuse, drug addiction, sexual exploitation, violence, unhappiness, hopelessness. It is not unreasonable for the poor, as well as the rich, to want the best of all worlds. This being so, it is reasonable to assume that people in the Second and Third Worlds might think twice before choosing the global capitalist project.

A more likely preference, but perhaps not in the short run, is a Third Way, combining some of the efficiencies of the market, forms of private enterprise in the peripheral areas of the economy and the commitment to the rule of law that have developed under capitalism, with some of the welfare structures, restrictions on the abuse of private economic power and the commitment to grassroots democracy that have developed in some socialist societies, even where the national polity is quite undemocratic. There is a growing band of people (in socialist as well as non-socialist societies) who believe that some form of the market can be created which will be efficient without being exploitative.

This version of the Third Way clearly has more in common with socialism, specifically democratic feminist socialism, than with free enterprise capitalism. It cannot be conclusively demonstrated that the global capitalist system would necessarily disappear entirely in a world where all transnational practices were based on such principles. Global capitalism has always been remarkably flexible and responsive to the crises which threaten its survival. There is no guarantee that it would fail to find a way of coexisting with global socialism.

All the experience of the last few decades strongly suggests that where socialism permits the coexistence of global capitalism, as opposed to the inclusion of selected capitalist practices that are reconstituted to fit in with the socialist project, it is socialism, not capitalism, that will be undermined. The reason for this is that in the absence of a capitalist development of the productive forces, socialism cannot meet the demands of the masses in the Second or Third Worlds for the standard of living that is demonstrably available for most people in the First World.

The triumph of global capitalism is the triumph of the transnational capitalist classes in selling the culture-ideology of consumerism and delivering the goods through the transnational corporations and other economic institutions. It is ironic that this can be observed as clearly in the socialist as in the capitalist world as the twentieth century comes to an end. In these respects China, the African socialist states and some of the countries of East Europe have surprised us more than once, and they will certainly surprise us again.

I have tried to show how developmental strategies driven from the outside by the demands of the global capitalist system have created transnational capitalist classes. But these classes are not simply effects of the system, for they themselves also embody their own histories, cultures and practices, and they can turn the developmental strategies of global capitalism to their own purposes and even, on occasion, challenge those who wield central power in the system. In doing this they create their own contradictions, throw up opposing classes, provoke class struggles, set in train economic, political and cultural-ideological changes. History, far from being at an end, has hardly begun!

References

(Unless otherwise stated, place of publication is London.)

Abbott, J. (1987) *Agricultural Marketing Enterprises for the Developing World*, Cambridge: Cambridge University Press.

Abel, C. and Lewis, C. (eds.) (1985) *Latin America, Economic Imperialism and the State*, Athlone Press.

Adikibi, O. (1983) 'The transfer of technology to Nigeria: the case of tire production', in Kirkpatrick, C. and Nixson, F. (eds.) *The Industrialization of Less Developed Countries*, Manchester: Manchester University Press.

Ake, C. (ed.) (1985) *Political Economy of Nigeria*, Longman.

Akinsanya, A. (1984) *Multinationals in a Changing Environment: A study of business–government relations in the Third World*, New York: Praeger.

Alger, C. (1988) 'Perceiving, analysing and coping with the local–global nexus', *International Social Science Journal*, **117**, August, pp. 321–40.

Anderson, M. (1984) *Madison Avenue in Asia*, Associated University Presses.

Andrae, G. and Beckman, B. (1985) *The Wheat Trap*, Zed.

Anker, R. and Hein, C. (eds.) (1986) *Sex Inequalities in Urban Employment in the Third World*, Macmillan.

Armstrong, W. and McGee, T. (1985) *Theatres of Accumulation: studies in Asian and Latin American urbanization*, Methuen.

Arnfred, S. (1988) 'Women in Mozambique: gender struggle and gender politics', *Review of African Political Economy*, **41**, September, pp.5–16.

Atwood, R. and McAnany, E. (eds.) (1986) *Communication and Latin American Society: Trends in critical research, 1960–1985*, Madison: University of Wisconsin Press.

Bagdikian, B. (1989) 'The lords of the global village', *The Nation*, **12**, June, pp.805–20.

240

Baird, P. and McCaughan, E. (1975) *Hit and Run: U.S. runaway shops on the Mexican border*, NACLA Report, **9**, July–August.

Baker, W. and Rappaport, A. (1989) 'The global teenager', *Whole Earth Review*, Winter, pp.2–39.

Barnathan, J. (1989) 'News in the Soviet Union', *Television/Radio Age*, 4 September, pp.42–4.

Barnet, R. and Müller, R. (1974) *Global Reach: the power of the multinational corporation*, New York: Simon & Schuster.

Bassett, T. (1988) 'Development theory and reality: the World Bank in northern Ivory Coast', *Review of African Political Economy*, **41**, September, pp.45–59.

Bassiry, G. and Dekmejian, R. (1985) 'MNCs and the Iranian revolution: an empirical study', *Management International Review*, **25**, 2, pp.67–75.

Beamish, P. (1985) 'The characteristics of joint ventures in developed and developing countries', *Columbia Journal of World Business*, Fall, pp.13–19.

Becker, D. (1987) 'Development, democracy and dependency in Latin America: a postimperialist view', in Becker, D. *et al.* (1987), ch.3.

Becker, D., Frieden, J., Schatz, S. and Sklar, R. (1987) *Postimperialism: International capitalism and development in the late twentieth century*, Boulder, CO: Lynne Rienner.

Becker, D. and Sklar, R. (1987) 'Why postimperialism?', in Becker, D. *et al.* (1987), ch.1.

Becker, J. (1988) 'China's experiment with capitalism comes up against free market vices', *The Guardian*, 5 September.

Becker, J., Hedebro, G. and Paldan, L. (eds.) (1986) *Communication and Domination*, Norwood, NJ: Ablex.

Belk, R. (1988a) 'Third World consumer culture', *Research in Marketing, Supplement 4*, pp.103–27.

Belk, R. (1988b) 'Possessions and the extended self', *Journal of Consumer Research*, **15**, September, pp.139–68.

Bennett, D. and Sharp, K. (1985) *Transnational Corporations versus the State: The political economy of the Mexican automobile industry*, Princeton, NJ: Princeton University Press.

Berardi, G. (ed.) (1985) *World Food, Population and Development*, Totowa, NJ.: Rowman and Allanheld.

Bergesen, A. (ed.) (1980) *Studies of the Modern World-System*, New York: Academic Press.

Bergesen, A. (1982) 'The emerging science of the world-system', *International Social Science Journal*, **34**, 1, pp.23–36.

Bergesen, H.O. (1980) 'A new food regime: necessary but impossible', *International Organization*, **34**, Spring, pp.285–302.

Bergson, C., Horst, T. and Moran, T. (1978) *American Multinationals and American Interests*, Washington: Brookings.

Bettelheim, C. (1988) 'Economic reform in China', in Fitzgerald and Wuyts (1988), pp.15–49.

Bhatt, B. and Jain, S. (1984) 'A framework for assessing the Third World response to multinational companies', *Advances in International Comparative Management*, **1**, pp.155–76.

Biersteker, T. (1980) 'The illusion of state power: transnational corporations and the neutralization of host-country legislation', *Journal of Peace Research*, **17**, 3, pp.207–21.

Biersteker, T. (1987a) *Multinationals, the State, and Control of the Nigerian Economy*, Princeton, NJ: Princeton University Press.

Biersteker, T. (1987b) 'Indigenization and the Nigerian bourgeoisie: dependent development in an African context', in Lubeck (1987), ch 8.

Birman, I. (1989) *Personal Consumption in the USSR and the USA*, Macmillan.

Blake, D. and Walters, R. (1987) *The Politics of Global Economic Relations*, 3rd edn, Englewood Cliffs, NJ: Prentice Hall.

Boddewyn, J. (1988) *Advertising Self-regulation*, New York: Quorum.

Bonnell, V. (1989) 'Moscow: a view from below', *Dissent*, Summer, pp.311–17.

Boorstin, D. (1968) 'The consumption community', in McClellan, G. (ed.) (1968) *The Consuming Public*, New York: Wilson.

Booth, D. (1985) 'Marxism and development sociology: interpreting the impasse', *World Development*, **13**, pp.761–87.

Bornschier, V. and Chase-Dunn, C. (1985) *Transnational Corporations and Underdevelopment*, New York: Praeger.

Boserup, E. (1970) *Woman's Role in Economic Development*, New York: St Martin's Press.

Boyd, R., Cohen, R. and Gutkind, P. (eds.) (1987) *International Labour and the Third World: The Making of a New Working Class*, Aldershot: Avebury.

Brenner, R. (1977) 'The origins of capitalist development: a critique of neo-Smithian Marxism', *New Left Review*, **104**, pp.25–92.

Brewer, A. (1980) *Marxist Theories of Imperialism*, Routledge and Kegan Paul.

Brown, D. (1986) *Partnership with China*, Boulder, CO: Westview.

Bryceson, D. (1981) 'The prolerarianization of women in Tanzania', *Review of African Political Economy*, **17**, January–April, pp.4-27.

Brydon, L. and Chant, S. (1989) *Women in the Third World*, Edward Elgar.

Burbach, R. and Flynn, P. (1980) *Agribusiness in the Americas*, New York: Monthly Review Press.

Burki, S. and Ul Haq, M. (1981) 'Meeting basic needs: an overview', *World Development*, **9**, pp.167–82.

Burnell, P. (1986) *Economic Nationalism in the Third World*, Brighton: Wheatsheaf.

Burton, J. (1972) *World Society*, Cambridge: Cambridge University Press.

Callaway, B. (1976) 'Women in Ghana', in Iglitzin and Ross (1976), ch.11.

Campbell, B. (1987) 'The state and capitalist development in the Ivory Coast', in Lubeck (1987), ch.9.

Caplan, R. (1989) 'Tracking transnationals', *Multinational Monitor*, July–August, pp.12–14,

Caporaso, J. (ed.) (1987), *Changing International Division of Labor*, Boulder, CO: Lynne Rienner.

Cardoso, F. and Faletto, E. (1979) *Dependency and Development in Latin America*, Berkeley: University of California Press.

Caulkin, S. (1989) 'Crippled by computers', *Management Today*, July, pp.84–8.

Chakravarty, S. (1989) 'How Pepsi broke into India', *Forbes*, 7 November, pp.43–4.

Chan, S. (1987) *Issues in International Relations: A view from Africa*, Macmillan.

Chase-Dunn, C. (ed.) (1982) *Socialist States in the World System*, Beverly Hills, CA: Sage.

Chase-Dunn, C. (1989) *Global Formation*, Oxford: Blackwell.

Cherry, C. (1978) *World Communication: Threat or promise*, revised edn, Chichester: John Wiley.

Chetley, A. (1986) *The Politics of Baby Food*, Pinter.

Chossudovsky, M. (1986) *Towards Capitalist Restoration? Chinese socialism after Mao*, Macmillan.

Chu, G. and Alfian (1980) 'Programming for development in Indonesia', *Journal of Communication*, Autumn, pp.50–74.

Clairmonte, F. and Cavanagh, J. (1988) *Merchants of Drink: Transnational control of world beverages*, Penang: Third World Network.

Cohen, R. (1987) *The New Helots: Migrants in the international division of labour*, Aldershot: Avebury.

Cole, J. (1988) 'The global distribution of natural resources', in Norwine and Gonzalez (1988), ch.5.

Consumers Association of Penang (1981) *The Other Baby Killer*, Penang: Consumers Association.

Cook, P. and Fitzpatrick, C. (eds.) (1988) *Privatisation in Less Developed Countries*, Harvester Wheatsheaf.

Copetas, A. (1989) 'Perestroika's yankee partner', *New York Times Magazine*, Part 2, 11 June, pp.20–2, 30, 32.

Corbridge, S. (1986) *Capitalist World Development: A critique of radical development geography*, Macmillan.

Crabtree, J. (1987) *The Great Tin Crash: Bolivia and the world tin market*, Latin America Bureau.

Croll, L. (1984) *Chinese Women since Mao*, Zed.

Djilas, M. (1957) *The New Class*, Thames and Hudson.

Doran, C., Modelski, F. and Clark, C. (eds.) (1983) *North/South Relations, Studies of dependency reversal*, New York: Praeger.

Dorfman, A. (1983) *The Empire's Old Clothes: What the Lone Ranger, Babar and other innocent heroes do to our minds ...*, Pluto Press.

Dorfman, A. and Mattelart, A. (1975) *How to Read Donald Duck: Imperialist ideology in the Disney comic*, International General.

Dror, D. (1984) 'Aspects of labour law and relations in selected export processing zones', *International Labour Review*, **123**, November–December, pp.705–22.

Dowden, R. (1987) 'Disturbing echoes of the pre-colonial era in Africa', *The Independent*, 14 October.

Dunning, J. (1981) *International Production and the Multinational Enterprise*, Allen & Unwin.

Eckstein, S. (1980) 'Capitalist constraints on Cuban socialist development', *Comparative Politics*, April, pp.253–74.

Editors of *Fortune* (1973) *Consumerism: Things Ralph Nader never told you*, New York: Harper and Row.

Edgren, G. (1982) 'Export Processing Zones , Spearheads of industrialisation or sweatshops in the sun', Geneva, ILO, mimeo.

Edwards, C. (1985) *The Fragmented World*, Methuen.

Eisenstadt, S. (ed.) (1970) *Readings in Social Evolution and Development*, Oxford: Pergamon.

Elliott, D. (1984) 'Why Beijing is hungry for US food companies', *Business Week*, 24 December, p.43.

Elson, D. and Pearson, R. (eds.) (1989), *Women's Employment and Multinationals in Europe*, Macmillan.

Enderwick, P. (1985), *Multinational Business and Labour*, Croom Helm.

ESCAP/UNCTC (1986) 'The socio-economic impact of transnational corporations in the fast food industry: some findings from a case study of McDonald's Corporation in the Philippines', *Asia-Pacific TNC Review*, January, pp.40–7.

Esteinou Madrid, J. (1986) 'Means of communication and construction of hegemony', in Atwood and McAnany (1986), ch.6.

Estes, R. (1988) 'Toward a "quality-of-life" index: empirical approaches to assessing human welfare internationally', in Norwine and Gonzalez (1988), ch.3.

Evans, P. (1979) *Dependent Development: The alliance of multinational, state and local capital in Brazil*, Princeton, NJ: Princeton University Press.

Evans P. and Bastos Tigre, P. (1989) 'Paths to participation in high-tech industry: a comparative analysis of computers in Brazil and Korea', University of California San Diego, Center for US–Mexican Studies, mimeo.

Evans, P., Rueschmeyer, D. and Skocpol, T. (eds.) (1985), *Bringing the State Back In*, Cambridge: Cambridge University Press.

Ewen, S. (1976) *Captains of Consciousness*, New York: McGraw-Hill.

Ewen, S. (1988) *All Consuming Images: The politics of style in contemporary culture*, New York: Basic Books.

Farr, M. (1990) 'East is open for business', *The Guardian*, 12 March.

Fath, J. (1985) 'Women and the growth of agro-industries in developing countries', Vienna, UNIDO, mimeo.

Featherstone, M. (1987) 'Consumer culture, symbolic power and universalism', in Stauth and Zubaida (1987), pp.17–45.

Feder, E. (1978) *Strawberry Imperialism*, America Latina.

Fejes, F. (1980) 'The growth of multinational advertising agencies in Latin America', *Journal of Communication*, **30**, Autumn, 36–49.

Field, J. (1973) 'Transnationalism and the New Tribe', in Keohane and Nye (1973), pp.3-22.

Fieldhouse, D. (1986) 'The multinational corporation: critique of a concept', in Teichova *et al.* (1986), ch.1.

Fitzgerald, E. and Wuyts, M. (eds.) (1988) *Markets within Planning: Socialist economic management in the Third World*, Cass.

Flora, C. and Flora, J. (1978) 'The fotonovela as a tool for class and cultural domination', *Latin American Perspectives*, V, 1, Winter, pp.134-49.

Forbes, D. and Thrift, N. (eds.) (1987) *The Socialist Third World: Urban development and territorial planning*, Oxford: Blackwell.

Frank, A.G. (1967) *Capitalism and Underdevelopment in Latin America*, Monthly Review Press.

Frank, A.G. (1977) 'Long live transideological enterprise! The socialist economies in the capitalist international division of labour', *Review*, **1**, Summer, pp.91–140.

Frank, A.G. (1984) *Critique and Anti-Critique*, Macmillan.

Fröbel, F., Heinrichs, J. and Kreye, O. (1980) *The New International Division of Labour: Structural unemployment in industrialized countries and industrialization in developing countries*, Cambridge: Cambridge University Press.

Fuentes, A. and Ehrenreich, B. (1984) *Women in the Global Factory*, Boston: South End Press.

Gabb, A. (1989) 'Heinz meanz brandz', *Management Today*, July, pp.64–70.

Gadant, M. (ed.) (1986) *Women of the Mediterranean*, Zed.

Gail, B. (1978) 'The West's jugular vein: Arab oil', *Armed Forces Journal International*, August, pp.18–32.

Ganley, G. and Ganley, O. (1987) *Global Political Fallout: The first decade of the VCR, 1976–1985*, Norwood, NJ: Ablex.

Garnsey, E. and Paukert, L. (1987) *Industrial Change and Women's Employment: Trends in the new international division of labour*, Geneva: International Institute for Labour Studies.

Gatehouse, M. (1989) 'Soft drink, hard labour', in Press and Thomson (1989), ch.3.

George, S. (1985) *Ill Fares the Land: Essays on food, hunger, and power*, Writers and Readers.

Gereffi, G. (1983) *The Pharmaceutical Industry and Dependency in the Third World*, Princeton, NJ: Princeton University Press.

Gereffi, G. and Wyman, D. (1987) 'Determinants of development strategies in Latin America and East Asia', *Pacific Focus*, **II**, Spring, pp.5–33.

Gershenberg, I. (1987) 'The training and spread of managerial know-how: a comparative analysis of multinational and other firms in Kenya', *World Development*, 15, July, pp.931–9.

Geyikdagi, Y. (1984) 'Attitudes towards multinationals: the Middle East in the world context', *Management Decision*, **22**, 3, pp.14–21.

Giffard, C. (1984) 'Inter Press Service: News from the Third World', *Journal of Communication,* Autumn, pp.41–59.

Gillespie, K. (1984) *The Tripartite Relationship*, New York: Praeger.

Girvan, N. (1976) *Corporate Imperialism: Conflict and Expropriation*, New York: Monthly Review Press.

Gladwin, T. and Walter, I. (1980) *Multinationals under Fire*, New York: John Wiley.

Goldman, R. (ed.) (1983) *Transnational Parties: Organizing the world's precincts*, Lanham, MD: University Press of America.

Gonzalez, A. (1988) 'Indexes of socioeconomic development', in Norwine and Gonzalez (1988), ch.4.

Goodman, L. (1987) *Small States, Giant Firms*, New York: Holmes and Meier.

Gorbachev, M. (1988) *Perestroika: New thinking for our country and the world*, Collins.

Gordon, D. (1988) 'The global economy: new edifice or crumbling foundation', *New Left Review*, **168**, March–April, pp.24–65.

Gorostiaga, X. (1984) *The Role of the International Financial Centres in Underdeveloped Countries*, Croom Helm.

Gorst, I. (1989) 'Growing force of "green" movement', *Petroleum Economist*, August, pp.247–8.

Gott, R. (1990) 'The blue pimpernels', *The Guardian*, 15 January.

Gould, P. and Lyew-Ayee, A. (1985) 'Television in the Third World: A High Wind on Jamaica', in Burgess, J. and Gold, J. (eds.) (1985) *Geography, the Media, and Popular Culture*, Croom Helm.

Graham, R. (1982) *The Aluminium Industry and the Third World*, Zed.

Grieco, J. (1984) *Between Dependence and Autonomy: India's experience with the international computer industry*, Berkeley and Los Angeles: University of California Press.

Grosse, R. (1982) 'Codes of conduct for multinational enterprises', *Journal of World Trade Law*, **16**, September–October, pp.414–33.

Grou, P. (1985) *The Financial Structure of Multinational Capital*, Leamington Spa: Berg.

Grunwald, J. and Flamm, K. (1985) *The Global Factory*, Washington: Brookings.

Guback, T. and Varis, T. (1982) *Transnational Communication and Cultural Industries*, Paris: UNESCO.

Halal, W. (1989) 'One world: the union of a new capitalism and a new socialism', in *The Future: Opportunity not destiny*, Washington: World Future Society.

Hamelink, C. (1984) *Transnational Data Flows in the Information Age*, Lund: Studentliteratur.

Hamelink, C. (1988) *Cultural Autonomy in Global Communication*, Centre for the Study of Communication and Culture.

Han Guojian (1990) 'Kinescope firm highlights China's investment climate', *Beijing Review*, 15–21 January, pp.23–5.

Hansen, P. (1974) *Advertising and Socialism*, Macmillan.

Hansen, P. (1989) 'Kremlin studies proposals for free economic zones', *The Guardian*, 5 March.

Harrison, D. (1988) *The Sociology of Modernization and Development*, Macmillan.

Harvey, M. (1985) 'The executive family: an overlooked variable in international assignments', *Columbia Journal of World Business*, Spring, pp.18–26.

Hauck, D., Voorhes, C. and Goldberg, C. (1983) *Two Decades of Debate: The controversy over U.S. companies in South Africa*, Washington: Investor Responsibility Research Center.

Havnevik, K. (ed.) (1987) *The IMF and the World Bank in Africa*, Uppsala: Nordiska Africainstitutet.

Hemphill, G. (1986) 'Selling the world. Soft drink potential is staggering', *Beverage Industry*, September, pp.1,124.

Henderson, J. (1989) *The Globalisation of High Technology Production*, Routledge.

Hicks, N. and Streeton, P. (1979) 'Indicators of development: the search for a basic needs yardstick', *World Development*, July, pp.567–80.

Higgott, R. and Robison, R. (eds.) (1985) *South-East Asia: Essays in the political economy of structural change*, Routledge.

Hill, H. (1982) 'Vertical inter-firm linkages in LDCs: A note on the Philippines', *Oxford Bulletin of Economics and Statistics*, 44, August, pp.261–71.

Hill, J. and Boya, U. (1987) 'Consumer goods promotions in developing countries', *International Journal of Advertising*, 6, pp.249–64.

Hill, J. and Still, R. (1984a) 'Adapting products to LDC tastes', *Harvard Business Review*, March–April, pp.92–101.

Hill, J. and Still, R. (1984b) 'Effects of urbanization on multinational product planning: markets in lesser-developed countries', *Columbia Journal of World Business*, Summer, pp.62–7.

Hill, P. (1986) *Development Economics on Trial*, Cambridge: Cambridge University Press.

Hirschman, A. (1958) *The Strategy of Economic Development*, New Haven, CT: Yale University Press.

Holland, B. (ed.) (1985) *Soviet Sisterhood*, Fourth Estate.

Hong, E. (1985) *See the Third World While it Lasts*, Penang: Consumers Association of Penang.

Hood, N. and Young, S. (1982) *Multinationals in Retreat: the Scottish experience*, Edinburgh: Edinburgh University Press.

Hoogvelt, A. (1979) 'Indigenization and foreign capital: industrialization in Nigeria', *Review of African Political Economy*, **14**, January–April, pp.56–68.

Horn, N. (ed.) (1980) *Legal Problems of Codes of Conduct for Multinational Enterprises*, Antwerp: Kluwer.

Hoskins, C. and Mirus, R. (1988) 'Reasons for the US dominance of the international trade in television programmes', *Media, Culture and Society*, **10**, pp.499–515.

Howard, D. and Mayo, M. (1988) 'Developing a defensive product management philosophy for Third World markets', *International Marketing Review*, **5**, Spring, pp.31–40.

Hymer, S. (1979) 'The multinational corporation and the law of uneven development', in Modelski (1979), ch.24.

Idris-Soven, A., Idris-Soven, I. and Vaughan, M. (eds.) (1978) *The World as a Company Town*, Mouton: The Hague.

Iglitzin, L. and Ross, R. (eds.) (1976) *Women in the World: A comparative study*, Santa Barbara, CA: Clio.

Ihonvbere, J. and Shaw, T. (1988) *Towards a Political Economy of Nigeria: Petroleum and politics at the (semi-)periphery*, Aldershot: Avebury.

International Confederation of Free Trade Unions (ICFTU) (1983) 'Trade unions and the transnationals, Export Processing Zones', Brussels: Information Bulletin, March, Special Issue no. 3, mimeo.

International Labour Organisation (1984) *Technical Choice and Employment Generation by Multinational Enterprises in Developing Countries*, Geneva: ILO.

Ivanov, I. (1987) 'Joint ventures in the Soviet Union', *The TNC Reporter*, **23**, Spring, pp.49–51.

Ives, J. (ed.) (1985), *The Export of Hazard*, Routledge.

Jabbonsky, L. (1986) 'Double Cola seeks a place in the Third World', *Beverage World*, September, pp.186,190.

James, J. (1983) *Consumer Choice in the Third World*, Macmillan.

James, J. and Stewart, F. (1981) 'New products: a discussion of the welfare effects of the introduction of new products in developing countries', *Oxford Economic Papers*, 33, March, pp.81–107.

Janus, N. (1986) 'Transnational advertising: some considerations on the impact on peripheral societies', in Atwood and McAnany (1986), ch.7.

Jawayardena, K. (1986) *Feminism and Nationalism in the Third World*, Zed.

Jayaweera, N. (1986) 'The Third World and the political economy of the communication revolution', in Becker, J. *et al.* (1986), ch.4.

Jefkins, F. and Ugboajah, F. (1986) *Communications in Industrializing Countries*, Macmillan.

Jenkins, R. (1984) *Transnational Corporations and Industrial Transformation in Latin America*, Macmillan.

Jodice, D. (1980) 'Sources of change in Third World regimes for foreign direct investment', *International Organization*, **34**, Spring, pp.177–206.

Jones, D. (ed.) (1989) 'Special issue on economic and industrial democracy in Eastern Europe', *Economic and Industrial Democracy*, **10**, August.

Journal of Communication (1985) 'What now? Telecommunications development. The U.S. effort', **35**, Spring, pp.8–51.

Journal of Communication (1989) 'The information gap. How computers and other new communications technologies affect the social distribution of power', Summer, special issue.

Kacker, M. (1988) 'The role of global retailers in world development', in Kaynak (1988), ch.3.

Kagarlitsky, B. (1989) 'The market instead of democracy?', *International Socialism*, 45, Winter, pp.93–104.

Kaplinsky, R. (1979) 'Inappropriate products and technique: breakfast food in Kenya', *Review of African Political Economy*, **14**, January–April, pp.90–6.

Kaplinsky, R. (ed.) (1984) *Third World Industrialisation in the 1980s: Open economies in a closing world*, Cass.

Karim, M. (1986) *The Green Revolution: An international bibliography*, New York: Greenwood Press.

Kaufman, E. (1988) *Crisis in Allende's Chile*, New York: Praeger.

Kaynak, E. (1985) 'Some thoughts on consumerism in developed and less developed countries', *International Marketing Review*, Summer, pp.15–30.

Kaynak, E. (ed.) (1988) *Transnational Retailing*, Berlin: Walter de Gruyter.

Kaynak, E. and Lee, K.-H. (eds.) (1989) *Global Business: Asia–Pacific dimensions*, Routledge.

Keller, E. (1987) 'Afro-Marxist Regimes', in Keller and Rothchild (1987), ch.1.

Keller, E. and Rothchild, D. (eds.) (1987) *Afro-Marxist Regimes: ideology and public policy*, Boulder, CO: Lynne Rienner.

Keohane, R. and Nye, J. (eds.) (1973) *Transnational Relations and World Politics*, Cambridge, MA: Harvard University Press.

Khaing, M.M. (1986) 'Entrepreneurs within a socialist economy – Burma', *Southeast Asian Business*, **11**, Fall, pp.36–41.

King, B. (1984) 'The Hollywood star system', PhD thesis, London School of Economics.

King, R. (1986) 'Aggressive promotion of imported consumer products by a socialist state enterprise', *Proceedings of the 1986 Conference of the American Academy of Advertising*, R7–R10.

Kirim, A. (1986) 'Transnational corporations and local capital: comparative conduct and performance in the Turkish pharmaceutical industry', *World Development*, **14**, April, pp.503–21.

Kis, J. (1989) 'Turning point in Hungary', *Dissent*, Spring, pp.235–41.

Kitching, G. (1987) 'The role of a national bourgeoisie in the current phase of capitalist development: some reflections', in Lubeck (1987), ch.2.

Kivikuru, U. (1988) 'From import to modelling: Finland – an example of old periphery dependency', *European Journal of Communication*, **3**, pp.9–34.

Knight, D. (1988) *Mozambique: caught in the trap*, Christian Aid.

Kobrin, S. (1980) 'Foreign investment and forced divestment in LDCs', *International Organization*, **34**, Winter, pp.65–88.

Korbonski, A. (1989) 'The politics of economic reforms in Eastern Europe: the last thirty years', *Soviet Studies*, 41, pp.1–19.

Kowaleski, D. (1982) *Transnational Corporations and Caribbean Inequalities*, New York: Praeger.

Kumar, K. (ed.) (1980) *Transnational Enterprises: Their impact on Third World societies and cultures*, Boulder, CO: Westview.

Kunzle, D. (1978) 'Chile's *La Firme* versus ITT', *Latin American Perspectives*, **16**, Winter, pp.119–33.

Laiodi, Z. (ed.) (1988) *The Third World and the Soviet Union*, Zed.

Lall, S. (ed.) (1983) *The New Multinationals: the spread of Third World enterprises*, Chichester: Wiley.

Lall, S. (1985) *Multinationals, Technology, and Exports*, Macmillan.

Lasserre, P. (1982) 'Training: key to technological transfer', *Long Range Planning*, **15**, 3, pp.51–60.

Lee Cheuk-yan (1987) 'Hong Kong clothing union: job saving campaign', *TUEC Bulletin* (Hong Kong), **3**, pp.2–3.

Lee Chin-Chuan (1980) *Media Imperialism Reconsidered: The homogenizing of television culture*, Beverly Hills, CA: Sage.

Leonard, R. (1986) 'After Bhopal: multinationals and the management of hazardous products and processes', *Multinational Business*, **2**, pp.1–9.

Leopold, M. (1985) 'The transnational food companies and their global strategies', *International Social Science Journal*, **105**, pp.315–30,

Levitt, T. (1983) 'The globalization of markets', *Harvard Business Review*, May–June, pp.92–102.

Lewis, J. and Kallab, V. (eds.) (1986) *Development Strategies Reconsidered*, New Brunswick, NJ: Transaction.

Lim, L. (1985) *Women Workers in Multinational Enterprises in Developing Countries*, Geneva: ILO.

Lim, L. and Foo, G. (1987) 'Poverty, ideology and women export factory workers', mimeo.

Lim L. and Pang, E. (1982) 'Vertical linkages and multinational enterprises in developing countries', *World Development*, **10**, July, pp.585–95.

Lim, P. (1988) 'Credit goes charging into China', *China Trade Communique*, June, pp.4–16.

Lloyd, P. (1982) *A Third World Proletariat?*, Allen & Unwin.

Long, F. (1981) *Restrictive Business Practices, Transnational Corporations and Development*, Dordrecht: Martinus Nijhoff.

Long, F. (1986) 'Employment effects of multinational enterprises in export processing zones in the Caribbean', Geneva: ILO/UNCTC Multinational Enterprises Programme, Working Paper no. 42.

Loxley, J. and Saul, J. (1975) 'Multinationals, workers and the parastatals in Tanzania', *Review of African Political Economy*, **2**, January–April, pp.54–67.

Lubeck, P. (ed.) (1987) *The African Bourgeoisie: Capitalist development in Nigeria, Kenya, and the Ivory Coast*, Boulder, CO: Lynne Rienner.

MacBride Commission (1980) *Many Voices, One World*, Paris, UNESCO.

Madden, C. (ed.) (1977) *The Case for the Multinational Corporation*, New York: Praeger.

Maex, R. (1983) *Employment and Multinationals in Asian Exporting Zones*, Geneva: ILO.

Mander, J. (1978) *Four Arguments for the Elimination of Television*, New York: Quill.

Manoff, R. (1984) 'Learning a lesson from Nestlé', *Advertising Age*, 13 February, pp.16,20.

Mansbach, R. and Vasquez, J. (1981) *In Search of Theory: A new paradigm for global politics*, New York: Columbia University Press.

Marcuse, H. (1964) *One Dimensional Man*, Routledge and Kegan Paul.

Martonyi, J. (1987) 'The legal framework for joint ventures in Hungary', *The CTC Reporter*, **23**, Spring, pp.52–3.

Mattelart, A. (1978) 'The nature of communications practice in a dependent society', *Latin American Perspectives*, **V**, 1, Winter, pp.13–34.

Mattelart, A. (1983) *Transnationals and the Third World: The struggle for culture*, South Hadley, MA: Bergin and Garvey.

Mattelart, A., Delcourt, X. and Mattelart, M. (1984) *International Image Markets: In search of an alternative perspective*, Comedia.

Mattelart, M. (1986) *Women, Media and Crisis*, Comedia.

Maxwell, S. and Singer, H. (1979) 'Food aid to developing countries: a survey', *World Development*, July, pp.225–47.

McKee, D. (1988) *Growth, Development, and the Service Economy in the Third World*, New York: Praeger.

McKendrick, N., Brewer, J. and Plumb, J. (1982) *The Birth of a Consumer Society*, Hutchinson.

McMillan, C. (1987) *Multinationals from the Second World*, Macmillan.

McPhail, T. (1987) *Electronic Colonialism*, Newling Park, CA: Sage.

Medawar, C. (1979) *Insult or Injury*, Social Audit.

Medawar, C. (1984) *Drugs and World Health*, Social Audit.

Medawar, C. and Freese, B. (1982) *Drug Diplomacy*, Social Audit.

Melrose, D. (1981) *The Great Health Robbery: Baby milk and medicines in Yemen*, Oxford: Oxfam.

Melrose, D. (1982) *Bitter Pills: Medicines and the Third World poor*, Oxford: Oxfam.

Merrill, J. (ed.) (1983) *Global Journalism*, New York: Longman.

Mertz, H. Jr. (1984) *Peace and Affluence through the Multinational Corporations*, Bryn Mawr: Dorrance.

Meyer, W. (1988) *Transnational Media and Third World Development. Structure and Impact of Imperialism*, New York: Greenwood.

Mezger, D. (1978) 'How the mining companies undermine liberation', *Review of African Political Economy*, **12**, May–August, pp.53–66.

Micou, A. (1985) 'The invisible hand at work in developing countries', *Across the Board*, March, pp.8–17.

Mikesell, R. and Whitney, J. (1987) *The World Mining Industry*, Boston: Allen & Unwin.

Miller, F. (1983), *Out of the Mouths of Babes: The infant formula controversy*, Bowling Green, OH: Bowling Green State University, Social Philosophy & Policy Centre.

Mirza, H. (1986) *Multinationals and the Growth of the Singapore Economy*, Croom Helm.

Mittelman, J. (1981) *Underdevelopment and the Transition to Socialism*, New York: Academic Press.

Mitter, S. (1986) *Common Fate, Common Bond*, Pluto Press.

Moaddel, M. (1989) 'State-centred vs. class-centred perspectives on international politics: The case of US and British participation in the 1953 coup against Premier Mossadeq in Iran', *Studies in Comparative International Development*, **24**, Summer, pp.3–23.

Modelski, G. (ed.) (1979) *Transnational Corporations and World Order: Readings in international political economy*, San Francisco: Freeman.

Montoya Martin del Campo, A. and Rebeil Corella, M. (1986) 'Commercial television as an educational and political institution', in Atwood and McAnany (1986), ch.8.

Moore-Lappe, F. and Beccar-Varela, A. (1980) *Mozambique and Tanzania: Asking the big questions*, San Francisco: Institute for Food and Development Policy.

Moran, T. (1974) *Multinational Corporations and the Politics of Dependence: Copper in Chile*, Princeton, NJ: Princeton University Press.

Moran, T. (ed.) (1985) *Multinational Corporations: The political economy of foreign direct investment*, Lexington, MA: D.C. Heath.

Morokvasic, M. (1986) 'Being a woman in Yugoslavia: past, present and institutional equality', in Gadant (1986), pp.120–38.

Morris, M. (1979) *Measuring the Condition of the World's Poor*, Washington: Pergamon.

Mouzelis, N. (1986) *The Politics of the Semi-Periphery*, Macmillan.

Mouzelis, N. (1988) 'Sociology of development: reflections on the present Crisis', *Sociology*, **22**, pp.23–44.

Mowlana, H. (1985) *International Flow of Information*, Paris: UNESCO.

Mun, K.-C. (1988) 'Chinese retailing in a changing environment', in Kaynak (1988), ch.15.

Murray, N. (1979) 'Socialism and feminism: women and the Cuban revolution', *Feminist Review*, (2 parts), no. 2, pp.57–73; no. 3, pp.99–108.

Murray, R. (ed.) (1981) *Multinationals beyond the Market: Intra-firm trade and the control of transfer pricing*, Brighton: Harvester.

Muskie, E. and Greenwald, D. (1986) 'The Nestlé Infant Formula Audit Commission as a model', *Journal of Business Strategy*, Spring, pp.19–23.

Nair, B. (1980) *Mass Media and the TNC: A study of media–corporate relationship and its consequences for the Third World*, Singapore: Singapore University Press.

Nash, J. and Fernandez-Kelly, M. (eds.) (1983) *Women, Men and the International Division of Labor*, Albany: State University of New York Press.

Nath, U. (1986) *Smoking: Third World alert*, Oxford: Oxford University Press.

Nawrocki, I. (1987) 'Foreign enterprises in Poland: ten years of experience', *The TNC Reporter*, **24**, Autumn, pp.49–50.

Nayyar, D. (ed.) (1977) *Economic Relations between Socialist Countries and the Third World*, Macmillan.

Nestlé (1975) *Nestlé in the Developing Countries*, Vevey.

Nestlé (1985) *The Dilemma of Third World Nutrition*, Vevey.

Newfarmer, R. (ed.) (1985) *Profits, Progress, and Poverty*, Notre Dame, IN: Notre Dame University Press.

Nicholson, P. (1988) 'Asia's space invadors', *South*, May, pp.12–13.

Nordenstreng, K. (1984) 'Bitter lessons', *Journal of Communication*, Winter, pp.138–42.

Norris, R. (ed.) (1982) *Pills, Pesticides and Profits: The international trade in toxic substances*, New York: North River Press.

Norwine, J. and Gonzalez, A. (eds.) (1988) *The Third World: States of mind and being*, Boston: Unwin Hyman.

Nwoke, C. (1987) *Third World Minerals and Global Pricing: A new theory*, Zed.

Oculi, O. (1987) 'Green capitalism in Nigeria', in Lubeck (1987), ch.6.

O'Donnell, G. (1979) *Modernization and Bureaucratic-Authoritarianism: Studies in South American politics*, Berkeley: University of California Press.

Ogan, C. (1988) 'Media imperialism and the videocassette recorder: the case of Turkey', *Journal of Communication*, **38**, 2, Spring, pp.93–106.

Okada, Y. (1983) 'The dilemma of Indonesian dependency on foreign direct investments', *Development and Change*, **14**, pp.115–32.

Onimode, B., Ohorhenvan, T. and Adeniran, T. (1983) *MNCs in Nigeria*, Ibadan: Les Shyraden Nigeria Ltd.

Otobo, D. (1987) *Foreign Interests and Nigerian Trade Unions*, Oxford: Malthouse.

Owen, R. and Sutcliffe, B. (eds.) (1972) *Studies in the Theory of Imperialism*, Longman.

Packenham, R. (1986) 'Capitalist vs. socialist dependency: the case of Cuba', *Journal of Interamerican Studies and World Affairs*, **28**, Spring, pp.59–92.

Pagan, R. (1986) 'The Nestlé boycott: implications for strategic business planning', *Journal of Business Strategy*, Spring, pp.12–18.

Palmer, J. (1985) 'Consumer service industry exports', *Columbia Journal of World Business*, Spring, pp.69–74.

Palmer, R. (1987) 'Africa in the media', *African Affairs*, **86**, April, pp.241–7.

Parsons, T. (1977) *The Evolution of Societies*, Englewood Cliffs, NJ: Prentice Hall.

Pendakur, M. (1985) 'Dynamics of cultural policy making: The U.S. film industry in India', *Journal of Communication*, **35**, Autumn, pp.52–72.

Peretz, S. (1984) 'Providing drugs to the Third World: an industry view', *Multinational Business*, **2**, pp.20-9.

Petritsch, M. (1985) 'Women's participation in manufacturing in developing countries, with emphasis on agro-industries', Vienna: UNIDO, mimeo.

Petro, N. (1989) 'The outer limit of glasnost?', *Orbis*, Spring, pp.266–71.

Post, K. and Wright, P. (1989) *Socialism and underdevelopment*, Routledge.

Press, M. and Thomson, D. (eds.) (1989) *Solidarity for Survival: the Don Thomson reader on trade union internationalism*, Nottingham: Spokesman.

Price, D. and Blair, A. (1989) *The Changing Geography of the Service Sector*, Pinter.

Radetzki, M. (1977) 'Where should developing countries' minerals be processed? The country view versus the multinational corporation view', *World Development*, May, pp.325–34.

Raikes, P. (1984) 'Food policy and production in Mozambique since independence', *Review of African Political Economy*, 29, July, pp.95–107.

Reynolds, B. (ed.) (1987) *Reform in China*, Armonk: M.E. Sharpe.

Richardson, E. (1987) 'Observations on the round-table', *The CTC Reporter*, 24, Autumn, p.25.

Riddell, A. (1976) 'Female political elites in Mexico: 1974', in Iglitzin and Ross (1976), ch.16.

Roca, S. (ed.) (1988) *Socialist Cuba: Past interpretations and future challenges*, Boulder, CO: Westview.

Rogers, E. and Antola, L. (1985) 'Telenovelas: A Latin American success story', *Journal of Communication*, 35, Autumn, pp.25–35.

Roncagliolo, R. (1986) 'Transnational communication and culture', in Atwood and McAnany (1986), ch.4.

Rosati, D. and Mizsei, K. (1989) 'Adjustment through opening of socialist economies', United Nations University, mimeo.

Rosen, S. (ed.) (1987/1988) 'The Private Economy', *Chinese Economic Studies*, 2 parts, XXI, Fall and Winter.

Rosset, P. and Vandermeer, J. (eds.) (1986) *Nicaragua: Unfinished revolution*, New York: Grove Press.

Rothchild, D. and Foley, M. (1987) 'Ideology and policy in Afro-Marxist regimes: the effort to cope with domestic and international constraints', in Keller and Rothchild (1987), ch.12.

Rowan, R., Northrup, H. and O'Brien, R. (1980) *Multinational Union Organizations in the Manufacturing Industries*, Wharton School: University of Pennsylvania.

Ruiz, V. and Tiano, S. (eds.) (1987) *Women on the U.S.–Mexico Border: Responses to change*, Boston: Allen & Unwin.

Rugman, A. (ed.) (1982) *New Theories of the Multinational Enterprise*, Croom Helm.

Russett, B. (1984) 'Resource dependence and analysis', *International Organization*, 38, 3, pp.481–99.

Ryback, T. (1989) *Rock around the Bloc*, New York: Oxford University Press.

Salinas Bascur, R. (1985) 'Information in the Third World: adjusting technologies or strategies', *Media, Culture and Society*, 7, pp.355–68.

Salmon. C. (ed.) (1990) *The Formula Pushers*, Minneapolis: Action for Corporate Responsibility.

Samarajiwa, R. (1984) 'Third-World entry to the world market in news: Problems and possible solutions', *Media, Culture and Society*, **6**, pp.119–36.

Sanderson, S. (ed.) (1985) *The Americas in the New International Division of Labor*, New York: Holmes and Meier.

Sanderson, S. (1986) 'The emergence of the "World Steer": internationalization and foreign domination in Latin American cattle production', in Tullis and Hollist (1986), ch.5.

Sano, H. (1983) *The Political Economy of Food in Nigeria 1960–1982: A discussion on peasants, state and world economy*, Uppsala: Scandinavian Institute of African Studies.

Sauvant, K. (1981) *The Group of 77*, New York: Oceana.

Sauvant, K. and Mennis, B. (1980) 'Socio-cultural investments and the international political economy of North–South relations: the role of transnational enterprises', in Kumar (1980), ch.11.

Schell, O. (1988) 'Capitalist birds in a socialist bird cage', *California Business*, July, pp.34–47.

Schiller, H. (1981), *Who Knows: Information in the age of the Fortune 500*, Norwood, NJ: Ablex.

Schiller, H. (1989) 'Farewell to cultural sovereignty', mimeo.

Schlesinger, P. (1987) 'On national identity: some conceptions and misconceptions criticized', *Social Science Information*, **26**, 2, pp.219–64.

Schuftan, C. (1983) 'De-Westernizing health planning and delivery through consumer participation: some lessons from Chile and Tanzania', in Morgan, J. (ed.) *Third World Medicine and Social Change*, Lanham, MD: University Press of America.

Scott, C. (1985) 'Transnational corporations, comparative advantage and food security in Latin America', in Abel and Lewis (1985), pp.483-99.

Seidman, A., Seidman, R., Ndlela, D. and Makamure, K. (eds.) (1986) *Transnationals in Southern Africa*, Harare: Zimbabwe Publishing House.

Servan-Schreiber, J.-J. (1968) *The American Challenge*, Harmondsworth: Penguin.

Sethi, S. (1977) *Advocacy Advertising and Large Corporations*, New York: Heath.

Sethi, S., Etemad, H. and Luther, K. (1986) 'New sociopolitical forces: the globalization of conflict', *Journal of Business Strategy*, Spring, pp.24–31.

Sheldon, R. and Arens, E. (1932) *Consumer Engineering: A new technique for prosperity*, New York: Harper Brothers.

Shenton, B. and Freund, B. (1978) 'The incorporation of northern Nigeria into the world capitalist system', *Review of African Political Economy*, **13**, May–August, pp.8–20.

Shivji, I. (1976) *Class Struggles in Tanzania*, Monthly Review Press.

Sigmund, P. (1980) *Multinationals in Latin America*, Madison: University of Wisconsin Press.

Silverman, M., Lee, P. and Lydecker, M. (1982) *Prescriptions for Death: The drugging of the Third World*, Berkeley and Los Angeles: University of California Press.

Sinclair, J. (1987) *Images Incorporated: Advertising as industry and ideology*, Croom Helm.

Sklair, L. (1988a) 'Transcending the impasse: metatheory, theory and empirical research in the sociology of development and underdevelopment', *World Development*, **16**, June, pp.697–709.

Sklair, L. (1988b) 'Foreign investment, Irish development and the international division of labour', *Progress in Planning* **29**, 3, pp.147–216 (whole issue).

Sklair, L. (1988c) 'The costs of foreign investment: the case of the Egyptian Free Zones', in Kedourie, E. and Haim, S. (eds.), *Essays on the Economic History of the Middle East: Second series*, Cass.

Sklair, L. (1989) *Assembling for Development: The maquila industry in Mexico and the United States*, Boston: Unwin Hyman.

Sklair, L. (forthcoming) 'Problems of socialist development: the significance of Shenzhen for China's open door development strategy', *International Journal of Urban and Regional Research*.

Sklar, H. (ed.) (1980) *Trilateralism*, Boston: South End Press.

Sklar, R. (1987) 'Postimperialism: a class analysis of multinational corporate expansion', in Becker *et al.* (1987), ch.2.

Smith, A. (1980) *The Geopolitics of Information. How Western Culture Dominates the World*, Faber.

Social Sciences in China (1989) 'Forum on DATW in a socialist commodity economy', March, pp.9–19.

Solinger, D. (1989) 'Capitalist measures with Chinese characteristics', *Problems of Communism*, January–February, pp.19–33.

Spraos, J. (1983) *Inequalising Trade? A study of traditional North/South specialisation in the context of terms of trade concepts*, New York: Oxford University Press/UNCTAD.

Sreberny-Mohammadi, A. (1984) 'The "World of News" study: results of international cooperation', *Journal of Communication*, 34, Winter, pp.120–34.

Stauffer, R. (1979) 'Transnational corporations and host nations: attitudes, ideologies and behaviours', University of Sydney, Transnational Corporations Research Project, mimeo.

Stauth, G. and Zubaida, S. (eds.) (1987) *Mass Culture, Popular Culture, and Social Life in the Middle East*, Boulder, CO: Westview.

Steif, W. (1989) 'Financial woes in Egypt', *Multinational Monitor*, March, pp.23–5.

Steinberg, D. (1982) *Burma: A socialist nation of Southeast Asia*, Boulder, CO: Westview.

Stevenson, R. (1984) 'Pseudo debate', *Journal of Communication*, **34**, Winter, pp.134–8.

Stewart, F. (1978) *Technology and Underdevelopment*, Macmillan.

Stoever, W. (1989) 'Foreign collaborations policy in India: a review', *Journal of Developing Areas*, **23**, July, pp.485–504.

Stoneman, C. (1978) 'Foreign capital and the reconstruction of Zimbabwe', *Review of African Political Economy*, **11**, January–April, pp.62–83.

Stover, W. (1984) *Information Technology in the Third World*, Boulder, CO: Westview.

Street, A. (1985) 'Multinationals square off against Central American workers', *Business and Society Review*, Winter, pp.45–9.

Sullivan, K. (1990) 'Fake festival of panty-givers', *The Guardian*, 14 March.

Sullivan, L. (1988) 'Assault on the reforms: conservative criticism of political and economic liberalization in China, 1985–86', *China Quarterly*, June, pp.198–222.

Summers, R. and Heston, A. (1988) 'A new set of international comparisons of real product and price levels estimates for 130 countries, 1950–1985', *Review of Income and Wealth*, **34**, March, pp.1–25.

Swainson, N. (1987) 'Indigenous capitalism in postcolonial Kenya', in Lubeck (1987), ch.5.

Szelenyi, I. (1988) *Socialist Entrepreneurs: Embourgeoisement in rural Hungary*, Oxford: Polity Press.

Taylor, J. (1979) *From Modernization to Modes of Production*, Macmillan.

Taylor, M. and Thrift, N. (1986) *Multinationals and the Restructuring of the World Economy*, Croom Helm.

Taylor, P. (1984) *The Smoke Ring: Tobacco, money and international politics*, Sphere.

Teichova, A., Levy-Leboyer, M. and Nussbaum, H. (eds.) (1986) *Multinational Enterprise in Historical Perspective*, Cambridge: Cambridge University Press.

Teng Weizao and Wang, N.T. (eds.) (1988) *Transnational Corporations and China's Open Door Policy*, Lexington, MA: Lexington Books.

Tharp, P. (1976) 'Transnational enterprises and international regulation: A survey of various approaches in international organizations', *International Organization*, **30**, Winter, pp.47–73.

Thomas, C. (1975) *Dependence and Transformation*, New York: Monthly Review Press.

Tiano, S. (1986) 'Women and industrial development in Latin America', *Latin America Research Review*, **XXI**, 3, pp.157–70.

Tomlinson, A. and Whannel, G. (1984) *Five-Ring Circus: Money, power and politics at the Olympic Games*, Pluto Press.

Torp, J., with Denny, L. and Ray, D. (1989) *Mozambique, São Tomé and Príncipe*, Pinter.

Transnationals Information Exchange (1985) *Meeting the Corporate Challenge*, Amsterdam: TIE Report 18/19.

Tsikata, F. (ed.) (1986) *Essays from the Ghana–Valco Renegotiations, 1982–85*, Accra: Ghana Publishing Corporation.

Tullis, F. and Hollist, W. (eds.) (1986) *Food, the State and International Political Economy. Dilemmas of Developing Countries*, Lincoln: University of Nebraska Press.

Tunstall, J. (1977) *The Media are American*, New York: Columbia University Press.

UNESCO (1976) *The Use of Socio-economic Indicators in Development Planning*, Paris: UNESCO.

Union of International Associations (1988–9) *The Yearbook of International Associations*, 3 vols., Munich: K.G. Saur.

United Nations Centre on Transnational Corporations (UNCTC) (1988) *Transnational Corporations in World Development*, New York: UNCTC.

United Nations Secretariat (1984) 'Mineral Processing in Developing Countries', *Natural Resources Journal*, special issue.

United States 93rd Congress (1973) *Multinational Corporations*, Washington: US Government Printing Office.

Urdang, S. (1989) *And Still they Dance: Women, war, and the struggle for change in Mozambique*, Earthscan.

Vaitsos, C. (1974) 'Employment effects of foreign direct investments in developing countries', in Edwards, E. (ed.), *Employment in Developing Nations*, New York: Columbia University Press.

Vaitsos, C. (1978) 'Crisis in regional economic cooperation (integration) among developing countries: a survey', *World Development*, June, pp.719–69.

Van Allen, J. (1976) 'African women, "modernization" and national liberation', in Iglitzin and Ross (1976), ch.2.

Vanden, H. and Queiser M., W. (1985) 'Nicaraguan Relations with the Non-aligned Movement', *Journal of Interamerican Studies*, **27**, Fall, pp.141–61.

Varis, T. (1984) 'The international flow of television programs', *Journal of Communication*, **34**, Winter, pp.143–52.

Vengroff, R. (1982) 'Food and dependency: P.L. 480 aid to black Africa', *Journal of Modern African Studies*, **20**, 1, pp.27–43.

Vernon, R. (1971) *Sovereignty at Bay*, New York: Basic Books.

Walker, A. (1989) 'The cult of Russia's new rich', *The Guardian*, 4–5 November, pp.1–4.

Walker, T. (ed.) (1987) *Reagan versus the Sandinistas: The undeclared war on Nicaragua*, Boulder, CO: Westview.

Wallerstein, I. (1974) *The Modern World-System*, New York: Academic Press.

Walton, J. (1987) 'Urban protest and the global political economy: The IMF riots', in Smith, M. and Feagin, J. (eds.) *The Capitalist City*, Oxford: Blackwell, ch.17.

Wang, N.T. (1984) *China's Modernization and Transnational Corporations*, Lexington, MA: Lexington Books.

Warner, M. (ed.) (1987) *Management Reforms in China*, London: Frances Pinter.

Warren, B. (1980) *Imperialism: Pioneer of capitalism*, New Left Books.

Webster, F. (1987) 'Advertising the American dream', *Media, Culture and Society*, **9**, pp.111–17.

Wells, A. (1972) *Picture-Tube Imperialism? The impact of U.S. television on Latin America*, Maryknoll, NY: Orbis.

West Africa (1980) 'Imperialism and the Volta Dam', 24 March, pp.518–23; 31 March, pp.571–3; 7 April, pp.611–14; 14 April, pp.655–60.

White, G. (1988) 'State and market in China's labour reforms', in Fitzgerald and Wuyts (1988), pp.180–202.

White, G., Murray, R. and White, C. (eds.) (1983) *Revolutionary Socialist Development in the Third World*, Brighton: Wheatsheaf.

Whiting, V. (1985) 'Transnational enterprise in the food processing industry', in Newfarmer (1985), ch.10.

Willetts, P. (ed.) (1982) *Pressure Groups in the Global System*, Pinter.

Wong, K. and Chu, D. (eds.) (1985) *Modernization in China: The case of Shenzhen SEZ*, Hong Kong: Oxford University Press.

World Bank (1978-) *World Development Report*, New York: Oxford University Press.

World Bank (1979) *Recognizing the 'Invisible' Woman in Development: The World Bank's experiences*, Washington: World Bank.

Worsley, P. (1973) *The Third World*, Weidenfeld and Nicolson.

Worsley, P. (1984) *The Three Worlds*, Weidenfeld and Nicolson.

Xia Xiaoxun and Li Jun (1987) 'Consumption expansion: a grave challenge to reform and development', in Reynolds (1987), ch.6.

Yoffie, D. (1983) *Power and Protectionism*, New York: Columbia University Press.

Youngson, A. (ed.) (1983) *Hong Kong and China: The economic nexus*, Hong Kong: Oxford University Press.

Zamet, J. and Bovarnick M. (1986) 'Employee relations for multinational companies in China', *Columbia Journal of World Business*, **21**, Spring, pp.13–19.

Zamiti-Horchani, M. (1986) 'Tunisian women, their rights and their ideas about these rights', in Gadant (1986), pp.11–19.

Zayed, A. (1987) 'Popular culture and consumerism in underdeveloped urban areas: a study of the Cairene quarter of Al-Sharrabiyya', in Stauth and Zubaida (1987), pp.287–312.

Zhang Ge (1988) 'The formation and growth of an open belt along China's coast', *New China Quarterly*, August, pp.69–71.

Zheng Yiyong (1988), *Business Guide to China's Coastal Cities*, Beijing: Foreign Languages Press.

Zimbalist, A. (ed.) (1988) *Cuban Political Economy: Controversies in Cubanology*, Boulder, CO: Westview.

Zimmerman, A. (1986) 'Marketing in the PRC', *Issues in International Business*, **3**, Summer–Fall, pp.27–34.

Index

Abbott, J. 108, 112
Abel, C. and Lewis, C. 28
Adikibi, O. 105
Advertising Age 151, 167n, 206, 224n
advertising industry 26, 44, 77, 132, 141,
    148–50, 154, 160–1, 164, 167n,
    168n, 200, 204n
  in China 166n, 200–1
  in Latin America 148–9
AFL-CIO 64
Africa 9, 13, 25n, 72, 97, 108, 127n, 130,
    142, 149, 207, 225n, 234, 235
  Afro-Marxism in 171, 216, 222–3
  bourgeoisie in 50n, 120–5
  socialism in 170, 215–23, 238
agribusiness 44, 110–17, 218, 228
Ake, C. 124
Akinsanya, A. 127n
Albania 173
Alger, C. 25n
Algeria 171, 216
Allende, S. 41, 137, 149
aluminium industry 32, 88–9
American Chambers of Commerce 63
American Express 83n, 197
Americas 40, 42, 87, 139
Amin, Idi 218
Anderson, M. 44, 148, 200
Andrae, G. and Beckman, B. 112
Angola 12, 171, 202n, 216, 217, 222–3
Anker, R. and Hein, C. 97
apparel industry 97, 102–3, 130, 186,
    197

Applied Engineering Systems 208
Aquino, B. 167n
Argentina 115, 148, 149, 150, 151, 167n
Armstrong, W. and McGee, T. 91
Arnfred, S. 222
Aron, R. 3
ARTEP 100
Asia 9, 50n, 56, 97, 116, 127n, 130, 135,
    164, 197, 207, 225n
AT&T 145
Atwood, R. and McAnany, E. 167n
Australia 133, 164
Austria 210

baby bottle feed case 155–7
Bagdikian, B. 75, 141
Bai Nanfeng 197
Baird, P. and McCaughan, E. 62
Baker, W. and Rappaport, A. 167n
Bangladesh 160
Barbados 92–3
barefoot doctors 161
Barnathan, J. 134
Barnet, R. and Müller, R. 25n, 44, 48,
    84n
basic needs approach 19, 25n
Bassett, T. 110–11
Bassiry, G. and Dekmejian, R. 83n,
    119, 230
Bata 153
Beamish, R. 107
Becker, Jasper 199
Becker, Jorg *et al.* 133, 141, 146

Becker, D. *et al.* 37, 38
Becker, D. and Sklar, R. 62
Belk, R. 83n, 132
Benin 216
Bennett, D. and Sharp, K. 60
Berardi, G. 112
Bergesen, A. 50n
Bergesen, H.O. 127n
Bergson, F. *et al.* 16
Berlin Wall 136
Bettelheim, C. 187
Bhatt, B. and Jain, S. 127n
Bhutan 11
Biersteker, T. 25n, 122, 123, 124
Birman, I. 175, 205
Blake, D. and Walters, R. 82n
blocs 20–2, 142, 172
Boddewyn, J. 168n
Bolivia 53, 167n
Bonnell, V. 212
Booth, D. 39
Boorstin, D. 83n
Bornschier, V. and Chase-Dunn, C. 44
Boserup, E. 13, 108, 109
Boyd, R. *et al.* 39, 65
brain drain 66–7, 218
Brazil 37, 38, 39, 106, 115, 125, 127n,
    134, 148, 149
Brenner, R. 33
Brewer, A. 50n
Britain 7, 8, 10, 19, 28, 40, 64, 81, 211
British Aluminium 89
British Petroleum 183
Brown, D. 127n
Bryceson, D. 219
Brydon, L. and Chant, S. 40, 97, 108,
    219
Bukharin, N. 27
Bulgaria 206
Burbach, R. and Flynn, P. 112, 127n
bureaucracy 4, 125, 176, 188, 189, 216,
    233
bureaucratic authoritarianism 36–7
Burki, S. and Ul Haq, M. 25n
Burma 111, 225n, 226n
Burnell, P. 114, 127n
Burton, J. 2–3

Cairo 64, 139
Callaway, B. 234
Campbell, B. 122
Canada 133
Canton (Guangzhou) 164, 183, 195, 200

Caplan, R. 46
Caporaso, J. 34, 225n
Cardoso, F. and Faletto, E. 31
Cardova, E. 155
Cargill Inc. 127n
Caribbean 40, 44, 49, 89, 95
Castro, F. 212–13
Caulkin, S. 103, 167n
Chakravarty, S. 164
Chan, S. 25n, 117
Chase-Dunn, C. 50n, 174, 202n
cheap labour 9, 34, 103, 193
Cherry, C. 73, 74
Chetley, A. 168n
child labour 199
Chile 41, 48, 86, 89, 137, 149
China 9, 12, 20, 34, 64, 100, 111, 117,
    130, 161, 172–5, 177, 178–202,
    211, 217, 225n, 235, 238
    'classes' in 125, 187–94
    consumption patterns in 164, 179,
        180, 191, 195–202, 204n
    foreign investment in 44, 58, 83n, 90,
        181–4, 193, 196–7, 199, 228
    labour in 182, 184–6, 194
    open door policy in 180–4, 194, 198–
        9, 203n
China Merchants Company 127n, 191
Chossudovsky, M. 190, 203n
Chu, G. and Alfian 143
Clairmonte, F. and Cavanagh, J. 163,
    168n
class 23, 29, 115, 171, 177, 192, 230–1,
    233, 235
    capitalist 4, 37–8, 41, 63, 154
    comprador 8, 37–8, 76, 106, 117–18,
        126, 144, 230
    struggle 33, 35, 68, 194, 216–17, 218,
        231, 239
    working 39, 63, 171, 177
    see also transnational capitalist class
Coca–Cola 47, 83n, 127n, 162–5, 196,
    200, 204n
Cohen, R. 34, 41
cola wars 162–5, 197
Cole, J. 18
COMECON 21, 170, 205–8, 212–14,
    215, 223, 225n
communications industry 49, 73–5,
    140–53, 236
communism 9, 20–1, 38, 45, 63, 114,
    170–1, 174–5, 223, 231
comparative advantage 92

comparative sociology 1
comprador mentality 63, 68–9, 117
computerization 38–9, 77–8, 102–3, 147, 167n
Congo 216
consumer engineering 84n, 127n
consumer movement 72, 83n, 155–6, 168n
consumerism 72, 83n, 129–32, 210, 230, 237
consumption 18, 39, 49, 80–1, 139, 220
Cook, P. and Fitzpatrick, C. 175, 228
Copetas, A. 209
copper industry 32, 48, 89
Corbridge, S. 33, 50n
core capitalist states 15, 88, 134
corruption 118, 183, 188–9, 193, 217
Costa Rica 19, 160, 167n
counter movements 69
Crabtree, J. 53
credit cards 26, 197, 212
Croll, L. 203n, 235
Cuba 12, 137, 170, 212–14, 215, 225n, 235
culture-ideology of consumerism 6, 38, 41–2, 51n, 53, 132, 135, 139, 150, 175, 236–8
  in First World 133–5, 162–3
  in Second World 136, 173, 197–8, 206, 223–4, 225n
  in Third World 91–3, 129–32, 139, 148–53, 155–66, 231
cultural/media imperialism 132–6, 167n
Czechoslovakia 206

Daiei 49
debt, Third World 5, 16, 219
democratic feminist socialism 24, 232–8
democracy 36–7, 41, 177, 232–3
Deng Xiaoping 186, 199
Dentsu 200
dependency 9, 31–2, 35, 49, 116, 118, 137, 213–14
dependency reversal 32, 35, 81
dependent development 31–3
development 8–9, 18, 90, 229–31, 238–9
Disneyland 27
Djilas, M. 176
dollars, US 11, 57, 212
Dominican Republic 113, 167n
Doran, C. *et al.* 50n
Dorfman, A. 169n
Dorfman, A. and Mattelart, A. 169n

Dougan, L. 145
Dowden, R. 225n
Dror, D. 100, 101
Dunning, J. 44, 83n

Eapan, E. 146
Eastern Europe 19, 64, 83n, 136, 168n, 170, 172, 174, 202n, 203n, 205–12, 223–4, 233–4, 236, 238
Eckstein, S. 214
ecoglasnost 83n
Edgren, G. 95
Editors of *Fortune* 83n
education 19, 146, 164
Edwards, C. 15, 35
Egypt 17, 37, 58, 90, 112, 113, 125, 207, 212, 225n
Eisenstadt, S. 50n
electronics industry 44, 50n, 56, 74, 97, 102, 127n, 141, 186, 197
ELIFFIT 102, 127n
Ellinghaus, W. 145
Elliot, D. 197
Elson, D. and Pearson, R. 39, 45, 103, 127n, 203n
Enderwick, P. 102
Engels, F. 21, 234
entrepreneurs 29, 129, 176–7, 179, 189–90, 193, 203n, 210, 217
Esteinou Madrid, J. 75–6
Estes, R. 19
Ethiopia 112, 171, 212, 216
ethnicity 7, 24, 99, 231, 233
European Community 21, 63, 185
Evans, P. 5, 31, 37, 38, 125, 126
Evans, P. and Bastos, P. 39
Ewen, S. 76, 83n, 84n, 149
export-orientation 16, 36, 122, 125, 127n, 176, 182, 224n, 229–30
  developmental criteria for 50n, 58, 90
export processing zones 57, 58, 90, 93–6, 99, 100–1, 127n, 209
expropriation 48, 51n, 122, 218

Farr, M. 224
fast food 151–3, 196–7
Fath, J. 107, 110
Featherstone, M. 76
Feder, E. 127n
Fejes, F. 149, 167n
feminism 233–5
Fernandez-Kelly, M. 99, 100

Fiat 208–9
Field, J. 60
Fieldhouse, D. 43
film industry 135, 146, 150–1
Finland 133
Fitzgerald, E. and Wuyts, M. 216
Flora, C. and Flora, J. 84n
food aid 112–14, 127n
food riots 72, 112, 127n
food systems 13, 17–18, 107–17, 154, 196–7, 220–1
Forbes, D. and Thrift, N. 171, 216
Foreign Agriculture 112–13
foreign trade 15–16, 55, 71, 182–3, 196, 207–8, 212–14
Forrester, L. 145
Fortune 500 43, 44, 50n, 86, 94, 103
France 64, 127n
franchising 151–3, 196–7, 210
Frank, A.G. 31, 50n, 118, 202n, 206
Frelimo 220, 222
Fröbel, F. *et al.* 34, 95, 100, 101
Fuentes, A. and Ehrenreich, B. 94

Gabb, A. 168n
Gadant, M. 235
Gail, B. 17
'Gang of Four' 131, 178, 186, 198
Ganley, G. and Ganley, O. 147, 167n
Gardner, M. 145
Garnsey, E. and Paukert, L. 97, 98, 127n, 168n
Gatehouse, M. 127n
GATT 120
General Motors 223
Gensior, S. and Scholer, B. 203n
George, S. 112
Gerber 148
Gereffi, G. 44, 157
Gereffi, G. and Wyman, D. 36
Germany 21, 173, 203n, 206, 209
Gershenberg, I. 66, 105
Geyikdagi, Y. 119
Ghana 216, 225n, 234
    Volta Dam project 87–9, 91
Giffard, C. 143
Gillespie, K. 37, 125
Girvan, N. 49, 88, 89, 202n
Gladwin, T. and Walter, I. 51n
glasnost 135, 205, 212, 231
Goldman, R. 63
Gonzalez, A. 19
Goodman, L. 25n

Gorbachev, M. 206, 224n
Gordon. D. 34
Gorostiaga, X. 44
Gorst, I. 83n
Gott, R. 224
Gould, P. and Lyew–Ayee, A. 167n
Graham, R. 127n
Gramsci, A. 73, 149
green movement 47, 71–2, 83n
green revolution 116, 127n
Grieco, J. 56
Gromyko, A. 171
Grosse, R. 46
Grou, P. 83n
Grunwald, J. and Flamm, K. 94
Guangzhou (Canton) 164, 183, 195, 200
Guatemala 47, 127n
Guback, T. and Varis, T. 150
Guinea 216

Halal, W. 231
Hamelink, C. 78–9, 80, 92, 137, 147
Han Guojian 203n
Hansen, P. 204n, 209
hard currency 32, 57, 182, 192, 196, 207, 210
Harrison, D. 50n
Harvey, M. 104
Hauck, D. *et al.* 217
Havnevik, K. 127n
health care 19, 146, 157–62
hegemon 6–7, 26, 133
Hein, C. 97
Heinz 168n
Hemphill, G. 163
Henderson, J. 44, 50n
Hicks, N. and Streeton, P. 19
Hilferding, R. 28
Higgott, R. and Robison, R. 50
Hill, H. 89
Hill, J. and Boya, U. 153
Hill, J. and Still, R. 91
Hill, P. 25n
Hirata, H. 127n
Hirschmann, A. 58
Hobson, J. 28
Holland, B. 235
Hollywood 76–7, 135, 150
Hong, E. 169n
Hong Kong 125, 127n, 130, 179, 181, 182–3, 184, 186, 188, 190–2, 196–7, 201, 203n
Hood, N. and Young, S. 70–1

Hoogvelt, A. 124
Horn, N. 83n
Hoskins, C. and Mirus, R. 166n
Howard, D. and Mayo, M. 168n
Hua Sheng 189
Huang Ping 202n
Hungary 12, 173, 176, 206, 210, 225n
Hymer, S. 44

IBM 56, 164
ICFTU 64, 96, 100
Idris-Soven, A. *et al.* 83n
Iglitzin, L. and Ross, R. 233
Ihonvbere, J. and Shaw, T. 37, 123, 125
Illich, I. 168n
ILO 96, 100, 106
IMF 5, 53, 112, 127n, 221
imperialism 6, 28–30
import substitution 15–16, 120
income per capita 4–5, 11–14
India 12, 40, 56, 64, 87, 90, 100, 106,
        113, 117, 146, 147, 160, 164, 207,
        225n
Indonesia 66, 104, 106, 107, 113, 143,
        179
informatics 77–81, 147
Intelsat 146
Interfaith Center on Corporate
        Responsibility 47
International Organization of
        Consumer Unions 47
international relations 2–3, 25n
International Social Science Journal
        25n, 50n
Iran 17, 25n, 83n, 119, 207, 230
Iraq 212, 225n
Ireland 12, 33, 55, 58, 90
Israel 12, 167n
Italy 12, 64
Ivanov, I. 208
Ives, J. 159
Ivory Coast 110–11, 122

Jabbonsky, L. 165
Jamaica 113, 167n
James, J. 92–3
James, J. and Stewart, F. 167
Janus, N. 148, 149
Japan 6, 18, 57, 64, 112, 130, 150, 151,
        196, 197
Jardines 127n
Jayawardena, K. 234
Jayaweera, N. 166

Jefkins, F. and Ugboajah, F. 92, 140,
        149, 150
Jenkins, R. 34, 44
Jinadu, L. 225n
Jodice, D. 51n
joint ventures 95, 106–7, 125, 208–10,
        221
Jones, D. 236
Journal of Communication 78, 144–5

Kacker, M. 153–4
Kagarlitsky, B. 35, 211
Kaiser Corporation 88, 89
Kaplinsky, R. 127n, 168n
Karim, M. 127n
Kaufman, E. 50n
Kayapos 134
Kaynak, E. 72, 152, 153, 210
Kaynak, E. and Lee, K-H. 50n
Keller, E. 216
Keller, E. and Rothchild, D. 170, 216,
        225n
Kentucky Fried Chicken 196
Kenya 66, 105, 106, 122, 160, 168n, 216
Keohane, R. and Nye, J. 3
Khaing, M.M. 226n
King, B. 135
King, R. 225n
Kirim, A. 161
Kis, J. 225n
Kitching, G. 121
Kivikuru, U. 133
Knight, D. 202n
Kobrin, S. 51n, 122
Kodak 83n
Korbonski, A. 205
Kowaleski, D. 44
Kumar, K. 140
Kunzle, D. 137
Kuwait 11

Laiodi, Z. 225n
Lall, S. 90, 118
Lasserre, P. 106–7
Latin America 9, 44, 48, 51n, 56, 97,
        112, 116, 131, 135–9, 148–9, 153,
        164, 167n, 207, 215, 225n
Lebanon 207
Lee, Cheuk-yang 186
Lee, Chin-Chuan 133, 134, 167n
Lenin, V. 28, 30
Leogrande, W. 213
Leonard, R. 159

Leopold, M. 108
Levitt, T. 91
Lewis, J. and Kallab, V. 36
Li Hao 188
Lilienthal, D. 43
Lim, L. 39, 45, 97, 127n
Lim, L. and Foo, G. 99
Lim, L. and Pang, E. 89
Lim, P. 197
linkages 55, 58–60, 83n, 89–90, 103–4,
    152
literacy 19, 146
Lloyd, P. 39
Long, F. 51n, 95
Lonrho 221, 225n
Loxley, J. and Saul, J. 217
Lubeck, P. 50n, 120, 121
Luxemburg, R. 28

Macao 191
MacBride Commission 79
Madagascar 216
Madden, C. 45
Madison Avenue 77
Maex, R. 100, 101
Maitland Commission 145
Malaysia 99, 100, 106, 152, 162, 179
Mali 216
managers 66, 98, 104, 185, 194, 203n,
    217
Mander, J. 47, 51n
Manoff, R. 156, 157
Mansbach, R. and Vasquez, J. 25n
Mao Zedong 178, 179, 187, 198
manufactured goods 15, 70, 219
Marcuse, H. 131
Marks and Spencer 211
Martonyi, J. 210
Marx, K. 21, 28, 30, 35, 73, 177, 236
Marxism 4, 28, 35, 68, 73, 172, 176,
    202n, 234, 236
mass luxuries 165, 201–2
mass media 53, 75, 132–47, 150–1, 201,
    233, 236
Mastercard 197
Matsushita 203n
Mattelart, A. 133, 136, 141, 149, 150,
    167n
Mattelart, M. 84n
Mauritius 97, 100
Maxwell, S. and Singer, H. 127n
McDonald's 27, 49, 152–3, 168n, 196
McKee, D. 169n

McKendrick, N. *et al.* 83n
McKinsey 217
McLuhan, M. 26, 27, 74, 76
McMillan, C. 206–7
McPhail, T. 74, 147, 150
Medawar, C. 158, 160, 162
Medawar, C. and Freese, D. 159
Melrose, D. 156, 161
Merrill, J. 167n
Mertz, H. 45
Mesa-Lago, C. 213
Mexico 17, 58, 90, 97, 98, 99, 101, 160,
    207, 235
    food industry in 110, 113, 115, 127n
    maquila industry in 34, 62, 95, 97,
        100, 103–4, 127n, 203n
    media in 136, 144, 148
Meyer, W. 140, 167n
Mezger, D. 225n
Micou, A. 45
Middle East 119, 139
migration 40–1
Mikesell, R. and Whitney, J. 50n
Miller, F. 156
mining industry 32, 44, 49, 50n, 53,
    225n
Mirza, H. 127n
Mittelman, J. 218, 225n
Mitter, S. 98, 100
Moaddel, M. 25n
Modelski, G. 44, 50n, 82n
modernization 30–1, 49, 69, 81, 109,
    129, 130, 135, 184, 206, 230, 234
modes of production 35–6
Montoya, M. and Rebeil, C. 144
Moore-Lappe, F. and Beccar–Varela,
    A. 225n
Moran, T. 44, 48
Morocco 113, 207, 235
Morokvasik, M. 235
Morris, M. 19
Moscow 168n, 170, 209, 212
Mouzelis, N. 33, 39
Mowlana, H. 78, 147, 167n
Mozambique 160, 171, 174, 202n, 216,
    217, 220–3, 225n, 235
Mun, K.-C. 195
Murray, N. 235
Murray, R. 51n
Muskie, E. and Greenwald, D. 168n

Nabisco 110
Nair, B. 140

Naor, J. 210
Nash, J. and Fernandez–Kelly, M. 34, 45, 97, 98
Nasser, G. 212
Nath, U.R. 169n
    see also state–centrism
nationalism 24, 231, 233, 237
nation state 2, 7, 138, 237
NATO 21
natural resources 9, 15, 16–18
Nawrocki, I. 209
Nayyar, D. 207, 225n
Negandhi, A. and Palia, A. 50n
neo-evolutionism *see* modernization
neo-Marxism 5, 30–2, 35–6, 133
Nestlé 47, 110, 148, 155–7, 168n
new international division of labour 34, 65, 95, 166
New Internationalist 127n
New York Stock Exchange 145, 180
New York Times 142
New Zealand 89
Newfarmer, R. 44
Ngouabi, M. 216
Nicaragua 151, 160, 174, 202n, 214, 224
Nicholson, P. 167n
NICs 31, 33, 59, 70, 95, 118, 126, 225n
Nigeria 17, 25n, 44, 83n, 92, 105, 106, 120, 150, 207, 225n
    class in 37, 126
    food in 112, 116
    indigenization in 48, 107, 122–5
Nixon, R. 178
Non-Aligned Movement 22, 214–15
Nordenstreng, K. 142
Norris, R. 159, 160
North Korea 12, 173
Norway 160
Norwine, J. and Gonzalez, A. 25n
Nwoke, C. 44
Nyerere, J. 218

Oculi, O. 123
O'Donnell, G. 36
OECD 19, 21, 46
Ogan, C. 134
Ogilvy and Mather 157, 200
oil 11, 17, 21, 32, 123, 225n
Okada, Y. 66, 105, 107
Olympic Games 74, 83n
Onimode, B. *et al.* 44, 123
OPEC 17, 21
Ortega, D. 215

Otobo, D. 83n
Owen, R. and Sutcliffe, B. 50n

Packenham, R. 213, 225n
Pagan, R. 168n
Pakistan 100, 225n
Palmer, J. 151–2
Palmer, R. 142
Panama 167n
Parsons, T. 30
Pearl River Delta 181, 182, 186
peasantry 40, 110–11, 115, 177, 180, 202n, 218–19, 220–1
Pendakur, M. 146
PepsiCo 149, 162–5, 183, 196, 204n
Peru 38, 113, 135, 207
perestroika 205, 210, 212, 224n, 231
Peretz, S. 160
Petritsch, M. 109
Petro, N. 224n
pharmaceuticals industry 44, 157–62
Phelan, J. 180
Philippines 89, 95, 100, 106, 152–3, 167n
Pizza Hut 196
Poland 12, 173, 205, 206, 209, 225n
politics of development 36–40
    see also transnational capitalist class
poorest countries 17
population 14, 179
Portugal 33, 117
    in Africa 216, 220
Post, K. and Wright, P. 202n
Pravda 142
Press, M. and Thomson, D. 83n
Price, D. and Blair, A. 44
privatization 175, 187, 219, 226n
producerism 130–1
product cycle 89
production sharing 39, 95, 102
protectionism 70–1, 83n, 120

quality of life 18–20

Radetzki, M. 83n
Raikes, P. 220
religion 7, 24, 29, 129, 132, 139, 231
resources 25n, 72
retail sector 153–4, 195–6, 210
Reynolds, B. 197, 203n
Reynolds Corporation 88
Richardson, E. 193
Riddell, A. 235

Roca, S. 225n
rock music 202n
Rogers, E. and Antola, L. 135–6
Romania 12, 206, 210
Roncagliolo, R. 137–9
Rosati, D. and Mizsei, K. 224n
Rosen, S. 203n
Rosset, P. and Vandermeer, J. 214, 215
Rotary Club 63
Rothchild, D. and Foley, M. 171–2,
    222–3
Rousseau, J.–J. 131
Rowan, R. *et al.* 65
Rugman, A. 83n
Ruiz, V. and Tiano, S. 99
Russett, B. 25n
Ryback, T. 202n
Ryle, J. 167n

Safeways 153
Salinas Bascur, R. 167n
Salmon, C. 168n
Samarajiwa, R. 167n
Sample, G. 77
Sanderson, S. 34, 115
Sandinistas 202n, 214–15
Sano, H.–O. 106, 116
Sanyo 183
Sauvant, K. 22
Sauvant, K. and Mennis, B. 81
Schell, O. 180, 200
Schiller, H. 74, 78, 133
Schlesinger, P. 167n
Schuftan, C. 161
Scotland 71, 72, 88, 89
Scott, C. 111
Searle 159
Sears, Roebuck 49, 153, 154
Seidman, A. *et al.* 225n
Servan–Schreiber, J.J. 46
service sector 44
Sethi, S. 47, 168n
sexual division of labour 13, 96–101,
    108–9, 127n, 194, 204n, 219, 222,
    234–5
Shannon Free Zone 55, 58–9
Shekou Industrial Zone 183, 189, 190,
    191, 203n
Sheldon, R. and Arens, E. 84n, 127n
Shenton, B. and Freund, B. 123
Shenzhen SEZ 94, 127n, 164, 181–3,
    184, 186, 188, 190–2, 194, 199,
    203n

Shih, T.–L. 191
Shivji, I. 218
Sigmund, P. 48, 51n
Silverman, M. *et al.* 159
Sinclair, J. 83n, 132, 133, 144, 148, 167n
Singapore 89, 90, 99, 106, 127n, 179,
    207
Singer 135, 153
Skak, J. 225n
Sklar, H. 64, 202n
Sklar, R. 37–8
Smith, A. 135, 167n
soap opera 77, 135–6
social democracy 231–3
Social Sciences in China 202n
socialism 24–5, 170–1, 173–8, 202n,
    235–8
Solinger, D. 187–8
Somalia 216
Sopron 210
Sorokin, P. v
South Korea 39, 47, 100, 113, 130, 151
Southern Africa 12, 40, 86, 174, 202n,
    217–23, 225n
Soviet Union 9, 16, 21, 64, 75, 83n, 134,
    162, 174, 176, 178, 187, 205–6,
    208–9, 211–14, 223, 225n, 234
Spain 12
Spraos, J. 25n
Sreberny-Mohammadi, A. 142
Sri Lanka 100
Stalinism 173–4, 224
standard of living 10
    under capitalism 24, 49, 154, 205,
        220, 231, 237–8
    under socialism 205–6, 220–1, 238
state-centrism 4–5, 6, 23, 25n, 27, 39,
    48, 79–80, 90, 114, 118, 126, 131,
    133, 136, 138, 144, 175
Stauffer, R. 45
Stauth, G. and Zubaida, S. 139
Steif, W. 112
Steinberg, D. 225n
Stevenson, R. 142
Stewart, F. 106
Stoever, W. 90
Stoneman, C. 226n
Stover, C. 140, 147, 150, 155
Street, A. 127n
Sullivan, K. 150
Sullivan, L. 186
Summers, R. and Heston, A. 11
Swainson, D. 122

Syria 212, 225n
Szelenyi, I. 176–7, 211

Taga, M. 150
Taiwan 12, 113, 190
Tanzania 171, 215, 216, 217–19, 220, 225n
Taylor, J. 35
Taylor, M. and Thrift, N. 83n
Taylor, P. 169n
technology 32, 67, 69, 89, 95, 104, 105–7, 119, 141, 146–7, 150, 178, 185, 229
Teichova, A. *et al.* 83n
telenovelas 135–6
television 51n, 75, 131, 134, 135–6, 143–4, 150–1, 167n, 200, 201
Teng Weizao and Wang, N.T. 183
Thailand 106, 111, 150, 151, 152, 179
Tharp, T. 46
Third Way 172, 177, 211, 231, 232–8
Thomas, C. 25n
Tiano, S. 96, 99
tobacco industry 169n
Tomlinson, A. and Whannel, G. 74
Tong K.-S. 127n
Torp, J. 221–2
tourism 26, 83n, 141, 169n, 180, 210
training 57, 67, 105–7, 152
transfer pricing 48, 59
transnational capitalist class(es) 6, 8, 36, 38, 48, 53, 60–2, 116–26, 144, 150, 173, 193, 200, 217, 223–4, 227, 236, 238
Transnational corporations 6, 25n, 26, 32, 34, 41, 43, 53, 78–9, 140–53, 227–31
   and consumerism 81, 155–66, 196–7, 204n
   in First World 45–6, 70–1, 86, 101, 131, 141–2, 162–3
   and foreign investment 34–8, 45–7, 55–6, 85–6, 95
   and jobs 40, 55–7, 60, 71, 82n, 93–6, 102, 106, 152, 186, 203n, 228, 230
   politics of 36–8, 63, 119, 122, 199, 228
   research on 43–5, 82n, 83n
   in Second World 183–6, 193, 201–3, 206, 208–10, 214, 221
   in Third World 36–9, 46, 68–9, 91–6, 109, 110–17, 118, 152–3, 155–66, 207, 217–18

and women 39, 45, 57, 96–101, 194
transnational practices 5–9, 20, 34, 52–4, 81–2, 85, 115–16, 172, 176, 210, 229, 237
   cultural–ideological 41–2, 75–81
   economic 40, 54–60, 86–91, 183, 186
   political 41, 60–75
Transnationals Information Exchange 46–7
transnational relations approach 3–4
Traynor, I. 225n
Trilateral Commission 64
triple alliance 37, 125–6
Tsikata, F. 89, 127n
Tullis, F. and Hollist, W. 44, 112, 114, 127n
Tunisia 113, 235
Tunstall, J. 133, 150
Turkey 134, 154, 161, 225

Uganda 218
UN 11, 19, 22, 46, 61, 73, 110, 155, 178, 193, 215
UN Secretariat 50n
UNCTC 46, 209
underdevelopment 9, 31, 49
unemployment 40
UNESCO 19, 79, 140, 145, 150
Unilever 77, 87, 92–3, 127n
Union of International Organizations 60
unions 54, 64–5, 83n, 95, 100, 101, 186, 193–4
Urdang, S. 222, 235
USA 7, 8, 10, 14, 16, 17, 19, 26, 40–1, 45–7, 64, 71, 81, 84n, 101, 112–14, 127n, 130, 131, 133–6, 143, 150–1, 163, 165, 178, 197, 211, 213
USAID 64

Vaitsos, C. 25n, 94, 101
Van Allen, J. 234, 235
Vanden, H. and Queiser Morales, W. 215
Varis, T. 143
Venezuela 167n
Vengroff, R. 127n
Vernon, R. 44, 48, 89
video industry 134, 147
Vietnam 170, 212, 225n
Visa 83n, 197
Volkswagen 209

wages 57, 93, 94, 96–7, 100–1, 184, 186
Walker, A. 211–12
Walker, T. 174
Wallerstein, I. 7, 33, 34, 50, 118
Walton, J. 127n
Wang, N.T. 44
Warner, M. 185, 186, 202n
Warren, B. 28, 35
Warsaw Pact 21
Waterman, P. and Klatter, M. 65
Weber, M. 29, 129
Webster, F. 83n
Wedgwood, J. 83n
Wells, A. 129–30, 131
West Africa 88, 127n
Western Europe 21, 43, 45–7, 64, 130, 134, 151, 164, 197, 203n
WFTU 64
White, G. 171, 193, 216
Whiting, V. 110
WHO 156–7, 160, 161
Willetts, P. 61
Wong, K. and Chu, D. 183
Woolworths 153
World Bank 5, 11–14, 20, 25n, 48, 53, 70, 110–11, 120, 127n, 218, 219, 221–2

World Council of Labour 64
world steer 115
world-systems theory 33–4, 90
Worsley, P. 9, 167n

Xia X. and Li J. 198
Xinhua 191

Yang, G. 203n
Yemen 156
Yoffie, D. 83n
Young and Rubicam 200
Youngson, A.J. 182
Yugoslavia 209, 235

Zahony 225n
Zamet, J. and Bovarnick, M. 203n
Zamiti-Horchani, M. 235
Zayed, A. 139
Zhang Ge 181
Zhang H. and Qin, S. 189
Zhao Ziyang 200
Zheng Yiyong 180
Zimbabwe 160, 216, 217, 226n
Zimbalist, A. 225n
Zimmerman, A. 202